Cyberspace Romance

Cyberspace Romance: The Psychology of Online Relationships

Monica T. Whitty
Queen's University Belfast, Northern Ireland, UK

and

Adrian N. Carr
University of Western Sydney, Australia

First published 2006 by
PALGRAVE MACMILLAN
Houndmills, Basingstoke, Hampshire RG21 6XS and
175 Fifth Avenue, New York, N.Y. 10010
Companies and representatives throughout the world

PALGRAVE MACMILLAN is the global academic imprint of the Palgrave Macmillan division of St. Martin's Press, LLC and of Palgrave Macmillan Ltd. Macmillan® is a registered trademark in the United States, United Kingdom and other countries. Palgrave is a registered trademark in the European Union and other countries.

ISBN-13: 978–1–4039–4514–3
ISBN-10: 1–4039–4514–4

This book is printed on paper suitable for recycling and made from fully managed and sustained forest sources.

A catalogue record for this book is available from the British Library.

A catalog record for this book is available from the Library of Congress.

10 9 8 7 6 5 4 3 2 1
15 14 13 12 11 10 09 08 07 06

Printed in China

Monica's Dedication

To my parents, Anthony and Mary Whitty – in token of my gratitude for their constant love and support

Adrian's Dedication

In memoriam – Florence Lillian Carr (nee Gaches) (1910–1983) and Thomas Ronald Carr (1910–1998)

Contents

Contents

List of Tables

Foreword

From Hydraulics to Cybernetics, and Back Again: Relationships at Play in the Electric Ether

Numerous pundits, scholars, and charlatans have proffered their views on how the world of the so-called 'new media' will alter our consciousness, our basic literacies, and our relationships to the world and to one another. Extensive research continues on the topic of 'online relationships'. However, to date, such research has been scattered across a frustratingly diverse range of disciplines, publications, and levels of quality of conceptualisation and methodology. Furthermore, most of the more serious works, such as books on the future of the new media world, have focused more on the *individual* and *societal* implications of such media. This book is the first to consider at length the *relational* implications of new media. In what ways do online relationships substitute for, complement, conflict with, amplify, or innovate new types of relationships? The answers to this question require that a more fundamental question be raised first.

What is a relationship? There have been many attempts to define relationships, and their close 'relation', the 'close' or 'personal' relationship. Relationships, we are told, entail interdependence of goals, contingency of action, overlap of meaning, persistence over time, and so forth. All of these characteristics are, to some degree or another, measures of a communication process. That is, without communication, there is no such thing as a relationship; or as an academic might put it – communication is the *sine qua non* of relationships. Without communication, a 'relationship' is really something more akin to a hallucination, a neurosis, or a psychopathological state such as erotomania – the belief that someone loves you when in reality that person may not even know you (a phenomenon often found in celebrity stalkers, for example). If communication is vital to the initiation, development, maintenance, deterioration, and ending of relationships, it follows axiomatically that anything that significantly alters the *way* we communicate should have influences on how we relate to one another.

Traditional approaches have generally viewed new media as somehow impoverished media through which to negotiate the full spectrum of the rich relational experience. The tapestry of vocal nuance, the subtlety of an eyebrow flash, the steadied patient silences of a romantic moment, the smell of a perfume that awakens ancient senses, and the immediacy of 'butterflies in the stomach' that remind one of the physicality of relationships, all seem difficult to translate in an online environment. Add to these limitations on non-verbal communication the enhanced possibilities of deception, the impersonality of the 'one-to-many' capabilities of the medium, the reproducibility of standardised rather than personalised icons and messages, and the asynchronous constraints of the keyboard or keypad, and it is easy to understand the early pessimism surrounding the possibilities of relating via the web and other computer-assisted devices.

The authors are not deterred by such dire anticipations of intimate dystopia. In a wonderfully self-reflexive move, they 'playfully' examine the concept of 'play' in the online environment. They show that we are human, after all, and when a medium presents us with disabling technological cul du sacs, we display an amazing capacity for getting through them, around them, and even finding ways of opening them into more enabling avenues of pursuit. The authors creatively investigate the ways in which we embody ourselves electronically, and the ways in which the identities we create online not only offer a space in which we play without our sense of self, they enable new senses of self in the process.

The internet did not develop in order to facilitate relationships, any more than newspapers were invented to publish personal ads. Like the panda's thumb, evolution, whether natural or technological, takes unanticipated directions. We are restless creatures when it comes to pursuing our relationships with others, and when presented with a new medium for communicating with others, its potential for facilitating relationship objectives will inevitably be explored in ways never anticipated by its inventors.

The authors provide an outstanding ability to draw bridges across the centuries to show that time too is a space in which courtship is changing. Whereas cyberspace may be a new courtship context, our behaviours in that medium bear resemblances to courtship in Victorian times and before. At the same time, as the fundamental nature of intimacy and courtship has changed with urbanisation and greater economic and political equality among the sexes, so the collapse of space, time, and the purely physical in online environments heralds fundamental changes in the ways we perform intimacy and courtship.

The ingenuity of the authors in envisioning the nature of these changes is seen in their ability to bridge not only space and time, but their ability to bridge the hydraulic metaphors of Freud's models of mind with the cybernetic worlds of the digital and the technological. Cyberspace becomes a place in which the id gets a longer leash from the generally firm grip of the ego and the superego. Despite some of the darker spaces into which some users may delve when given such slack (e.g., internet addiction, online predators, etc.), most of us find such space at least somewhat liberating. We get to play with less concern for the regulative pressures of 'realspace', and as such, we get to explore facets of ourselves and others we might not otherwise encounter.

In the context of considering what is a relationship and what roles do our communication media play in constituting a relationship, other questions arise. What is sex? What is the self? What is physical? The authors deftly avoid the infinite regress into the issue of 'what is real', and instead take as assumed the real nature of our interactions online. In the process, they richly illustrate their concepts and analyses with examples from popular culture and real correspondents. These illustrations entertain, but they also demonstrate, at a very 'real' level, the creative and intriguing theoretical perambulations the authors pursue in pursuing the processes of online pursuits.

Almost every book about the trends in new media risks instant obsolescence. As the authors illustrate, early theorists of new media tended to view either the media or people's individual personalities, as having 'strong effects' on relationships. Media strong effects theories predicted that relationships would be impoverished by the relative communication poverty of the media. Personality strong effects theories predicted that it was the type of person using the medium that made the difference. A relational perspective, though informed by aspects of both the former theories, is much more concerned with how we co-evolve with the capabilities of the medium in our relationships with self and others. Neither the medium nor the person are constants – they are active agents in the process of constructing our relationship to others. As such, although the details of this book may change across future editions (e.g., to include new technologies and examples), the basic conceptual perspectives developed herein should stand the test of time well.

Some less technologically immersed readers will read this book with voyeuristic curiosity, others more technologically inculcated will often blush at seeing themselves in the online foibles and flirtations so richly characterised. Either way, the reader is in for an intellectual treat.

Finally, if you had no answer to the question 'what is a relationship?' I ask that you return to it upon reading this book. What is a relationship? You may or may not be any closer to having an answer you consider defensible, but I will predict that if nothing else, you will feel like you have a relationship with the authors themselves. Their writing is playful, and you sense the vivid relationship they have with the material, the subject, and their audience. After all is said and done, perhaps that is what a relationship is: feeling like you connect with someone, even if you have not met them face-to-face. And if getting connected to a book about connecting through media, then what better metaphor for a book on online relationships?

BRIAN H. SPITZBERG, PH.D

Acknowledgements

In bringing this book to fruition there are many people to thank and acknowledge. First and foremost amongst the people to thank are our respective families who have unconditionally supported our intellectual journey. We would like to also thank colleagues (many of which are also good friends) that have helped us in a variety of ways both personal and intellectual, in particular: Matt Allen, Kate Anthony, Mark Andrejevic, Andrea Baker, Azy Barak, Trudy Barber, Tom Buchanan, Mark Griffiths, Bob Hsiung, Adam Joinson, Uwe Matzat, Janet Morahan-Martin, Sheizaf Rafaeli, Ulf Reips, Noel Sheehy, and the staff at Queen's, Brian Spitzberg, John Suler, Sonja Utz, Alexander Voiskounsky, Barry Wellman, Guy Adams, Richard Bates, David Boje, Keith Bennett, Jane Coulter, Alexis Downs, Yiannis Gabriel, Cheryl Lapp, Sharon Mason, Burkard Sievers, and Hank Stam. Our thanks would also like to go to the following friends who have supported us through this journey, including: Jeff, Og, Stuart, James, Anna, Lisa, Jill, Joanne, Rowena, Charles, Linda, Rozulmo, Mark, Katrina, Steve, Subhajit, Joe, Lilian, David, Anthony, Sebastian, Connor, Amy, and Ryan. We would like to thank Jaime Marshall, Andrew McAleer, Anna Van Boxel, and the other people at Palgrave for their expertise in supporting this project.

The authors and publishers are grateful to the following for permission to reproduce copyright material, specifically the following journals and publishers: *Computers in Human Behavior* (Elsevier); *CyberPsychology & Behavior* (Mary Ann Liebert); *Human Relations* (Sage); *Human Resource Development International* (Routledge); Idea Group Inc., *Theory & Psychology* (Sage); *Journal of Psycho-Social Studies* and *Journal of Managerial Psychology* (Emerald); *Social Science Computer Review* (Sage); *The Journal of Change Management* (Emerald); and *M@n@gement* (E-journal).

CHAPTER 1

Cyber-Relationships, the Story so Far

The recent Hollywood techno-thriller "The Matrix" features a sequence in which the menace of technology takes on a decidedly human character. Cyber-emotions are unleashed in a confrontation between the character Morpheus – the human hero – and his arch-rival, an "intelligent agent" in the service of the computer network which has taken over the planet. The agent, Mr. Smith, is intent on "hacking" into Morpheus's brain in order to learn the computer codes that will betray the human resistance to its digital foes. Morpheus – human that he is – is proving particularly intractable to Smith's interrogation. After asking his fellow agents to leave the room, presumably to spare them the rather un-computer-like display of emotion that is to follow, Smith turns to his prisoner and vents his violent aversion to humanity. "I hate this place, this zoo, this prison, this reality," he hisses, as he gestures toward the world outside – a computer construct in which human minds are imprisoned so their bodies can be farmed for energy. "It's the smell *– if there is such a thing," Smith continues. "I feel saturated by it. I can taste your stink . . . I must get out of here. I must get* free*".*

(Andrejevic, 2000)

Presenting stories about online gender-switching and cannibals seeking out their prey, the media would have us believe that cyberspace is full of an assortment of geeks and freaks. As with the offline world, there are of course unusual people interacting online, but this does not mean that the majority of people seeking to interact online are oddballs or sexy individuals clad in black pvc. Nevertheless, we believe that cyberspace is a unique space. It is a space where one can be playful with presentations of self. It is also a space where one can *'play at love'*.

1

This chapter provides an overview of the research to date on online relationships and how researchers have compared cyber-relationships with offline relationships. First, it provides an outline of the early theories on cyber-relationships, which suggested that there is little hope that online relationships can be rich or fulfilling. We follow this by outlining theories which provide a contrasting view – that despite the lack of online cues, online relationships can be just as personal and intimate, if not more so, than face-to-face relationships. We also make the argument that cyberspace is not one generic space and that people have many different motivations for meeting others online. We follow this line of argument throughout the book as we consider online relationships in more detail.

A brief history of the internet: From the defence force to human relationships

The internet, as we know it today, looked very different in its original form. The US Defense Department is responsible for the beginnings of the internet. In the 1960s, they originally built a system where their workers could share data. They called this system the *Arpanet*. Ironically, the intention was to link computers rather than people; however, the individuals using the system quickly re-shaped it to meet their personal needs. Email was developed relatively early on by the users of the Arpanet, and so the original Arpanet gradually grew into what we know as the internet. By about 1985, the internet was well established as a technology that supported a broad community, including those involved in research and development. Electronic mails (though not in the form we know them today) were being used to send messages across several communities, often with different systems. The World Wide Web was developed in the early 1990s and the commercial release of web browsers started in 1993.

Tim Berners-Lee a graduate of Queen's college at Oxford University is credited with the development of the very first web browser in 1990. Most would also acknowledge that Tim Berners-Lee is credited with helping the web to grow. Berners-Lee was successful at persuading the large research organisation he was working for (CERN) to provide a certification on April 30, 1993 that stated that web technology and program codes were in the public domain. This allowed anyone to use and improve them. Since then people have improved on the technology, and they continue to do so today. The first of the public web browsers, MOSAIC, was released in 1993, the first version of Netscape was released in 1994, and the first version of Internet Explorer was released in 1995.

Although the internet was not originally developed with the intention of linking people, as this chapter illustrates, people began to embrace the technology as a means of communication as well as a way to initiate and develop relationships. This book is interested in how people form online relationships, the trajectory of these relationships, and how successful and meaningful these relationships are. In order to do so we do not treat cyberspace as one generic space, but rather consider a number of different '*spaces*' available online. It should also be noted that these spaces are not limited to text, but rather can combine photographs, pictures, video (including live video via webcams), and sound (both live and recorded). Some of the spaces we will be considering in this book include:

- *Email*: Email is short for electronic mail and is the transmission of messages over communication networks. It is an asynchronous form of communication where one-on-one as well as communication amongst many is possible (e.g., through discussion lists). An email message usually has three parts – a header, a message, and attachments (which are documents or computer-readable files). Typically, one can identify from the header the source of the email.
- *Newsgroup*: A newsgroup is a continuous public discussion about a particular topic. These are not maintained on a single server. This is a form of asynchronous communication.
- *Discussion boards/Bulletin boards*: Similar to newsgroups, discussion and bulletin boards are websites, or part of a website, that allow individuals to post messages, but does not have the capacity for interactive messaging. These are typically kept on a single server. This is a form of asynchronous communication.
- *Chat rooms*: In chat rooms the conversation is synchronous. When one enters a chat room, they can type a message that will be visible to all other individuals in the chat room at the time. Most chat rooms have a particular theme, although this is not necessary. IRC (Internet Relay Chat) and ICQ (I seek you) are examples of chat systems.
- *IM (Instant Messenger)*: IM is also a synchronous communication between two or more users over communication networks. Individuals

can have private conversations or group discussions. Unlike chat rooms, individuals often chat to people they already know offline in this space. The instant messaging system usually alerts users when someone on their private list is online.

- *MUDs/MOOs*: Multiple-user dungeons, more commonly understood these days to mean multi-user dimensions or domains. In 1979, Roy Trubshaw, a student at the University of Essex in the UK, is credited for coining the phrase MUD (Cuciz, n.d.). These were originally spaces where interactive role-playing games could be played, very similar to Dungeons and Dragons. MUDs and MOOs are another form of synchronous communication and are typically text-based virtual environments. Participants appear as characters and communicate with other characters online. Many MUDs have hundreds of players logged in at the same time.

- *MMORPGs*: Massively multiplayer online games are an extension of MUDs/MOOs. Most MMORPGs are commercial and require the player to pay a fee in order to play. Like MUDs, the virtual worlds that are created are 'persistent worlds', in that the world continues regardless of whether the player is logged in or not. Similar to MUDs, people appear as characters; however, in MMORPGs their characters are usually represented by an *avatar*, which is a graphical representation of the character they play.

- *Online dating sites*: Online dating sites began appearing in the 1980s and are still increasing in popularity as an alternative or addition to offline dating. Similar to newspaper personals (but with much more information), individuals construct a profile, describing themselves and often providing photographs of themselves and sometimes sound bites and video. Users typically have to pay to use this service and once they identify a person whose profile they like, online contact is made through the system to gauge whether the other individual might also be interested. From there, individuals typically organise to meet face-to-face.

- *Weblog/Blog*: A blog is essentially a personal journal or diary that is placed online. Individuals regularly update their blogs. Individuals who keep a blog are known as bloggers. Bloggers are motivated to keep their journals for a number of reasons – sometimes to gain notoriety, sometimes for personal reasons (e.g., to keep friends up-to-date), and sometimes for professional reasons (e.g., journalist purposes).

The virtual wedding

Romantic relationships started to blossom online in places, such as MUDs, MOOs, and bulletin boards. It did not take long for MUD players to create the idea of the *'virtual wedding'*; that is, through the text, their characters would *'act out'* a virtual wedding. For example, Taxén (2002) described the following virtual wedding:

> I observed the following events at an in-game wedding I attended. . . . Among the guests was an orc character belonging to one of the ERPA guilds. Orcs are regarded as barbarians and are typically rude and quite evil. In this case, the guest was tolerated and was allowed to sit next to a lady, but his presence led to a funny sequence of events. The priest is addressing the wedding couple, and at one point, the bride takes the groom's hand in her own:

> *Priest*: As the many stars that glitter in the firmament make the heavens as a whole.
> *Bride*: *squeezes [groom's] hand*
> *Priest*: So too does the life that flows through our veins render us as one.
> *Orc*: *puts paw on [lady's] lap*
> *Lady*: *slaps it*
> *Orc*: *quickly removes*
> *Male guest*: *stifles a chuckle*
> *Priest*: Now, let the light of the countless stars caress all here in its sacred embrace that we might feel the oneness of creation.
> *Orc*: *fartz*

> Here, the player of the orc character very quickly saw the opportunity for creating a funny situation by mirroring the bride's action in a way consistent with his/her character. The male guest acknowledges the role-playing abilities of the orc player by his *stifles a chuckle* emote.

There are other stories of people 'play acting' weddings online and then becoming romantically involved in the real word. Others who are already romantically involved offline might also act out a wedding online. For example, Curtis (1992) described the following romance that began in LambaMOO:

> In the specific case of the upcoming LambdaMOO wedding, the participants first met on LambdaMOO, became quite friendly, and eventually decided to

meet in real life. They have subsequently become romantically involved in the real world and are using the MUD wedding as a celebration of that fact. This phenomenon of couples meeting in virtual reality and then pursuing a real-life relationship, is not uncommon; in one notable case, they did this even though one of them lived in Australia and the other in Pittsburgh!

Cyberspace: A small world after all

One might think of the internet as a vast space where everyone is a stranger; however, this is not always the case. The following story illustrates that even the World Wide Web can sometimes be a small world:

A budding romance between a Jordanian man and woman turned into an ugly public divorce when the couple found out that they were in fact man and wife, state media reported on Sunday.

Separated for several months, boredom and chance briefly reunited Bakr Melhem and his wife Sanaa in an internet chat room, the official Petra news agency said.

Bakr, who passed himself off as Adnan, fell head over heels for Sanaa, who signed off as Jamila (beautiful) and described herself as a cultured, unmarried woman – a devout Muslim whose hobby was reading, Petra said.

Cyber love blossomed between the pair for three months and soon they were making wedding plans. To pledge their troth in person, they agreed to meet in the flesh near a bus depot in the town of Zarqa, northeast of Amman.

The shock of finding out their true identities was too much for the pair.

Upon seeing Sanaa-alias-Jamila, Bakr-alias-Adnan turned white and screamed at the top of his lungs: "*You are divorced, divorced, divorced*" – the traditional manner of officially ending a marriage in Islam.

"*You are a liar*", Sanaa retorted before fainting, the agency said. (Jordan, 2005)

Online relationships: Cueless, shallow, and hostile or close and friendly?

In the earlier days of research into cyber-relationships, some theorists contended that the lack of non-verbal cues online (that are typically present in face-to-face encounters) made cyberspace a relatively impersonal medium (e.g., Kiesler, Siegel, & McGuire, 1984) and, as a result, *'real'*, genuine relationships could not be formed. While theorists have moved on from this view, we must also be aware that the construction of cyberspace has also changed (and continues to change) since these theories were first conceived. Moreover, the way people engage with this technology has also altered the way people use this space. However, before considering current theories on cyber-relating, we provide an outline of the theories that lead researchers to their current way of thinking about internet relationships.

Social context cues theory

The social context cues theory, first proposed by Sproull and Kiesler (1986), states that online and face-to-face communication differ in the amount of social information available. Social context cues, such as those conveyed by aspects in the physical environment as well as non-verbal behaviours, are not typically available online. Sproull and Kiesler (1986) argued, at the time, that because these social context cues are absent online there is an increase in excited and uninhibited online communication (e.g., in the form of flaming). This theory was one of a few that argued that online relationships are less intimate and more aggressive than face-to-face relationships.

Social presence theory

Social presence theory, although first devised to explain interactions via teleconferencing, was one of the first theories to be applied to CMC (Computer-mediated communication). This theory contends that social presence is the feeling that one has that other individuals are involved in a communication exchange. Since CMC involves fewer non-verbal cues (such as facial expression, posture, dress, and so forth) and auditory cues in comparison to face-to-face communication, it is said to be extremely low in social presence (Hiltz, Johnson, & Turoff, 1986; Rice & Love, 1987). According to this theory, as social presence declines communication becomes more impersonal. In contrast, when more information is available about how one physically looks this leads to greater positive regard. Hence, given that there is less social presence online compared to other media (including videoconferencing) CMC is less personal and intimate.

Media richness theory

Media richness theory takes a similar stance to the previous two theories in that it focuses on what CMC lacks when compared to face-to-face interactions. This theory contends that individuals want to overcome equivocality and uncertainty in organisations and that different types of media typically used in organisations work better for certain tasks when compared to others. As explained by Daft and Lengel (1986):

> Information richness is defined as the ability of information to change understanding within a time interval. Communication transactions that can overcome different frames of reference or clarify ambiguous issues to change understanding in a timely manner are considered rich. Communications that require a long time to enable understanding or that cannot overcome different perspectives are lower in richness. (p. 560)

The types of criteria that Daft and Lengel (1986) used to define media richness include: (a) availability of instant feedback; (b) capacity of the medium to transmit multiple cues; (c) the use of 'natural language'; and (d) the personal focus of the medium. According to this theory, face-to-face communication is the richest type of media as it provides immediate feedback and utilises more channels (e.g., Trevino, Lengel, & Daft, 1987). The telephone would be less rich, followed by other types of media, such as IM and email (Hancock, Thom-Santelli, & Ritchie, 2004).

Cyberspace: A place for the lonely to hang out?

Given this view of CMC it is not so surprising that early research considered what types of negative effects the internet might have on an individual. In what has become a well-known study, Kraut and his colleagues (1998) made the claim that greater use of the Internet was associated with negative effects on an individual, such as decreases in the size of one's social circle and increases in depression and loneliness. In Kraut et al.'s longitudinal study, households who had never accessed the internet were provided with a computer, a free telephone line, and free access to the internet. During the course of the study, they tracked changes in psychological states over time. As stated above, this study found a significant relationship between heavy internet usage and loneliness. Kraut et al. argued that since initial loneliness failed to predict subsequent loneliness, the most likely explanation was that the increased use of the internet was what caused the increase in loneliness. In other words, internet usage was taking up time that could be better used for more psychologically beneficial interactions offline. Kraut et al. made the claim that *'weak ties'* were being established online which were of poorer quality compared to the types of relationships and strong ties already established offline.

Kraut et al.'s (1998) 'HomeNet Study' has been widely criticised. One of the major criticisms made was that they used only three items from the UCLA loneliness scale to measure loneliness and their Cronbach's alpha of 0.54 was clearly poor (Grohol, 1998). Morahan-Martin (1999) also points out that the sample size was too small and not randomly selected. Perhaps a more important criticism, however, is that Kraut et al.'s findings might only explain novice internet users (LaRose, Eastin, & Gregg, 2001). Moreover, as LaRose et al. (2001) have maintained, self-efficacy might be an important variable to consider. The individuals that spent more time online in Kraut et al.'s study might have been simply ineffective users of the internet and the stress in trying to work out how to use this new technology might have caused them to become more depressed (Whitty & McLaughlin, in press).

Interestingly, in the 3-year follow-up to the HomeNet study the same researchers found that almost all of the previously reported negative effects had dissipated (Kraut et al., 2002). Instead, higher levels of internet use were positively correlated with measures of social involvement and psychological well-being. Perhaps such results might be explained by LaRose et al.'s (2001) claim that it is also important to consider self-efficacy. Could it be that the participants in the HomeNet study became more internet savvy over time which, in turn, altered the way they used the internet?

A contrasting view to the one that posits the internet causes loneliness is that lonely people may have a greater desire to use the internet and can even benefit from doing so. As Morahan-Martin and Schumacher (2003) have stated:

> The Internet provides an ideal social environment for lonely people to interact with others. Not only does it provide a vastly expanded social network, but also it provides altered social interaction patterns online that may be particularly attractive to those who are lonely. (p. 662)

Others have also argued that individuals can benefit from weak ties. For example, Barry Wellman (1997) argued that although strong ties provide more social support than weak ties, weak ties are not useless. As he stated 'their very weakness means that they tend to connect people who are more socially dissimilar than those connected through strong ties. Consequently, weak ties tend to link people to other social worlds, providing new sources of information and other resources' (p. 196). In addition, Constant, Sproull, and Kiesler (1997) found that information providers on a computer network (that is, those people who volunteered information when individuals requested it) gave useful advice and solved many of the problems of information seekers. Interestingly, individuals willingly provided information even when they had no personal connection with the seekers.

Too much too soon: Boom or bust phenomena

According to some theorists, there are other negative aspects of CMC that researchers need to consider. The late Al Cooper and his colleagues considered the pace at which online relationships develop. Although these researchers have pointed out many positive aspects of online relationships and sexuality, they have stated that online relationships are vulnerable to a 'boom or bust phenomenon' (Cooper & Sportolari, 1997). The boom or bust phenomenon is where a rapid process of intimate self-disclosure leads budding relationships to become 'quite intense quite quickly'. As argued by Cooper and Sportolari (1997):

> Such an accelerated process of revelation may increase the chance that the relationship will feel exhilarating at first, and become quickly eroticized, but then not be able to be sustained because the underlying trust and true knowledge of the other are not there to support it. (p. 12)

Real relationships in cyberspace

In contrast to the negative view of online interactions, research has demonstrated that 'real' relationships can be initiated online and can move successfully offline. Parks and Floyd (1996), for instance, found in their research on newsgroups that almost two-thirds of their sample (60.7%) admitted to forming a personal relationship with someone they had met for the first time in a newsgroup. Of these, 7.9 per cent stated that this was a romantic relationship. They found that women were more likely than men to have formed a personal relationship online. It is also noteworthy that those who participated in more newsgroups were more likely to have developed personal relationships. Parks and Floyd claimed that their results challenged previous theories which take the view that genuine relationships cannot be formed online. In addition, they found that many of the relationships that began online also moved to interactions in other channels, including, for some, face-to-face.

In 1998, Parks and Roberts attempted to replicate the results yielded in the Parks and Floyd (1996) study by investigating a different space online. Instead, these researchers examined relationships initiated and developed in MOOs. They found that most of the participants they surveyed (93.6%) reported forming at least one ongoing personal relationship during their time on MOOs. A variety of kinds of relationships was identified, including close friendships (40.6%), friendships (26.3%), or romantic relationships (26.3%). Parks and Roberts (1998) remark that 'the formation of personal relationships on MOOs can be seen as the norm rather than the exception' (p. 529). Interestingly, the majority of the online relationships were with members of the opposite sex. This finding was consistent across ages and relationship status. As Parks and Roberts point out, this result is quite different to real life where same-sex friendships are far more common than cross-sex friendships. Parks and Roberts explained this result saying 'that MOOs break down the structural and normative constraints on cross-sex friendships off line' (p. 531). The structural constraints they refer to include the lack of opportunities for men and women to interact on an ongoing basis as well as the status differences that exist between men and women, especially in the workplace. These theorists conclude that 'MOOs provide users with the perception of a safe environment for social interaction in which individuals can explore all types of relationships without fear of repercussions in their physical lives' (Parks & Roberts, 1998, p. 531).

A similar space to MOOs is MUDs. Sonja Utz has examined the interactions that take place in this space. In Utz's (2000) study of MUD users, she found that 76.7 per cent of her respondents reported forming a relationship online that developed offline, of which 24.5 per cent stated this was a romantic relationship. In addition, she found that with time people do learn how to 'verbalise non-verbal cues'. The MUDders she surveyed typically utilised emoticons to denote feelings and emotions. Interestingly, Utz also found that not all those who spend a great deal of time playing MUDs necessarily formed friendships. Utz argued that this might be because not everyone playing MUDs believed that they were going to form friendships in this space, nor do all MUDders play in order to develop friendships.

In their examination of interactions in chat rooms, Whitty and Gavin (2001) also found ample evidence that individuals form friendships and romantic relationships in this space. Unlike what social presence theorists and the like would predict, the participants in this study found that the absence of traditional cues actually encouraged and enhanced online relations, especially for young men. Moreover, rather than finding evidence of less 'real' or less satisfying relationships online, some of the participants in this study reported that their relationships seemed to work better solely on the internet. As this 18-year-old women reports:

> It [the relationship] *developed through an interesting chat on IRC and a series of about 500 e-mails. The attraction was merely someone who cared and listened. He was very sensitive and caring, and his picture was hot! {laughs} . . . we exchanged addresses and he sent me presents on Valentines Day and Easter. We would write a two page e-mail every day, send sounds to each other, and eventually after six months we talked on the phone. Our phone conversation was very weak so we decided to stick to e-mail . . . We met after eight months of exchanging e-mails. He was a great guy, and it would have worked but he lived in email. It was a good experience though and he was exactly like his photo.* (Whitty & Gavin, 2001, p. 628)

Cyberspace: More radical opportunities for relationship development

Theories have been developed to explain why real and meaningful relationships can initiate online and successfully progress offline. A strong counterargument to the reduced social cues theories is the view that the lack of available online social cues offers more radical opportunities in relationship development (Lea & Spears, 1995). As Lea and Spears (1995) have stated: 'The visual anonymity of the communicators and the lack of co-presence – indeed the physical isolation – of the communicators add to the interaction possibilities, and for some this is the "magic" of on-line relationships' (p. 202). While it is acknowledged that online communication lacks many of the physical and non-verbal cues made available in face-to-face communication, most theorists would now subscribe to the view that this 'lack' does not necessarily represent an insurmountable obstacle to the development of close personal relationships. Instead, online relationships can be as intimate and personally fulfilling as any other (Lea & Spears, 1995; Parks & Floyd, 1996).

Parks and Floyd (1996) asked whether the conditions that exist offline are really necessary for the development of relationships? Just because offline is the norm does not mean that this is the only way people can go about initiating and developing healthy relationships. Lea and Spears (1995) express 'the fact that the interactants [those communicating via CMC] have not met face to face does not necessarily seem to mean that the relationships are any less "real" or significant for those involved' (p. 203). Importantly, researchers like Lea and Spears (1995) contend that we need to distinguish between what we know about the norm in forming relationships and what are the necessary requirements to forming relationships. As Lea and Spears (1995) have stated:

> it is important to draw the distinction between properties and processes that are simply the observed norm in relationships and those that are considered to be necessary prerequisites for relationships. The emergence of CMC as a pervasive communication medium that overcomes distance but denies physicality and nonverbal communication brings many of these underlying assumptions about relationship processes and definitions into focus, inviting their reappraisal. (p. 212)

Lea and Spears made the bold assertion in 1995 that 'less can mean more' (p. 218). This is quite a contrasting view to early theorists who were suggesting that reduced social cues meant relating online was less rich and fulfilling. Since this time, other researchers (such as Walther, discussed in more detail later in this chapter) have backed up this assertion with convincing empirical evidence. In the Whitty and Gavin (2001) study mentioned earlier, chat room users reported feeling less self-consciousness and less aware of being socially evaluated, which in turn allowed these individuals to reveal intimate details about themselves while maintaining distance and personal space. Ironically, many of the male participants in this study believed that by disguising their identity they could be more emotionally honest and open.

More cues than meet the eye

Looking at all of this another way, research indicates that it is too simplistic to argue that CMC is altogether devoid of social cues. Rather, text-based communication is capable of providing complex and subtle social and cultural information. For example, researchers have found that complex gender information can be transmitted via text, with certain linguistic cues distinguishing men's conversations from women's (Lea & Spears, 1995). Thomson and Murachver (2001) have found that women are more likely to make references to emotional and personal information online. Moreover, these researchers found that participants in their experimental study were able to identify the gender of the person they were communicating with online. Witmer and Katzman (1997) found that women used '*graphic accents*' (which are essentially what most people refer to as emoticons) in their online conversations more than men did. It has also been found that men's and women's messages are treated differently online. For example, Susan Herring (1993) found that men were more likely to participate on discussion boards. Moreover, men's messages were mostly much longer than women's.

Given the strong support for the notion that 'real' relationships can develop online, theories have been developed to explain how they form. Theories, such as the Social Identification/Deindividuation (SIDE) model, attempt to explain how the self is viewed online as well as how others are perceived in this space. Other theories, such as the Social Information Processing theory (SIP), developed by Joe Walther (1995), consider the pace at which online relationships are developed when compared to offline relationships. Walther, Slovacek and Tidwell (2001) have also extended upon the SIP theory to argue that some relationships developed online are 'hyperpersonal'. We now turn to consider each of these theories in detail.

SIDE model

The SIDE model was first put together by Reicher (1994), and developed further by researchers, such as Lea and Spears (see, for example, Lea & Spears, 1995; Spears, Lea, & Lee, 1990). It is critical of theories described earlier in this chapter, which claim that interpersonal interaction is necessary for social presence to occur. Unlike theories, such as the social presence theory, the SIDE model contends that visual anonymity does not necessarily lead to negative behavioural consequences.

This theory extends upon self-categorisation theory, which assumes that the self is not a fixed entity but rather is comprised of a number of self-categories. Individuals perceive themselves and other groups in terms of different characteristics. Each social identity provides information about a social group. An example of a social identity might be an identity with one's netball team, or an identity with one's gender affiliation. What is important to understand is that the salience of social categories is determined by the social context; hence, individuals are more likely to behave in accordance with the social identity of a given moment. As Rogers and Lea (2005) explain: 'from this perspective, the group exists within the individual as a cognitive representation, rather than the individual existing within the external group' (p. 153).

Spears and Lea (1992) have argued that when interacting, an absence of traditional social cues does not necessarily imply an absence of cues per sé. SIDE theory purports that information about social categories is not difficult to communicate. Rogers and Lea (2005) provide the example of headers in emails that can provide cues, such as gender or an affiliation to a particular organisation (e.g., an email address ending in ac.uk indicates that the person is from a university in the UK). When it comes to CMC, Rogers and Lea (2005) explain that:

> The virtual group will also have a purpose to their communication and this shared purpose can form the basis of a shared social identity. The salience of category cues underlying social identification is therefore, to some extent, independent of interpersonal cues that are absent from many computer-mediated environments. Rather than the group being reduced to a set of interpersonal connections between group members, the group exists within the individual as a cognitive representation. Thus, a feeling of belongingness to a group, or identification with a particular group, can occur in environments with relatively few sensory channels. (p. 153)

The SIDE theory therefore states that because online personal or 'individuating' information is limited online, at least when individuals are visually anonymous, the salience of social identity can become more important. One does not have to be physically present in order to feel part of a group. Lea, Spears, and DeGroot (2001) have found evidence to support the notion that visual anonymity increases group identification, which in turn increases attraction to the group; hence, a lack of online social presence does not mean that interactions are less rich, important, or enjoyable than face-to-face encounters. The implication of this theory is that for a group member to be motivated to work for the group, their salient identity needs to be the same as the group identity (Rogers & Lea, 2005).

One of the major criticisms of the SIDE model, as Joinson (2003) points out, is its emphasis on visual anonymity. However, while visual anonymity might have been a popular online option for people online when the theory was first developed, this is becoming far less so. For example, on IM people often choose to have a photo of themselves online, and they might also use a webcam while they type (they also often know the person offline). Online daters will typically ignore a profile without photos (see Chapter 7 for a detailed discussion of online dating). Another limitation of the theory has been pointed out by Rogers and Lea (2005):

> the SIDE approach to presence in distributed groups does not predict that social presence based upon a shared social identity will always be beneficial and desirable.... Where groups consist of members with, for example, different roles, status positions or individual goals that may conflict with the overall aim of the group, emphasis on a shared social identity may be more problematic. (p. 157)

SIP: Social information processing theory

Walther (1995) has also criticised the early theories, such as social presence theory. He criticised the methodologies employed by researchers who supported such theories. While he still subscribed to the reduced social cues view, he believed that many of these studies did not account adequately for time. He pointed out that by examining only groups online, in the short-term one misses out on how these groups evolve in reality.

Moreover, Walther (1995) argued that many of these studies ignored the non-verbal cues present in the face-to-face comparison group. Hence, while Hiltz et al. (1986) might have found that there is more disagreement online because this is obvious in the way the text is used, Walther contended that offline disagreement might be displayed more subtly through non-verbal cues (e.g., shakes of the head). Given the shortcomings of previous research, Walther and his colleagues sought to develop a more thorough understanding of the exchanges that take place in CMC. In doing so, Walther came up with the 'social information processing theory'.

The SIP 'refers to the way by which communicators process social identity and relational cues (i.e., social information) using different media' (Walther, 1995, p. 190). This theory proposes that the main difference between face-to-face communication and CMC is the pace that relationships develop in each space rather than capability to develop relationships. Walther argued that although CMC may be more aggressive at first, with time this dissipates. Walther (1992, 1995, 1996) stressed in this theory that many of the differences between online relationships and face-to-face relationships diminish over time, and although restricted bandwidth may limit the rate of information exchange, this problem can be alleviated by allowing longer and/or more frequent communication. This theory had three main assumptions:

> (a) Communicators' affiliation motives induce them to develop impressions and relations despite hindrances that alternative media may impose. (b) Users adapt their efforts to present and acquire social information using whatever cue systems a medium provides. CMC users employ language, content, and timing to achieve social goals. (c) Relational processes take time, and CMC is relatively slower than FTF.... When greater periods of time are available and as CMC participants actively seek and present social and personal information about each other, knowledge accrues, CMC partners construct impressions of each other, and their relationships develop to normal interpersonal levels. (Walther et al., 2001, p. 108)

In testing his theory out, Walther (1995) compared online and offline groups over time. Coders were trained to code both videotapes and transcripts of the interactions. They were told to consider both the content and the non-verbal behaviour displayed by individuals in the face-to-face condition. In addition, they were told to complete the relational communication questionnaire (Burgoon & Hale, 1987, cited in Walther, 1995) after observing each of the participants in a group. Much to Walther's surprise, he found that rather than increasing in relational communication over time, CMC groups were significantly higher in most relational communication over time compared to face-to-face, regardless of the time scale. In fact, the CMC groups were rated as less task-oriented and more socially oriented than face-to-face groups during all the time slots. In the light of these results, Walther (1995) concluded that 'SIP underestimates the positive effect of computer-mediation on relational communication' (p. 198). Moreover, he states that the most striking finding of the study was that 'when CMC participants are interdependent over time, they adopt more intimate and sociable relational behaviour *from the inception of interaction* and throughout' (p. 198).

Hyperpersonal communication

Walther has extended his SIP theory to develop a hyperpersonal communication framework. This theory posits that 'CMC users sometimes experience intimacy, affection, and interpersonal assessments of their partners that exceed those occurring in parallel FTF activities or alternative CMC contexts' (Walther et al., 2001, p. 109). Walther and his colleagues believe that in some situations CMC users idealise their virtual partners. This theory also stresses that CMC users may be selective in their self-presentations. While of course, individuals do tend to be strategic in their presentation of self offline, Walther and his colleagues believe that in CMC impression management is more controllable and fluid. These researchers claim that 'online communicators may exploit the capabilities of text-based, nonvisual interaction to form levels of affinity that would be unexpected in parallel offline interactions' (Walther et al., 2001, p. 110).

According to this hyperpersonal communication framework, displays of online affiliative behaviours depend on whether the individual anticipates a long-term or short-term commitment with their partner. In addition, these hyperbolic projections are altered by the presence of a photograph. These researchers found that the presence of a photograph prior to and during CMC had a positive effect on intimacy/affection and social attractiveness for short-term CMC partners. Moreover, CMC partners who met online felt less intimacy/affection and social attraction once a photograph was introduced compared to individuals with long-term CMC partners who never saw each other's picture. Ironically, the same photographs 'that help defeat impersonal conditions also dampen hyperpersonal ones' (Walther et al., 2001, p. 122).

It is also noteworthy that this result does not occur for ratings of physical attractiveness. However, these researchers did find that when there was no photograph present, physical attractiveness perceptions depended on the success of one's self-presentation, whereas, when photographs were present self-presentation was negatively related to physical attractiveness and familiarity had a positive effect on physical attractiveness. As Walther et al. (2001) have explained:

> it appears that when partners' photographs are shown, the less physically attractive they are, the more they engage in successful self-presentation, perhaps in a compensatory manner. Or, the more physically attractive partners are, the less successful they believe their impression management efforts are. (Or they are wrong about their perceived success at self-presentation, and the more successfully they believe they self-presented, the less physically attractive they were rated.) (pp. 123–124)

Walther et al. (2001), quite rightly, state that the empirical evidence elicited in their work suggests that the SIDE model does not adequately explain all online interactions. Applying the SIDE model, a photograph should reduce social attraction to the group. However, in contrast, Walther et al. (2001) found that the presence of a picture prior to and during CMC had a positive affect on social attractiveness for short-term CMC partners.

Cyberspace: A place to be more liberated

Of course, no book on cyber-relationships should omit Sherry Turkle's (1995) work. In her book, 'Life on the screen', Turkle presents a utopian view of cyberspace. Turkle studied and participated in MUDs and MOOs. Like subscribers to the SIDE model, Turkle was interested in different selves online; however, unlike the SIDE model, Turkle was more interested in the construction of personal identities. In her understanding of the players she wrote that 'As players participate they become authors not only of text but of themselves, constructing new selves through social interaction' (p. 12).

We will consider Turkle's work in more detail in Chapter 3; however, an essential point to highlight here is her view that cyberspace presents opportunities for people to experiment with multiple identities. Turkle (1995) stated that:

> I am not implying that MUDs or computer bulletin boards are causally implicated in the dramatic increase of people who exhibit symptoms of multiple personality disorder (MPD), or that people on MUDs have MPD, or that MUDing is like having MPD. What I am saying is that the many manifestations of multiplicity in our culture, including the adoption of online personae, are contributing to a general reconsideration of traditional, unitary notions of identity. (p. 260)

Turkle perceived cyberspace as a place where people can discover a deeper truth about themselves. It is, however, important to understand that although Turkle believed that people can experiment with presenting different identities online that often individuals have a connection with both their online and offline identities. She illustrated this in the following example about a young man who did not fit in at school. This young chap found that MUDs provided him with a fresh start. As Turkle (1995) described:

> Since MUDs allowed him to create a new character at any time, he could always begin with a clean slate. When he changed his character he felt born again.
>
> On MUDs, Gordon has experimented with many characters, but they all have something in common. Each has qualities that Gordon is trying to develop in himself. He describes one current character as "an avatar of me. He is like me, but more effusive, more apt to be flowery and romantic with a sort of tongue-in-cheek attitude toward the whole thing". (p. 190)

Other empirical research also suggests that some individuals might feel more liberated online. For example, Scharlott and Christ (1995) claimed that many shy individuals used an online dating site to overcome inhibitions that would have ordinarily prevented them from attempting to initiate a relationship face-to-face. Moreover, they found that shier individuals were more likely to say that Matchmaker (an online dating site) allowed them to explore new aspects of their personalities. It is, however, important to point out that online daters were visually anonymous on this site – which is not typical of today's online dating sites. As further support, Joinson (2004) found that when compared to high self-esteem individuals, low self-esteem individuals showed a greater preference for email as a mode of communication for situations, such as asking someone for a date or asking for a pay rise.

Sex in cyberspace

In addition to providing a space to create new identities, theorists have argued that cyberspace provides a place to be more sexually liberated. Turkle (1995) writes that:

> Many people who engage in netsex say that they are constantly surprised by how emotionally and physically powerful it can be. They insist that it demonstrates that truth of the adage that ninety percent of sex takes place in the mind. This is certainly not a new idea, but netsex has made it commonplace among teenage boys, a social group not usually known for its sophistication about such matters. A seventeen-year-old high school student tells me that he tries to make his erotic communications on the net "exciting and thrilling and sort of imaginative". (p. 21)

There are a range of sexual activities one can engage in online. For example, cybersex is generally understood to be synchronous communication in cyberspace where two or more individuals engage in discourses about sexual fantasies. This is typically accompanied by masturbation. In contrast, hotchatting is when two or more individuals engage in discourses which move beyond light-hearted flirting. This does not have to be in real time (synchronous). 'TinySex' is a term used by MUD players and is an online activity where one or more of the characters engage in sexual activities.

Al Cooper and his colleagues have spoken at length about the problems and joys cyberspace has to offer individuals – especially when it comes to sex. Cooper, Scherer, and Marcus (2002) have stated that 'the Internet can equally threaten or aid a healthy, sex-positive, emotionally satisfying sex life' (p. 210). Cooper (1998) developed, what he named, the '*Triple A Engine*' to explain how the internet is a potent medium for sexual activity. He pointed out that it is easy to '*access*' the internet, it is '*affordable*' and one can be '*anonymous*' online. Given these aspects of the internet, sexual activities online are available at any time, cost little, or nothing and users can maintain anonymity, allowing them safety to engage in sexual activities without people knowing their 'true' identities. Cooper and Sportolari

(1997) contended that the internet can provide a more positive arena for individuals to express themselves in relation to sex. This they stated was especially true for women. As they have stated:

> In the anonymity and safety of Net-space, women may feel free to be more directly and explicitly sexual, without fear of potential real-life consequences (e.g., pregnancy, forced sex, or STD's [*sic*]) or the need to deal with men's more powerful physical presence. (p. 11)

More self-disclosure online

Highlighted earlier in this chapter was Lea and Spears' (1995) view that sometimes 'less can mean more'. Other theorists have also taken up this idea by examining how much people are prepared to self-disclose online. Parks and Roberts (1998) have claimed that the anonymous nature of cyberspace provides a place where people can open up about aspects of themselves that they might not feel so comfortable doing face-to-face. They compared this phenomenon to Thibaut and Kelley's (1959) 'stranger-on-the-train' theory, whereby, people feel more comfortable disclosing to someone that they will probably never meet again.

Being anonymous on the internet allows individuals to be more emotionally honest and open (Whitty & Gavin, 2001). John Suler (2004a) has discussed in detail the '*disinhibition effect*'. He writes that sometimes people can reveal secret emotions, fears, or wishes or they might be extremely kind online. This he names 'benign disinhibition'. In contrast, he says that others might be extremely rude or be very angry or look at material which they might not look at otherwise, such as pornography. This he calls 'toxic disinhibition'. Adam Joinson (2001), in his empirical research, has found that individuals disclose more information about themselves online than they do face-to-face. In addition, he found that when people are visually anonymous they are more likely to disclose information about themselves than those who are not.

Other researchers have considered what aspects of the self individuals might be more likely to self-disclose online when compared to offline. For example, as discussed in detail in the next section, some theorists contend that cyberspace allows one to disclose their 'true self'.

True self versus actual self

> Logically, those individuals who are able to find similar others in traditional settings, who are able to get past the usual gating features by force of personality, attractiveness, charm, or wit, and who have the social skills needed to communicate themselves well and effectively have little need to express their true selves or 'Real Me' over the Internet. The rest of us should be glad that the Internet exists. (McKenna, Green, & Gleason, 2002, p. 12)

John Bargh, Katelyn McKenna, and their colleagues have taken the stranger-on-the-train notion one step further. McKenna et al. (2002) point out that unlike the encounter with a stranger-on-a-train, 'people often have repeated interactions with those they get to know on-line, so that early self-disclosure lays the foundation for a continuing, close relationship' (p. 10). In particular, these theorists have focused on which online presentation of self is more likely to lead to closer relationships (Bargh, McKenna, & Fitzsimons, 2002; McKenna et al., 2002). Bargh, McKenna, and colleagues have drawn from Rogers' and Higgins' work on personality to come up with two aspects of the self that they believe are important to consider when focusing on the development of relationships online, these being the '*true self*' and '*actual self*'. Although, arguably, they present too simplistic a version of Higgins' work, their research has nonetheless made an important contribution to the field.

To briefly outline Higgins' and Rogers' views of the self, Higgins (1987) made a clear distinction between three aspects of the self: the '*actual self*', '*ideal self*', and '*ought to self*'. The 'actual self' is the representation of how you or another actually believes you are; the 'ideal self' is the representation of how you or another would like to see yourself, including hopes and wishes for you; and the 'ought to self' represents the attributes that you believe you should possess. To illustrate these different selves, Higgins (1987) provided a literary example to compare the difference between the 'ideal' and the 'ought to' self, where the hero in a story has to decide between his personal wishes and his sense of duty. He also provided a real-life example of a woman who desired success in her career, but who endured conflict with the 'ought self' that others might have of her to be a housewife. Rogers (1951), in contrast, developed a humanistic personality theory where the 'self' is a central construct. Rogers' believed that the self developed through interactions with others, and that the point of therapy was to help people to discover their true selves. Theoretically, an individual can do this if they experience 'unconditional positive regard'.

Bargh et al. (2002) and McKenna et al. (2002) drew from Rogers' work (1951), to define the *true* self (or what they also refer to as the '*Real Me*') as traits or characteristics that individuals possess and would like to express, but are not usually able to demonstrate to others. In contrast, drawing from Higgins' (1987) research, they defined the *actual* self as traits or characteristics that individuals possess and express to others in social settings. In line with Higgins, these researchers claim that as one develops trust and intimacy with one's partner they are more likely to disclose aspects of themselves that are not widely known to others.

Based on previous theoretical and empirical work (mentioned earlier in this chapter) that suggests that the internet provides a safer space to disclose intimate aspects about one's self, McKenna et al. (2002) reasoned that 'we would expect people who are lonely or are socially anxious in traditional, face-to-face interaction settings to be likely to feel better able to express their true self over the Internet and so to develop close and meaningful relationships' (p. 12). These researchers have argued that individuals who are more likely to express their true self online will consider the relationships they form in this space to be more identity-important compared to those individuals who are more likely to express their true selves in non-internet relationships. As McKenna et al. (2002) have expressed:

> Those who locate their true selves on-line, as opposed to off-line, will feel that their on-line relationships develop much more quickly than do their non-Internet relationships, these relationships will be close and meaningful, and they will be motivated to move these relationships into their face-to-face lives through a series of stages. These close relationships should also be durable and stable over time. (p. 13)

To test out the above ideas, Bargh, McKenna, and their colleagues conducted a number of experiments. Bargh et al. (2002) measured true and actual selves by asking participants to list a maximum of ten traits or characteristics that participants believed they actually possessed and expressed to others in social settings as well as what characteristics individuals possessed and would like to but are typically unable to express to others. Their series of experiments revealed that the individuals' true selves were more accessible in memory after interacting with a stranger online when compared to after a face-to-face interaction. Moreover, they found that participants tended to like each other more when they meet first online compared to face-to-face.

Taking this work a step further, McKenna et al. (2002) were interested in whether individuals who are better able to disclose their 'true' selves online than offline were more equipped to form close relationships online and then take these relationships offline successfully. They randomly selected 20 Usenet newsgroups to include in their study. Over a three-week period, questionnaires were emailed to every fifth poster in each of the newsgroups (excluding spam). Their first study found that when people convey their 'true' self online they develop strong internet relationships and bring these relationships into their 'real' lives. Two years after this initial study, 354 of the 568 participants were emailed a follow-up survey (the remainder of the sample had email addresses that were no longer valid). In line with these researchers' prediction, these relationships remained relatively stable and durable over the two-year period; however, one has to wonder about the fate of 38 per cent of the sample that were not followed. In this same research, McKenna et al. (2002) found that participants who were more socially anxious and lonely were somewhat more likely to believe they could express their true selves with others online than they could with people they knew offline. McKenna et al. (2002) concluded from this research that:

> rather than turning to the Internet as a way of hiding from real life and from forming real relationships, individuals use it as a means not only of maintaining ties with existing family and friends but also of forming close and meaningful new relationships in a relatively nonthreatening environment. The Internet may also be helpful for those who have difficulty forging relationships in face-to-face situations because of shyness, social anxiety, or a lack of social skills. (p. 30)

Moving it offline successfully

Other researchers have also been interested in how relationships that are initiated online might successfully move offline. Whitty and Gavin (2001) have examined how online relationships move offline. They interviewed 60 internet users, aged between 19 and 51 years about their online relationships. In order for these relationships to successfully progress, the participants in their study stated that they needed to move through increments of trust. In this particular study, it was found that allowing someone to know your email, then your phone number, and finally your address represented increasing levels of trust in the relationship and in one's online partner. This is nicely expressed by a 21-year-old women who participated in the study:

> *I've just always wanted to* [meet him] *since we first started talking to each other, on like the first time I met him we were just talking for hours and hours, and we were like 'I've got to meet you tomorrow'. We started meeting each other all the time in chat rooms, e-mailing each other all the time, and then started calling. We were like 'Do you want my phone number?', 'I want to meet you'. I was like coming to America next year, 'Do you want me to meet you?'. He said, like 'Yeah'.* [She did go to America and they met.]

Interestingly, after having progressed through these stages, several of the participants believed that the internet eventually becomes obsolete to these relationships. As expressed by this 23-year-old man:

> *Yes, I met someone on the net... It wasn't like I sat down at my computer and told myself I was going to look for a relationship... we were in* [internet] *contact for a while, spoke to each other for a while, then decided to meet one day. We were friends for a while and eventually it led to a relationship. It went... we were together for about two months. I think once you meet then it goes beyond the internet, so it becomes just like any other relationship... you get to the point where the internet becomes obsolete.*

The sociologist Andrea Baker (2000, 2002) has also considered the progression of romantic relationships online to offline. Baker asked couples who had met in cyberspace and either met face-to-face or intended to meet offline fill out an open-ended questionnaire. She also interviewed some of these couples by phone. Most of the sample were recruited by chance face-to-face meetings with people who revealed in conversation that they had been meeting people romantically online or by individuals who came across Baker's web page and volunteered from there to tell their stories. While admittedly, the methodology employed here has its limitations, making it difficult to generalise the results, Baker's transcripts do give some interesting ideas for future researchers to investigate.

Baker (2000, 2002) has also been very interested in what makes an online relationship successful. By successful, she means what makes these relationships last. The structural and situational factors she considered included where couples met, the obstacles involved, the timing, and how conflict is resolved. Importantly, Baker does not treat the internet as one generic space. Rather she purports that it is important to consider where individuals meet online. While research is yet to confirm her hunches, she believes, that meeting in a place online where people have similar interests is more likely to lead to a successful relationship. She provides the example of successful relationship of a couple who met in a Law Enforcement newsgroup compared with an unsuccessful relationship where the couple met in a more general newsgroup.

In this book, we also contend that the nature of the spaces online is important to consider when it comes to relationship formation. We extend Baker's notions by also considering the opportunities to play in different spaces online. Even when couples might find themselves attracted to one another online 'love does not necessarily always find a way'. Baker believes that there are critical obstacles to overcome if the relationship is to move offline. The obstacles she has highlighted include: how far an individual might have to move to be with their online love (including issues of moving children), whether it is financially possible (e.g., do they have enough money to move, are they skilled/educated enough to find work in another country), and whether one (if already in a relationship) is prepared to leave their relationship to be with their online love. Baker also believes that the length of online contact, prior to meeting face-to-face, can determine whether a relationship will be successful or not. Again, while more rigorous research needs to be conducted to confirm this view, Baker believes that couples who spend more time online in the absence of photographs or cybersex are more likely to develop a successful relationship online. In our book, we contend that this also depends on the spaces within which individuals are interacting. Moreover, we believe that even if people are not engaging in cybersex or exchanging photos we cannot disregard the importance of the body or physical attraction. Finally, as psychologists have found in their research on offline relationships, it perhaps comes as no surprise that Baker notes that good communication is an important determinant for a successful relationship first initiated online. Baker also notes that her transcripts suggest that conflict can arise much sooner online than offline and the ways people deal with this conflict also determine whether the relationship will be successful.

Keeping up with the times

The theories presented in this chapter are certainly not the beginning or end of the story. This book goes into more depth about how relationships are initiated and maintained online, and taken offline. We would still like to point out here that given the changing nature of the internet, theories on online relationships will no doubt change as time goes on. For example, many of the theories presented in this chapter assume that individuals are visually anonymous online. This, of course, is gradually changing. Individuals typically present a picture of themselves whilst interacting via IM and online dating sites. Hence, theories, such as the SIDE model, will lose their relevance over time. In fact, we believe that even when the physical body is not present, how we present the physical self online is still important for researchers to consider – as discussed in detail in the following chapter.

Developing a theory towards explaining cyber-relating

The work to date on cyber-relationships has made some ground in explaining how and why relationships develop online and sometimes progress offline. However, it is our view that these theories do not tell the whole story. In this book we argue that the cyber-world is both similar and different to the offline world. Unlike some other theorists, we make the claim that cyberspace should not be perceived as a conglomeration of bodiless selves. We believe that how the physical self is reconstructed and the choices individuals make in presentations of self should be of interest to social scientists. We make the argument that cyberspace can be a more playful space. This can be liberating for those anxious about forming relationships offline. However, the freedom of cyberspace can be problematic for some – especially when they venture too far into the realms of fantasy.

In the following chapter the point is made that it is important for researchers to consider the choices individuals make in constructing their online self. We move on to develop our theory further by drawing from object-relations theory. We argue that cyberspace shares the same qualities as Winnincott's notion of 'potential space'. In Chapter 3 we make the argument that like 'potential space', cyberspace provides a safer space than the offline world to play and experiment at flirting and developing relationships. Chapter 4 extends this argument by considering 'transitional objects'. In particular, we draw from Bollas' work that considers the relationships we have with objects and the trace they leave within us. Like other theorists, we believe that cyberspace can be a liberating space, however, in Chapters 5 and 6 we make the point that one's playful activities in this space are not always liberating. In these chapters we examine internet infidelity, internet addiction, paedophilia, cyber-harassment, cyberstalking, and misrepresentation of self online. Although we do believe that the online world and the offline world are not completely separate from one another, in Chapter 5 we draw from Klein's object-relations theory to argue that individuals sometimes split the cyber-world from the offline world. As mentioned earlier in this chapter, this book emphasises that the cyber-world is not one generic space. Chapter 7 illustrates this nicely by highlighting that the way individuals develop relationships through an online dating site is considerably different to the way relationships are developed within other spaces. In this chapter we draw from work on 'possible selves' to make the argument that individuals might feel more comfortable presenting different aspects of themselves in different spaces online. Chapter 8 considers theories on personality in more detail, including what character types tend to be attracted to cyberspace. Chapter 9 looks at our visions for the future of cyber-relationships and how individuals might conduct sexual relations online. This chapter also examines how cyberspace might be used to conduct counselling. Finally, we consider some of the ethical issues that arise when studying online relationships.

CHAPTER 2

From Courtly Love to Cyber-Flirting

The distinctiveness of the flirt lies in the fact that she awakens delight and desire by means of unique antithesis and synthesis: through the alternation or simultaneity of accommodation and denial.

(Simmel, 1984, p. 134)

In the previous chapter we summarised to date how cyber-relationships have been considered in the literature. We concluded the chapter by suggesting ways forward in theorising about online interactions. In this chapter we further develop our theory by placing cyber-dating within an historical context. We begin this chapter by taking a step backwards giving a brief history of the courting process. We consider the ways in which individuals have previously managed to meet romantic partners, got to know each other, who controlled the dating process, and what qualities individuals sought out in a partner.

Comparing online dating with previous forms of courtship helps elucidate how this new form of dating has evolved. This history helps to highlight the uniqueness of cyber-dating, but in turn demonstrates that the process of initiating relationships online can be very similar to the way we initiate relationships offline. We revisit old theories on cyber-relationships and argue that, rather than focusing on a 'body less' self online, new theories must focus on how the body is presented in cyberspace – even if it is not one's 'actual' body. In particular, we focus here on cyber-flirting and make the claim that, in spite of the lack of traditional non-verbal cues, individuals online find ways to reconstruct the body in order to successfully cyber-flirt. Rather than believing that it is merely

30

'personality that wins out' online, we argue that, as with offline attraction, physical attributes can also play a key role in attraction.

Vacillating from the home to the outside world

'Courtship takes many forms, depending mainly on the point in history and the culture in which it exists' (Cate & Lloyd, 1992, p. 13). We also acknowledge that different cultures go about the courting process differently, and in this book, we focus mostly on a Western perspective. However, even if we are to consider only Western culture (and it should be noted that much that has been documented has pertained to white middle-class individuals) we find that the history of how individuals have initiated romantic relationships and the spaces in which they have courted have changed over time – and we believe they continue to change.

In early 19th century Europe, marriages were arranged with little emphasis on romantic attraction (Murstein, 1974; Rice, 1996). As Rice explains: 'arranged marriages sought to merge the property and good name of the families to ensure economic well-being and the perpetuation of family status and prestige' (p. 96). Cate and Lloyd (1992) and Murstein (1974) have explained that at the same time in America, due to social (e.g., the need to populate) and economic conditions (e.g., women could not afford not to work), young people had more autonomy in their choice of a partner. The choice of a partner was based more on reason than love or affection. For instance, it was important for the man to demonstrate that he could financially support his wife and family, that the couple was of similar social standing, and that the families approved of the choice in partner. Individuals met in social settings, such as church, and parents would give the young couple privacy. Cate and Lloyd (1992) tell us that during this time some individuals engaged in the colonial practice of bundling. As Cate and Lloyd (1992) describe:

> Bundling consisted of a young woman inviting a suitor to go to bed with her, fully clothed, in some cases with a board placed between their bodies (Murstein, 1974; Stiles, 1871). Bundling was a privilege of the woman to bestow upon a favorite suitor (Rothman, 1984) and in situations where there was little room for privacy of the couple, bundling served as a time for the young people to get

to know one another (Murstein, 1974). Bundling obviously must have taken place with the sanction of the young women's parents. (p. 15)

In the mid-19th century, men's and women's social roles in America had changed. Women were back in the home and her domesticity was prized (Cate & Lloyd, 1992). Women were seen as the more virtuous sex, supposed to be able to tame the bestial nature of men (Coontz, 1988; Murstein, 1974). As a consequence of these social changes, courtship became more formalised. Cate and Lloyd (1992) state that it was at this time that the formal wedding ceremony emerged, together with the white wedding dress to symbolise the purity of the bride. This was also a time when romantic love began to flourish. As Cate and Lloyd (1992) describe:

> Romantic love contained elements of passion as well as mutuality, communion, sympathy, and candor (Coontz, 1988; Rothman, 1984); romantic love was very emotionally intimate and at the same time mysterious and unexplainable (Lystra, 1989). Romantic love centered around the concept of the "ideal self" (Lystra, 1989). The true inner person was to be revealed through extensive self disclosure and honesty with the loved one; thus romantic love embodied total self revelation and open communication. (p. 18)

Towards the end of the 19th century and the beginning of the 20th century courtship in America became increasingly more formalised. Courtship now began in the home. As Cate and Lloyd (1992) describe:

> A young man and young woman had to be formally introduced before they were allowed to speak to one another (Waller, 1951). After such an introduction, the young women's mother would ask the young man to call upon her daughter; later on the young lady could do the asking (Bailey, 1988). (pp. 20–21)

Koller (1951) studied the courting behaviours of three generations of Ohio women. He found that women from this time said that dating in the home, or what were known as parlour dates, gave women 'an opportunity to display their culinary and homemaking abilities before their potential mates...' (p. 368). Moreover, Koller (1951) points out that men have not always been the financers of dates and instead during these times the women took care of the financing of dates. Of further interest is the elaborate system of etiquette which was developed to signal to the young man whether or not he was welcome to call again (Cate & Lloyd, 1992).

In the early 20th century, courtship moved again to outside the home. This time the surveillance of the couple was mostly informal through community control (Cate & Lloyd, 1992; Koller, 1951). However, towards the mid-20th century, dating became more informal and the rules of dating were established by the peer group more than the community at large (Cate & Lloyd, 1992). Mongeau, Hale, Johnson, and Hillis (1993) have pointed out that, with this change in how individuals developed their relationships, there was a change to who traditionally made the first move. They contended that, since the turn of the 20th century, men began to initiate the courtship, generally because they had to pay for the date and arrange transportation. These theorists argued that this altered who was in control of the courting process. As Cate and Lloyd (1992) have explained:

> When courtship was centered in the home, the woman was more in control, but as courtship shifted to the public sphere and the need for money arose, control also shifted to the man. (p. 23)

Cate and Lloyd (1992) made the claim that, at this time in history, courting was more about competition than love.

From the mid-20th century to the 1960s, love was still the main reason for marriage (Cate & Lloyd, 1992). However, in this post-war era women moved back to the home, and according to Cate and Lloyd (1992) became more passive in the courting process. Of course the sexual revolution in the 1960s again changed courting for both men and women. Moreover, the end goal was not necessarily marriage, and cohabitation began to become a popular choice. Concern over HIV arose in the 1980s and consequently monogamous sexual relationships were once again more valued. In this new millennium, however, there have been further changes in the way we date, which is of course the focus of this book.

Romantic love in the postmodern era: How different is it?

The above brief history is important to the discussion in this book as it demonstrates how throughout time we have changed our practices and even the settings in which we initiate romantic relationships. Who watches over the interaction, decides where and when the first meeting should take place and whether or not the courting should continue have all altered. The motivation for the match has also varied: sometimes it was the result of 'romantic love', while at other times it was more rationally based. Moreover, once a relationship was established, how and what pace it developed and whether or not it would result in marriage have all also varied throughout time. Bearing in mind that these were all face-to-face interactions, how do they compare with how we initiate relationships in cyberspace?

Initiating the relationship at home might seem old fashioned but as the above history of American dating shows, this was how courtship was initiated in the mid-19th century. Nonetheless, we are now moving back into the home (as well as cafes and offices) to initiate romantic relationships, and so considering the history of courtship the home is not a unique place to initiate relationships. However, what is considerably different is how we now go about it and our motivations for doing so.

Historically then, couples have had their courting activities monitored. Moreover, who had the final say about what was an appropriate match has varied over time. O'Hara (2000) nicely illustrates this in her summary of courtship in Tudor England:

> The marriages of very few individuals, no matter how humble, could escape some or all of the compromises and impediments put in place. This was partly due to the marriage itself. The kinds of restructuring which a marriage entailed affected not only the couple, but a range of people in varying degrees. As a result marriage formation was also influenced by collective values and was an activity which implicated various, sometimes conflicting, interests. Family, friends, neighbours and the wider community of parish or town had vital interests in local marriages . . . Individuals hoping to marry were expected to undergo an increasingly public series of examinations and meetings. Many of these sometimes ritualised and formal gatherings drew on kin and neighbours to perform particular functions. (pp. 30–31)

Such concerns over who has a stake in the match are not so important in current times. Parents are more concerned that their children find someone that makes them happy, although, of course, concerns about social class are an issue for some. We also have a greater range of places to initiate romantic relationships. Some of these places include traditional places, such as the church and dances. Other places include the pub and places of work as well as cyberspace.

Potentially, cyberspace can provide a more private space for individuals' dating activities, which are likely to be less monitored than more traditional spaces. Nonetheless, it is interesting that some individuals have a desire to include others in this dating process. Moreover, others have family and friends who want to be involved in their online dating experiences. For example, in Monica Whitty's study, some of the participants interviewed from an Australian online dating site purported that they included their family and friends in this online dating process. Some asked their family (including their own children) for advice on how to present themselves online, while others also asked for advice on appropriate candidates for their affection. As an interesting twist, some of the younger family members decided they needed to assist some of the older family members with finding a date. This is nicely highlighted by a 44-year-old woman when she explained how she finished up having a profile on an online dating site:

A   *My 16 yr old niece did it for me, I needed a little help from my friends as I wasn't doing anything myself.*

I   *So, did she help you set up your profile?*

A   *She did it herself.*

I   *Did she tell you first?*

A   *No.*

I   *So how did that make you feel?*

A   *I know my niece and I know what to expect, she reminds me of myself when I was that age. I know her so I know what she is capable of doing.*

I   *So, it doesn't surprise you?*

A   *No it doesn't surprise me in the least.*

  (Alison)

In the history of courtship that we provided earlier in this chapter, we summarised various theorists' claims about which gender made the first move. It could be argued that as a consequence of the women's movement, women now have more power and control in the courting process than ever before. However, as also mentioned earlier in this chapter, some theorists, such as Cate and Lloyd (1992) and Mongeau et al. (1993), have made the claim that once courtship moved out of the home, the power shifted back to the male. They tell us that men again were the initiators of a romantic relationship. We believe that such theorists have missed an important step – that of flirtation (Whitty, 2003a). Therefore, women might have more control over the courting process in this postmodern era; however, if we pay close attention to the non-verbal cues (as researchers, such as Moore, 1985, do) then it is plausible to argue that women have had more control in the early phases of the courting process in the past (Whitty, 2003a). Perhaps more control than some of the aforementioned writers have acknowledged.

Eibl-Eibesfeldt (1971) is one of the first researchers credited with observing and documenting flirtatious behaviour. In a clever, but perhaps unethical manner, he devised a special camera that was fitted with right angle lenses, so that he could point the camera in one direction and actually photograph couples, without their knowledge, facing another direction. From his observations he noticed that an eyebrow flash combined with a smile were common behaviours elicited during courtship. Eibl-Eibesfeldt believed that these gestures represented primal behaviours. He also stated that these behaviours appeared to be childlike poses.

Following from his work, other researchers have been interested in observing and documenting the steps involved in the courtship process. Givens (1978), for instance, developed a five-stage model which highlights some of the important non-verbal and paralinguistic cues involved in flirting behaviour (the first three stages relate more to flirting). According to Givens, the first stage is the *attention phase*, where one typically uses primping, object caressing, and quick glances. Givens (1978) has provided us with a hypothetical scenario to illustrate this phase:

> Suppose that a woman, alone at a cafeteria table, is joined by a strange man who takes the seat diagonally across from her. They may acknowledge one another and nod civilly, then quickly break contact and begin to eat lunch privately as noninteracting individuals. Although the imagined women reads as she eats and does not glance at him, the man may find that he is attracted by certain attention-soliciting features. Her long hair, the colourful soft and fitted clothing. (p. 349)

Drawing from Crook's (1972) work, Givens argued that men are typically hesitant to approach a woman without some apparent interest from her.

In the second phase, the *recognition phase*, he stated that flirting behaviour consists of head cocking, pouting, primping, using eyebrow flashes, and smiling. Givens suggested that *interaction* does not occur until the third stage (the interaction stage), where conversation is initiated. During this stage, participants appear highly animated, displaying laughing or giggling. The fourth stage is the *sexual-arousal phase*, which is followed by the *resolution phase*.

Returning to the question of who makes the first move when courting – while theorists have documented a history of men making the first move, others would contend that women initiate romantic relationships through the flirt. For example, Perper (1985), like Givens (1978), believed that courtship goes through a series of stages; however, he makes the point that women were responsible for courtship initiation approximately 70 per cent of the time. He concluded this after observing unsuspecting men and women in singles' bars. Through a series of laboratory experiments, Grammer (1990) and his colleagues (Grammer, Kruck, Juette, & Fink, 2000) have also concluded that 'based on direct observation of behaviour in encounters of opposite-sexed strangers, that women initiate and "control" the outcome' (Grammer et al., 2000, p. 371). Monica Moore (1998) also emphatically believes that women are the active participants when it comes to the initiation of relationships, as she has described:

> Through the use of these nonverbal behaviors women can pace the course of courtship and have the prerogative to accept or decline proposals. By exhibiting or withholding displays, women are able to determine when and where they wish to survey mate potential. They can elicit a high number of male approaches, allowing them to choose from a number of available men. Or they may direct signals to a particular man. In this fashion, nonverbal behaviors functioning as attractants and advertisers of female interest give women some measure of control in choosing men for relationships. (p. 202)

As demonstrated above, there are a number of critical phases that preface the initiation of romantic relationships. The phases are quite subtle in nature – mostly because initial attraction is communicated via non-verbal cues. So, given the lack of opportunity for non-verbal cues online, how does one cyber-flirt? This chapter now considers what role the body has in online flirtatious behaviour.

Offline signals: The crucial place of non-verbal signals

There are a variety of reasons why people flirt. Downey and Vitulli (1987) have argued that flirtation can be defined in two ways:

> One implies an existing casual relationship where one or both persons are engaged in maintaining some suggestion or expectation of intimacy without intentions of increasing its level or allowing some type of "consummation" ... but another common meaning seems to refer simply to the initial actions one takes to convey a message of interest or attraction. (p. 899)

Feinberg (1996) has contended that flirting involves teasing and communication. She proposed that flirting is a short cut to intimacy. Feinberg (1996) stated that 'flirting transmits a hidden message the same as other types of teasing. The underlying communication is to find out how intimate a person wants to become or if she wants to become intimate at all' (p. 40).

Although evolutionary psychologists purport that flirting is a universal basic instinct necessary for the procreation of the species, there appear to be other motivations for flirting. It has been suggested that there are three main reasons for why people flirt: (1) to signal sexual interest; (2) to test the grounds to see if others still find them attractive; and/or (3) to simply pass the time of day (Feinberg, 1996). Similar to the above theorists, Aaron Ben-Ze'ev (2004) has defined flirting as:

> Flirting is not necessarily a prelude to sexual interaction; it is rather a subtle, sexual communication. Flirting may involve gentle physical contact, but often it does not involve sexual intercourse. Flirting may develop into sexual relationships, but then it stops being flirting in the sense described above. ... In flirting, we do not force ourselves on others; it is a kind of enjoyable play having the pleasant atmosphere that is typical of the promise of sexual activity. Flirting also involves the mystery and uncertainty associated with sex. (pp. 150–151)

In our view, an important point stressed by Ben-Ze'ev is that although flirting can eventuate into sexual relationships, if it does it ceases to be flirting.

As already highlighted in some of the work summarised in this chapter, flirting behaviour is, in the main, non-verbal behaviour. The lack of verbal cues evident in offline flirtatious behaviour is not so surprising given that verbally conveying feelings about sexual interest involves a high risk of embarrassment or possible rejection. Unlike the spoken word, body language can signal attraction without being too obvious. The non-verbal signals used in flirtation are typically ambiguous. This ambiguity protects people from humiliation or overt rejection if the person they are signalling attraction to does not share these sentiments.

In the offline world, individuals have a range of non-verbal gestures to choose from (even if this selection is not conscious) to convey feelings of sexual interest. As already summarised, some researchers have attempted to categorise these behaviours. One such researcher, Monica Moore (1985), provided an extensive list of behaviours from her covert observations of over 200 randomly selected adult female subjects in a singles bar. In her study, she identified 52 flirtatious facial expression and gestures displayed by these women. She followed her initial study up with another to validate her catalogue by observing another 40 randomly selected women in four spaces: a singles bar, a university snack bar, a university library, and a university Women's Centre. In the second study, she found that women, in what she called 'mate relevant' contexts, 'exhibited higher average frequencies of nonverbal displays directed at males. Additionally, women who signalled often were also those who were most often approached by a man; and this relationship was not context specific' (Moore, 1985, p. 237).

Some basic codes that are important to consider in flirting that emerged from Moore's (1985) research, together with other studies (e.g., Eibl-Eibesfeldt, 1971; Grammer, 1990; Grammer et al., 2000; Kendon, 1975), include kinetics, oculesics, physical appearance, olfactics, vocalics, proxemics, and haptics. Much of this research reveals that flirting usually consists of a combination of these basic codes. It is instructive to consider these codes a little further.

Kinetic gestures include phenomena such as tossing one's head so that an individual's face is titled upwards and the neck is exposed. Women often lick their lips, or pout to indicate attraction. To mirror another's body movements is often a sign of attraction. Smiling, laughing, and giggling can also signal attraction.

Oculesics, or eye movements, can reveal a great deal about a person's feelings. A person's pupils will dilate if they are attracted to another. Flirtatious behaviour often consists of demure glances downward, a short darting glance (glancing at a person one is attracted to for a few seconds, glancing away, then looking back again), and eyebrow flashes (the raising of both eyebrows for a couple of seconds, usually accompanied by a smile and eye contact).

Given that researchers have mostly agreed that first impressions leave a lasting impression (e.g., Asch, 1946; Dion, Bercheid, & Walster, 1972), it is no surprise that people take more care of their physical appearance when they hope to attract another. In Dion et al.'s (1972) classic study it was revealed that participants judged photographs of more attractive people as people who would be happier, make happier mates, and have higher status occupations than less attractive people.

In addition to looking good, individuals make attempts to smell good. However, store-bought perfume is more decorative than a love potion. Despite what the perfume and deodorant companies would have us believe, men prefer women with a light amount of perfume. Interestingly, women are attracted to men whose MHC (major histocompatibility complex – a segment of the DNA that we can smell, which determines what diseases individuals are inherently resistant to) is more varied from their own (Wedekind, Seebeck, Bettens, & Paepke, 1995).

The use of voice is a most telling indicator of the type of interaction that is taking place. Flirtatious speech is more animated with moderate amounts of laughter, decreased silences and pauses, with increased warmth and interest. Researchers have examined what types of voices men and women find to be more attractive (e.g., Collins & Missing, 2003; Zuckerman & Miyake, 1993). Collins and Missing (2003) found that most men believed that women with attractive faces also had attractive voices. Moreover, higher-frequency voices were attributed to belonging to younger women and were perceived to be more attractive. Anolli and Ciceri (2002) found that the male seductive voice is 'characterized by strong variations during the course of the seductive sequence' (p. 149). They found that when a man begins to seduce a woman his speech is usually at a higher pitch and an elevated intensity as well as a faster rate of articulation than normal speech; this they named the 'exhibition voice'. Following from this phase is the 'self-disclosure voice' which is when the voice gradually becomes lower, weaker, and warmer.

Proxemics is the amount of personal distance kept between individuals. Individuals who lean towards one another and who are at the same body angle are perceived as being more seductive than those individuals who lean away from each other. Flirtatious behaviour is further characterised by crossing legs towards one another and more face-to-face interaction.

Haptics, or the use of touch, is a common form of communication, particularly in flirtatious behaviour. Another sign of seductive behaviour is the use of clothing adjustment, for example playing with buttons, jewellery, a tie, or smoothing out one's skirt even when it does not require adjustment. Yet another indicator of attraction is called 'object caress', where individuals fondle with their keys or perhaps their wine glasses.

Sometimes a smile is just a smile

It is important to understand that offline, when individuals flirt they use a gamut of these behaviours. Hence, to toss one's hair is not necessarily meant as a flirting gesture. Freud is credited with once saying 'Sometimes a cigar is just a cigar'; likewise, when it comes to flirtation, *sometimes a smile is just a smile*. In other words, it is important to consider the repertoire of these behaviours in deciding if someone is indeed attempting to grab your attention. Moreover, as the above authors point out, one needs to be a skilled displayer of these gestures as well as a skilled interpreter of others' gestures.

Conceptualising cyberspace

> Case was twenty-four. At twenty-two, he'd been a cowboy, a rustler, one of the best in the sprawl... He'd operated on an almost permanent adrenaline high, a byproduct of youth and proficiency, jacked into a custom cyberspace deck that projected his disembodied consciousness in the consensual hallucination that was the matrix. (Gibson, 1986, pp. 11–12)

Before moving on to examine how people might flirt online, we need to consider what cyberspace actually is. The science fiction writer William Gibson is credited with coining the phrase 'cyberspace'. When Gibson wrote his book *Neuromancer*, he had little knowledge of computers or how interactions might actually occur in cyberspace. Nevertheless, his fictional writing has had some influence on our non-fictional perceptions about interactions over the internet. Gibson's fictional world of cyberspace is a place to play. For Gibson, cyberspace offers an ultimately liberating experience. In *Neuromancer*, the main character Case becomes addicted to cyberspace. Virtual reality (VR) is a space where one's dreams can be satisfied. In this space, one can excogitate new identities. The fictional characters of *Neuromancer* experience cyberspace as a place of rapture and erotic intensity. Within Gibson's matrix, entities attain a 'hyper-reality'. In comparison, ordinary experience appears dull and mundane. In his writings, Gibson (1986) also highlighted the erotic appeal of cyberspace:

> Now she straddled him again, took his hand, and closed it over her, his thumb along the cleft of her buttocks, his fingers spread across the labia. As she began to lower herself, the images came pulsing back, the faces, fragments of neon arriving and receding. She slid down around him and his back arched convulsively. (p. 45)

It is generally understood that cyberspace is the space generated by software within a computer that produces a VR. Although this is the commonly held definition, an alternative view is that cyberspace existed before the origins of the internet, via the space produced in telephone calls (Standage, 1987). Standage claimed that the equipment might be different but the impact that the telegraph had on people's lives is very similar. Standage (1987) described the telegraph in the following extract:

> During Queen Victoria's reign, a new communications technology was developed and allowed people to communicate almost instantly across distances, in effect shrinking the world faster and further than ever before. A worldwide communications network whose cables spanned continents and oceans, it revolutionized business practice, gave rise to new forms of crime, and inundated its users with a deluge of information. Romances blossomed over the wires. Secret codes were devised by some users and cracked by others. The benefits of the network were relentlessly hyped by its advocates and dismissed by the sceptics. Governments and regulators tried and failed to control the new medium. Attitudes toward everything from news gathering to diplomacy had to be completely rethought. Meanwhile, out on the wires, a technological subculture with its own customs and vocabulary was establishing itself. (pp. vii–viii)

Standage (1987) has made some important comparisons between the internet and the telegraph in his book *The Victorian Internet*. With respect to relationships, he pointed out that within a few months of being opened the telegraph was being used to conduct an 'online wedding'. As the story goes:

> The daughter of a wealthy Boston merchant had fallen in love with Mr. B., a clerk in her father's counting house. Although her father had promised her hand to someone else, she decided to disregard his intentions and marry Mr. B. instead. When her father found out, he put the young man on a ship and sent him away on business to England.
>
> The ship made a stopover in New York, where the young woman sent her intended a message, asking him to present himself at the telegraph office with a magistrate at an agreed-upon time. At the appointed hours she was at the other end of the wire in the Boston telegraph office, and, with the telegraph operators relaying their words to and fro in Morse code, the two were duly wed by the magistrate. (p. 128)

While Standage's work is helpful in conceptualising cyberspace, there are some important differences between the internet and the telegraph – for example, the accessibility and the range of ways individuals use the internet not just to communicate, but for a host of other activities, such as using the web as a resource tool and a means of entertainment.

Some researchers have placed great emphasis on cyberspace being a space where disembodied communication can take place. For example, Argyle and Shields (1996) contended that 'technology is often viewed as source of separation between people, a barrier' (p. 58). Clark (1997) proposed that in 'the virtual environment, we can exist in either a disembodied or a cyberspatial form' (p. 86). Stratton (1997) too contends that 'we might, then, define cyberspace simply as the space produced by human communication when it is mediated by technology in such a way that the body is absent' (p. 29). Levine (2000) has written that 'the beauty of the virtual medium is that flirting is based on words, charm, and seduction, not physical attraction and cues' (p. 565). Rollman, Krug, and Parente's (2000) comment that 'by eliminating time, distance, and body, the architects of the Internet have created an unhindered medium that connects the mind and spirit' (p. 161). In each of the examples, the importance of the presence of the person's body is downplayed.

When theorists discuss relationships developed in cyberspace they also often focus their writings on the absence of the body. In their discussions of cybersex, theorists often emphasise the idea that participants can engage in virtual sex without the *real presence* of bodies. In respect to internet romantic relationships one writer has commented that 'some Internet lovers come to the conclusion that they love each other before they even meet or without ever meeting. . .' (Gwinnell, 1998, p. 89). The implication here is that bodies can only meet offline. To give a further example, McRae (1996) has defined cybersex or virtual sex as 'a generic term for erotic interaction between individuals whose bodies may never touch. . .' (p. 243). Again, this writer is focusing on the lack of the body online.

McKenna et al.'s (2002) work, mentioned in Chapter 1, also emphasises the utility of the absence of the body online. As summarised earlier, they focus on which online presentation of self leads to the development of a successful relationship offline. These theorists concluded from their research that the absence of gating features and the ability to self-disclose more in an anonymous environment are important reasons why relationships on the internet develop quickly and are often close and intimate.

As we have argued in our earlier work, this view of cyberspace as being a place where there is no physical body is a very narrow construction of how we should conceive of cyberspace and the activity that occurs in this space (Whitty, 2003a; Whitty & Carr, 2003). In contrast to this very restricted view, which is somewhat of a metaphysical interpretation, we believe that in considering cyber-flirting, it is in fact the reconstruction of the body that is imperative to the success of many interpersonal interactions over the internet.

For example, Stone (1995) has discussed the importance of the body in telephone sex. Stone has pointed out that telephone sex is clearly a different kind of sex to physical or 'embodied' sex. Physical sex involves a range of senses, touch, sight, sound, smell, and hearing. In contrast, telephone sex workers are required to translate the physical experience of sex into an audible form. In turn, the receiver at the other end of the line needs to reconstitute these images. As Stone (1995) describes, 'what's being sent back and forth over the wires isn't merely information, it's bodies – not physical objects, but the information necessary to reconstruct the meaning of body to almost any desired depth and complexity' (p. 244).

In respect to cyberspace, while it cannot be denied that the physical body is not present in the textual exchanges, how the real physical body is reconstructed should be of interest to researchers as well as users of the internet. For although we do not have physical, tangible bodies in cyberspace, we do nonetheless have bodies represented in our online interactions. If one were to peruse the textual exchanges on bulletin boards, discussion boards, chat rooms, or IM, they would find ample evidence of reconstructed bodies in this cyberspace. For instance, people describe what their bodies look like and feel like. Moreover, individuals have the option of selecting photographs or video to represent their physical self – even if this is not always photos of their actual bodies. It is also interesting that although webcams are considerably cheap that these are still not a popular choice. Given the ways the body is reconstructed through text and the use of photos and video as well as avatars online, we make the argument here that although physical bodies are not physically present in cyberspace, the body still does matter.

Cyber-flirting: New rules

Although we have and will continue to argue in this book that online relationships are unique in many ways, we have previously identified some links with cyber-flirting and courtly love – which was conducted in medieval times (Whitty & Carr, 2003). In courtly love:

> the male lover presents himself as engrossed in a yearning desire for the love of an exceedingly beautiful and perfect woman whose strange emotional aloofness and high social status make her appear hopelessly distant. But the frustrated and sorrowful lover cannot overcome his fascination and renders faithful "love service" to this "high-minded" and exacting lady who reciprocates in a surprising manner: She does not grant him the amorous "reward" which he craves, but she gives him what immeasurably increases his "worth": She rewards him with approval and reassurance. (Moller, 1959, p. 137)

Courtly love is said to have its origins in the 12th century and was a luxury of the aristocrats (Askew, 1965). Andreas Capellanus (1969) in his book *The art of courtly love* attempted to systematically record the rules of courtly love. He described these relationships as idealised relationships that could not exist within the context of a *real life* marriage. Courtly lovers apparently spent a great deal of time talking to each other, mostly about the nature of love. The courtly lovers could not physically act out their passions, and if made public this love rarely endured. Finding it to be extremely oppressive to women, it may be of little surprise that feminist theorists are completely 'opposed' to courtly love (Baruch, 1991). Nonetheless, there are some similar aspects between courtly love and cyber-flirting that ought to be highlighted. For instance, cyber-flirting is unlike a real life marriage while it remains solely online. Conversations about love can abound online, but in a real physical sense cannot be consummated. Online relationships can also seem hopelessly distant, as with courtly love. Moreover, as we discuss in more detail in Chapter 5, it is possibly easier to idealise someone in cyberspace.

There are some more unique aspects of cyber-relationships that we would also like to consider. Some researchers have suggested that one of the distinctive aspects of online relationships is the greater value placed on conversations: not only how captivated individuals are in the conversation but also how well individuals write. For instance, Levine (2000) found that many individuals place great importance on others' spelling and grammar in their online interactions. Drawing again from the interviews carried out in Whitty's study (discussed in detail in Chapter 7) with the participants using an Australian online dating site, many of the individuals stated that they were attracted to someone who used correct spelling and grammar. As illustrated in the following quotes:

> [I'm looking for] *somebody who demonstrates a fairly high level of intelligence, who demonstrates that they've thought a bit about their profile and I can tell that I have something in common with them. No spelling mistakes, all of that turns me off immediately.* (Paul)

> [I'm looking for someone with] *a steady job for a start and I think you can also get a handle, I mean voices you cannot tell, you cannot tell what a person looks like from their voice and although I didn't do a voice thing, even the way the people when they typed to you, if there was a lot of spelling errors and all that well then I don't think that I would be attracted.* (Margaret)

However, we believe that there is much more going online than a simple '*meeting of minds*'. While we agree that online flirtation is a unique interaction and needs to be considered separately to offline flirtation, we nonetheless wish to point out that the body still plays an important role in these interactions. If one is to subscribe to our view that the body plays an important role online, the obvious question then arises as to how might the body translate to online flirting? How might we conceptualise cyber-flirting? If we are to just consider *textual exchanges* online for the moment, we need to acknowledge that none of the traditional offline flirting signals described earlier in this chapter are physically present. Obviously, the non-verbal cues presented above to define offline flirting are typically not physically present, as there is not a physically present body to convey these signals. However, this does not mean that these cues do not exist. We believe that for flirting to occur in cyberspace the body needs to be translated in some way – even if one only has (or chooses only to have) text available to interact through. In fact, we would go as far to say that the reconstruction of the body is imperative to the success of many interpersonal interactions over the internet (Whitty, 2003a; Whitty & Carr, 2003). Online people do describe what their bodies look like and feel like. This is exemplified in the following extract in an email sent from an individual to their internet lover:

> *Very quietly, because the night is so very quiet a hundred miles from all other humans, of the lake. We lean up against each other for warmth, I have my arm around you to hold you close. The sense of waiting becomes almost intolerable . . . We reach out to touch the reflections and out hands meet in the sparkling water. Breathless from the transformation of night to day, I turn to you and our lips meet.* (Gwinnell, 1998, p. 59)

In addition to describing how one actually looks, one can play with how they choose to represent their own bodies online. This is illustrated in the following extract from an interview conducted with a 22-year-old man who discussed how he flirted in chat rooms:

> *They all think I'm a six foot tall tanned lifesaver. I tell them certain things that are true, but other things are bullshit. I mean, I can get away with it so why not. What they don't know won't hurt them. I will admit that I am pretty sly when it comes to smooth talking certain ladies on the net.* (Whitty & Gavin, 2001, p. 629)

In this participant's case, arguably, it would be more difficult to play with being a six-foot tanned lifesaver in a face-to-face interaction, if his 'real' physical body was an obese, pale, five-foot tall individual (and, of course, it is easier to be creative with constructions of the body online with others that one does not know offline). This type of flirtation is clearly different to offline flirting. However, despite the differences, this example does illustrate the importance of considering the reconstruction of the body online rather than emphasising the absence of body. Hence, in what ways the body is reconstructed should be of interest to researchers. For instance, what does it mean for this young man to play with inhabiting a stereotypical Australian attractive body? How else has he re-created his body online? How has this altered his dialogue with others?

In addition to playing with the shape and form of one's own physical body, cyberspace provides an opportunity to play with other bodies – or how we would like to reconstruct other people's bodies. The following quote from an 18-year-old woman, illustrates how one might play with other bodies in chat rooms:

> *Usually I just block out the photo they have sent me if I don't like it and just pretend they look a certain way. It's more fun that way!* (Whitty, 2001)

This quote is again contrary to the view that the internet is simply a place for the meeting of minds. Rather, it demonstrates that even in cyberspace the body plays an important role. This is again supported in the following statement by a 21-year-old man in regards to his interactions in a chat room:

> *Well you always wanna know what the other person looks like and you're always hoping for it to be some good looking chic.* (Whitty, 2001)

Interestingly, in response to whether he would continue communicating with a woman who turned out to be unattractive this man stated:

> *Well then yeah in that case I would still talk to them but I know that I would change towards them . . . Like I wouldn't be flirty or anything like that.* (Whitty, 2001)

The importance of desiring a physical image and not a 'faceless' other is nicely demonstrated in the following extract:

> *I have been waiting to ask you this for a while now – would you mind telling me what you look like? It is hard to just write to a faceless someone, and I have to say I have made up a picture in my mind of what you look like.* (Gwinnell, 1998, p. 66)

This extract highlights that even when a physical body is not presented, a physical image can fill in this gap.

Therefore, we believe that if social scientists shift their focus to the reconstruction of the body online then we will be able to consider new ways that people might cyber-flirt. There are numerous ways individuals can go about this. For instance, rather than make an effort to look good, individuals can create a lasting first impression by describing how attractive they look. As illustrated in examples above, this is not necessarily a description of one's actual bodies. Cyberspace allows individuals, through text, to create new attractive bodies. Indeed, one can devise an entirely new attractive being, one that has a good job, a self that earns huge sums of money, and is well educated. Again, we would like to point out that, how creative one is with their presentation of their physical body online is constrained by whether they already know the person offline.

Emoticons, acronyms, and screen names: The universal language of online love

The traditional non-verbal gestures, used in flirting behaviour (outlined earlier in this chapter), can be substituted online. While demure glances and eyebrow flashes might not be easily replicated online, there are some alternatives to these non-verbal gestures. For example, emoticons, which are drawings made from grammatical symbols, might be a useful alternative. Individuals can use facial expressions, such as smiley faces, winks, and kisses as a substitute to body language. Examples of flirtatious facial expressions are shown in Table 2.1. Besides emoticons, individuals can also represent laughing and giggling using acronyms, such as LOL and BG (some software even has sound files to represent sounds, such as laughter). Examples of flirtatious acronyms are displayed in Table 2.2.

There is also some empirical evidence available to support our theoretical arguments. For instance, in a recent study it was found that those who were more likely to flirt online than offline were able to successfully translate the body through text (see Whitty, 2004a). For example, kinetics (in the form of acronyms, such as LOL), oculesics (in the form of emoticons, such as a wink), speech/laughter and haptics (through descriptions in the text) were popular ways to flirt online. Indeed, the representation of non-verbal cues and laughter appeared to be the most popular way for individuals to cyber-flirt.

Screen names are another devise people utilise in their repertoire of online flirting behaviours. A screen name can be an individual's real name, a variation of an individuals' name or a totally made-up pseudonym.

Table 2.1　Examples of flirtatious emoticons

Smiley face:	Kiss:
:-)	:-x
Wink:	Kisses:
;-)	:*
Devilish wink:	Blowing a kiss:
;->	:-{}
Laughing:	Hugs:
:-D	[ ]
Sticking out one's tongue:	Hug
:-P	{name here}
Wow:	Lots of hugs:
:-o	{{{name here}}}
High five:	Hugs and Kisses:
^5	(( )):**
Angelic, being an angel (at heart, at least)	Devil:
O :-)	>:-)~
Rose:	Goo-goo eyes, drooling over you
@-->-->---	8-P"

Screen names are especially required on the internet for applications, such as instant messaging, chat rooms, and online dating sites. Screen names can be flirtatious (as shown in Table 2.3) or one might want to represent something about their identity through their screen name (to attract someone of similar character). To be flirtatious, one wants a screen name that stands out, and so the cyber-flirter needs to be creative with their choice of screen names.

It is worthwhile noting that the acronyms people use online do not always represent the same words. For instance, LOL can take on a number of meanings, including laugh out loud, lots of love, or lots of luck. Given the large range of emoticons and acronyms available to flirt with and the deciphering required to obtain the correct meaning, it might be that the internet savvy individual is more likely to be a successful cyber-flirter. As Levine (2000) has written in regards to cyber-flirting: 'even though there are fewer paralinguistic cues, there is a learning curve and people who are seasoned communicators online become adept at using and interpreting textual signs and codes' (p. 568). That being said, a number of programmes, including IM and some online dating sites, have made flirting easier for the internet amateur. They provide a range of animated emoticons and sound files where they give a title for each emoticon for people to interpret more easily.

Table 2.2 Examples of flirtatious acronyms

AML: all my love	LNK: love and kisses
ASLP: age, sex, location, picture	LMHO: laughing my head off
A/S/L: age/sex/location	LOL: laughing out loud
BEG: big evil grin	PM: private message
BG: big grin	QT: cutie
BL: belly laughing	ROFLMAO: rolling on floor laughing my ass off
EG: evil grin	ROFLOLTSDMC: rolling on floor laughing out
FOFL: falling on the floor	loud tears streaming down my cheeks
laughing	ROFLOLWTIME: rolling on floor laughing out
FOTCL: falling of the chair	loud with tears in my eyes
laughing	ROTFL: rolling on the floor
GBH: great big hug	laughing
GBH&K: great big hug and kisses	SWAK: sealed with a kiss
GMAO: giggling my ass off	SWALK: sweet, with all love, kisses
H&K: hug and kiss	URAQT: you are a cutie
HH: holding hands	VBG: very big grin
ILU: I love you	VBS: very big smile
ILYFAE: I love you forever and	*G*: giggle or grin
ever	*H*: hug
JK: just kidding	*K*: kiss
JP: just playing	*S*: smile
KOTC: kiss on the cheek	*T*: tickle
KOTL: kiss on the lips	*W*: wink

Some offline flirting behaviours are not so easy to translate online. For example, it is difficult to find substitutes, or an equivalence, for olfactics, vocalics, and proxemics. Online participants do not know what the person they are chatting with smells like, nor are they allured by their sexy deep voice. Chatting with CAPITALS IS CONSIDERED TO BE SHOUTING! The subtleties of voice, such as pitch and tone, are not evident online.

Table 2.3 Examples of flirtatious screen names

CallMeBaBy
Winker
Cherub
Hot4u
DarkPrince
Sexybabe

Pauses in conversation might be attributed to a poor internet connection or bad typing skills, as opposed to a lack of interest. Individuals also cannot indicate attraction online by leaning closer to another or by mirroring their body movements. Nonetheless, individuals might still get around these hurdles by being imaginative and describing how they might smell, how they are talking, or how they might like to be physically interacting with another. We would like to suggest here though, in revisiting Given's (1978) phases of courting, we find that the stages that occur offline are not as distinctive online. Instead, these phases appear to merge into one phase, given that the reconstruction of the body that is occurring online is interwoven throughout the conversation that has already been initiated.

Cyber-flirting: Old rules

Although we have pointed out the many new ways individuals might flirt online we would also like to acknowledge that – '*the more things change, the more they stay the same*'. Evidence for this assertion can be found in Whitty's (2004a) study, where 5690 individuals completed a survey about their flirting behaviour both in face-to-face interactions and in chat rooms. It was found that women were more likely than men to cyber-flirt by utilising non-verbal substitutes, such as laughing and emphasising physical attractiveness. Men, in this study, were also more likely than women to initiate contact with women they were attracted to online. This is similar to the ways men and women flirt offline. However, in contrast, it was found that unlike offline flirting, men were more likely to describe touch online. Perhaps this was because the use of touch in face-to-face situations is a more subtle advance than actually describing touch online. This study suggests two important findings: (a) that there are some differences in the ways people flirt online and offline; and, (b) that gender roles cannot completely be transcended online.

Bodies on internet dating sites

We have emphasised in our previous work the importance of not treating the internet as one generic space. In the above examples of the reconstruction of the body online, we have mostly focused on how the body might be represented through text. However, of course, individuals can also represent their physical selves online through photographs, video, via webcams, and voice files. We turn now to how people use photos to attract others on an online dating site. Again, we do so by considering the interviews conducted with participants who used the Australian online dating site.

When it came to these participants' representations of themselves online, most (65%) decided to put a photograph on their profiles. Women (87%) were more likely to put a photo up compared to men (66%). Some stated that it was important to put a photo up given that they expected it from others, as expressed by this 46-year-old woman:

I   *Do you have a photograph of yourself up there?*

S   *Yes definitely. I think I really don't like it when somebody sends you a virtual kiss and they don't have a photograph attached. I just don't see the point in it.*

(Sharon)

Others talked about the importance of presenting a flattering photograph of themselves, as this 40-year-old man stated:

C   *And part of it too was that in some of the early photo's, early profiles, I had unflattering photos on there and like I don't believe in going out and getting glamour shots because that is not a true representation of yourself and it leads to disappointment if somebody meets you and you have got this fabulous glamour shot and you are not like that in real life. That is misleading, but the photo makes a huge difference. If you haven't got a flattering genuine photo, you will find it harder to get the quality of contacts you are looking for.*

I   *So you got a better photograph of you?*

C   *I got a few better photographs.*

(Christopher)

It was also interesting that 8 per cent of the sample said that they had a glamour shot – all of which were women. It is not surprising that it was only women going to such lengths with their photographs, given that men place greater importance on finding a partner who is physically attractive (Feingold, 1990, 1991). This 45-year-old woman stated:

I   *So, you said you recently put up a new photograph of yourself?*
J   *Yes.*
I   *How did you get that photograph done? Did you do a professional photograph?*
J   *I had a professional one done. The photo I had up there was about five years old and just wasn't a good reflection of how I am and didn't work for me very well. So I did have a professional one done and it has worked a treat.*

     (Jill)

This 41-year-old woman tells a similar story:

I   *Did you put a photograph up of yourself?*
J   *Yes.*
I   *And how did you decide what type of photograph to put up of yourself?*
J   *Well obviously you want something decent and I didn't have a lot of things around. So the photograph that I have got was a studio glamour photograph, where they did your makeup, and your hair, and made you look gorgeous, but that is the only decent photograph I had.*

     (Joan)

In respect to online dating, the participants interviewed from the Australian online dating site, in the main, expected a photograph of the individuals' profiles. In fact, most participants (85%) would not consider someone if they did not have a photograph on their profile. The importance of having a photograph displayed is nicely highlighted in an interview with a 37-year-old woman:

I   *What about photographs?*
K   *A must.*
I   *So, you wouldn't waste your time with anyone if they didn't have a photograph?*
K   *I have and I have been extremely disappointed a couple of times. And even with photographs, they tend to be misleading. I know myself, I take a photograph, I take a horrendous photo and people just always say to me, "you don't look anything like it". I have met guys who look at me and go "oh my God". You can see it is them in the photos but it's not really but people without photos I tend to stay away from.*

     (Kath)

Some of the men told a similar story. For example, this 50-year-old male described what he was drawn to when considering a profile:

G   *Initially, the eye contact of the photograph, then just their profile to start off*
     with. It's all governed by that really.
I   *So the photo is a big factor then?*
     (Grant)

This 46-year-old male also emphasised the importance of being able to clearly see the picture, so that he really knew what he was buying into:

The first thing I look for is there a picture. I'm very much a visual person. It is their
picture, I think it should be mandatory to have a picture and also the picture should
have a certain size. (Patrick)

We will discuss in Chapter 7 other sorts of characteristics these online daters sought when choosing out potential partners from the list of profiles they were presented. The following chapter, however, explains how cyberspace provides a unique and more playful space to play at love. We do so by drawing from psychodynamic theory.

CHAPTER 3

Playing at Love

Winnicott and Potential Space

> *Carnival is not a spectacle seen by the people; they live in it, and everyone participates... While carnival lasts, there is no other life outside it. During carnival time life is subject only to its laws, that is, the laws of its own freedom... Carnival celebrated temporary liberation from the prevailing truth and from the established order... it demanded ever changing, playful, undefined forms.*
>
> (Bakhtin – cited in Green, 2001, p. 159)

So far in this book, we have argued that although there are some important similarities between the ways relationships are developed and maintained face-to-face and in cyberspace, nonetheless there are some unique characteristics of cyberspace that need to be highlighted. We believe that playing at love in cyberspace can be both a liberating and a debilitating experience, and how much so depends on the individual and how he/she interacts within this space. For example, does one use this space to help free themselves of social anxieties? Does one idealise their online relationships too much? In the following chapters we discuss this notion in detail. We depart from the prevailing wisdom carried in the existing literature, and extend our previous argument (see Whitty, 2003a; Whitty & Carr, 2003, 2005a) that much of human relationships in cyberspace can be coherently comprehended through a conceptual lens of psychodynamics[1] specifically that school of psychology called object-relations theory. In this chapter, we summarise Winncott's object-relations theory and use it to explain online relating. In keeping with our opening citation from the work of Bakhtin, like the time and space that is the carnival, we argue that cyberspace appears to have its own regime of 'laws' and indigenous objects that influence the manner in which people

56

relate. Moreover, the notion of play is very instructive in explaining and predicting online behaviour. Object-relations theory calls attention to such rules and play. This psychodynamic perspective is also capable of appreciating that cyberspace is a different place for humans to relate and results in behaviours that, while not necessarily encountered in other relational spaces, have origins capable of coherent explanation. Indeed, it is through an object-relations appreciation of play that the behaviour of cyber-flirting, and a variety of other behaviours on the internet, we find to be readily understandable. It is to the psychodynamics related to play to which we now turn our attention.

The psychodynamics of play: The work of Donald Woods Winnicott

Play is an activity that humans perhaps most commonly associate with childhood. Certainly much of the study of play has focused upon children rather than adults (see Abramis, 1990) with many in psychology suggesting that childhood play is an essential part of human development. The Dutch historian Huizinga (1944/1980), in the opening pages of his book *Homo Ludens: A study of the play-element in culture*, recounts a story that was told to him by the father about his 4-year-old son. The father found his son 'sitting at the front of a row of chairs, playing "trains". As he hugged him his son said: "Don't kiss the engine, Daddy, or the carriages won't think it's real"' (p. 8). This story is indicative of a child at play, but at the same time this story reveals how fragile and ephemeral the quality of *illusion* in play. Modell (1990/1996) notes that 'the connection between playing and illusion has long been recognised and, as many have noted, is revealed by the etymology of the word *illusion*, which can be traced to *inlusio, illudere*, or *inludere*, which means literally "in play"' (p. 27, italics is original emphasis).

Those who champion a psychoanalytic approach to the understanding of play insist that play is all about illusion and that such illusion can only be sustained provided play can be kept within a frame of its own – a frame which seeks to separate it from ordinary life (see Freud, 1905–6/1985, 1908/1985; Modell, 1990/1996; Winnicott, 1971a–g). This frame represents a 'differentiated level of reality' (Modell, 1990/1996, pp. 25–30) and its separation from everyday life is achieved through a variety of means not least of which are factors related to time and space. Play, children's play in particular, can begin at one moment and be concluded at another when it is deemed that play is 'over'. In the case of certain games, the rules may declare that play occurs within a specific time limit within a specific space. Other games are simply 'played out' in time limits determined through how play takes its own course.

Rules are particularly important in creating the separation of play from ordinary life – have you ever noticed when two children play, how much time and argument occurs over the rules? The temporary world of play has rules to define the space in which the illusions can be generated and flourish. Play depends upon rules and other factors related to space and time, but in so doing we can note that an interesting paradox arises. On the one hand, the fundamental essence of play is the freedom, the license to create and be set apart from ordinary life. Yet, on the other hand, for this to be accomplished, constraint is required in the form of rules and other factors related to space and time. Thus, in an interesting twist of logic, freedom is created only through constraint.

In considering play as occurring within a frame of its own – a differentiated level of reality – a psychodynamic view of play notes that much of what happens in this transported world is very serious indeed.[2] The idea that play falls into some dichotomous world, or binary opposition, of serious and no-serious activity, is something firmly rejected in a psychodynamic view of play. Freud (1908/1985) makes this point strongly when he asserts:

> every child at play ... creates a world of his own. ... It would be wrong to think he does not take that world seriously; on the contrary, he takes his play very seriously and he expends large amounts of emotion on it. The opposite of play is not what is serious but what is real. In spite of all the emotion with which he cathects his world of play, the child distinguishes it quite well from reality; and he likes to link his imagined objects and situations to tangible and visible things of the real world. This linking is all that differentiates the child's 'play' from 'phantasying'. (p. 132)

The paediatrician and psychoanalyst Donald Woods Winnicott is credited, by many, with making a very significant contribution to a psychoanalytic understanding of play. His notions of *transitional objects* and that of *potential space* are particularly important in the context of understanding play. Winnicott (1971a), in keeping with Freud, argued that play transcended the serious and non-serious oppositional binary. He also viewed the play of infants as being spontaneous and occurring in an environment of trust and safety of parents – in particular, the mother. Highly significant for Winnicott was what he took to be the intermediate territory between the inner and the external world. He noticed, for example, how an infant would suck and hug a doll or blanket. He suggested that the doll or blanket did not represent a doll or blanket as such, but is rather an as-if object. The infant makes use of the illusion that although this is not the breast, treating it as such will allow an appreciation of what is 'me' and what is 'not-me' (Winnicott, 1971d, p. 41; 1971g, p. 107). Although referred to as a *transitional object*, 'it is not the object, of course that is transitional' (Winnicott, 1951/1971b, p. 14). The object is the initial manifestation of a different positioning of the infant in the world, as Wright (1998) observes:

> What is important is not what the object stands for but what it enables the child to do, namely, to enter the field of illusion, moving from the subjective (as created by the child) to the objective (as found in the environment). The transitional object has the "specific capacity to change the 'given' into the 'created' " [cited in Pontalis, 1981, p. 142]. (p. 84)

The doll or blanket, thus, connects to subjective experience, but is in the objective world.

The *potential space* between subject and object is where, for the infant, play takes place. The potential space is an area of intermediate experiencing that is between inner and outer worlds, 'between the subjective object and the object objectively perceived' (Winnicott, 1967/1971f, p. 100). Conceptually, this produces a number of paradoxes. Winnicott (1968/1971e) himself notes:

> The essential feature [of this area of experiencing in general and the transitional object in particular] is ... *the paradox and the acceptance of the paradox*: the baby creates the object, but the object was there waiting to be created. ... In the rules of the game we all know that we will never challenge the baby to elicit an answer to the question: did you create that or did you find it? (p. 89, italics is original emphasis)

While the notions of transitional objects and potential space are raised within a context of an infant, Winnicott (1951/1971b) insists, however, 'they are not simply confined to the experience of infants', but is something that 'throughout life is retained in the intense experiencing that belongs to the arts and to religion and to imaginative living, and to creative scientific work' (p. 24). We come to rely upon our own resources to experience culture to expand our understanding of the world. The individual develops his/her own capacity to generate potential space. As Winnicott (1967/1971f) notes: 'The place where cultural experience is located is in the *potential space* between the individual and the environment (originally the object). The same can be said of playing. Cultural experience begins with creative living first manifested in play.' (p. 100, italics is original emphasis).

Winnicott viewed play as creative communication and is inherently intersubjective. Play would not occur in the context of the subject alone. Play takes into account other subjectivities and an environment that responds to the subject. In addition, Winnicott viewed play as creating and sustaining illusion, which, as we noted earlier, can be maintained if kept within a frame of its own – a frame that separates it from ordinary life (see Carr & Downs, 2004a).

The implications of intersubjectivity, Winnicott was to note in the course of outlining his views on mental health and creativity. He argues that a person who lives in a realm of subjective omnipotence, with no bridge to objective reality, is self-absorbed and autistic. A person who lived only in the realm of objective reality, with no roots in subjective omnipotence, was viewed by Winnicott as superficially adjusted, but lacking passion and originality. As Mitchell and Black (1995) nicely summarise, it was 'precisely the ambiguity of the transitional realm that rooted experience in deep and spontaneous sources within the self and, at the same time, connected self-expression with a world of other subjectivities' (p. 128). This transitional realm provides relief 'from the strain of relating inner and outer reality... that no human is free from' (Winnicott, 1951/1971b, p. 24). The tension and strain between inner and outer worlds is not eliminated, but is bound in this space. Culture and cultural activity, in this context, is an expression of the 'inter-play between separateness and union' (Winnicott, 1951/1971b, p. 24).

The potential space is not pure fantasy, nor is it pure reality. 'In the absence of potential space, there is only fantasy; within potential space *imagination* can develop' (Ogden, 1985a, p. 133, italics is added emphasis). Winnicott believed that given a 'good enough' environment the interplay of the inner world and the external reality promotes the development of self and facilitates growth. It is a space where we can develop psychologically, to integrate love and hate and to create, destroy, and re-create ourselves (see Winnicott, 1971d, p. 41).

Winnicott and cyberspace

Critical to our understanding of the most fundamental aspects of cyberspace would appear to be Winnicott's notion of potential space which he argues is not inner psychic reality but rather 'is outside the individual, but is not the external world...Into this play area the child gathers objects or phenomena from external reality and uses these in the service of...inner or personal reality' (Winnicott, 1971d, p. 51). We would suggest that cyberspace can be productively understood as what Winnicott calls potential space – a space between the '*real individuals*' and the '*fantasy individuals*', 'a space that is somewhere outside the individual but is still not the external world' (Whitty, 2003a, p. 349). In being a potential space, cyberspace would hold the possibility for psychological growth in the manner alluded to in the previous paragraph.

The computer, and the other computer periphery objects, are the transitional objects that allow the individual to position themselves in this space and explore the 'me' and 'not-me' that we noted earlier in Winnicott's appraisal (1971d, p. 41) of the significance of these objects. Others have also made a similar assessment. For example, Turkle (1995) suggested that 'the computer can be similarly experienced as an object on the border between self and not-self...People are able to see themselves in the computer. The machine can seem a second self' (p. 30). Indeed, we invest emotion towards these objects and, as we will discuss in the next chapter, they leave a trace within us and serve as psychic keys to unlock emotions – in the case of cyberspace, even before we turn on the computer or log onto the internet. Object-relation theorists insist that objects are often symbolically charged, typically at an unconscious level. Indeed, as Carr and Downs (2004a, p. 353) have highlighted, Freud (1905/1977, 1933/1988) believed that 'objects are the targets towards which action or desire is directed in order to satisfy instinctual satisfaction'. Simply touching the computer or thinking about going online may trigger a range of emotional responses. For example, Lupton (1995) describes the effect of turning on the computer has on her:

> When I turn on my computer... it makes a little sound. This sound I sometimes playfully interpret as a cheerful 'Good morning' greeting, for the action of bringing my computer to life usually happens first thing in the morning... In conjunction with my cup of tea, the sound helps to prepare me emotionally and physically for the working day ahead, a day that will involve much tapping on the computer keyboard and staring into the pale blue face of the display monitor. (p. 97)

The rules for preserving the illusion such that one can 'play' on the internet are still evolving, but there are some clear forms of *Netiquette* to set 'boundaries' that also help in communication in an environment where there is a lack of the normal social cues.[3] A Winnicottian orientation to understanding behaviour on the internet is instructive in relation to our earlier chapters on internet relationships. We have argued that playing at love on the internet, although synonymous in some ways with offline flirting, is characterised here as a *unique activity* that is a form of play. There is greater opportunity online for *fantasy* than there is offline. Online participants can inhabit any body they desire, whether that is a youthful body, attractive body, or even the opposite sex. Research has found that men, in particular, switch their gender online (Whitty, 2002). Moreover, one can invent how their fantasy partner looks like, feels like, and feels about them. Participants can *fantasise* that they are attracted to others, and in turn, others are attracted to them. Therefore, as argued and illustrated in the previous chapter, while clearly the body is not physically present during online interactions, the body still does matter. In this 'potential space', participants are open to play with a variety of identities, including their physical identity.

Aitken and Herman (1997) have suggested that Winnicott's framework 'allows the possibility of a flexible manipulation of meanings and relationships' (p. 11). They argue that objects, cultural practices, and self-images may become elements of this space. Moreover, they suggest that these elements can be altered 'as an individual adjusts and updates knowledge throughout a lifetime' (p. 11). Indeed play can challenge society's rules.

In Winnicott's potential space, reality is plastic and meanings can be reconstituted. Applying this to cyberspace, stereotypical gender roles can be challenged by playing online. It could therefore be argued that this potential space provides opportunities for individuals to play and experiment with traditional cultural meanings of the self and the gender (although as demonstrated in Chapter 2, not everyone capitalises on these opportunities). An individual can play, by trying out different identities, to discover, to use Winnicott's terms, what is 'me' and what is 'not-me'. This type of play has significant implications for therapeutic outcomes and, of course, the potential for psychopathologies to develop from this activity cannot be discounted. Of course, as mentioned in Chapter 2, trying out different identities in cyberspace is easier to do when the people one is interacting with are unknown to the person offline.

Germane to Winnicott's argument is that potential space is a safe space, a place where one can be spontaneous and experimentation can take place. He argues that in order for one to play there needs to be trust. For example, he argues that if psychotherapy is to be successful 'playing has to be spontaneous, and not compliant or acquiescent' (Winnicott, 1971d, p. 51). In line with these qualities of potential space, cyberspace potentially provides a safer space than offline space, to play and experiment at flirting, presentation of self, and developing relationships. 'The friendly and safer atmosphere surrounding the formation of online relationships increase the likelihood that people will choose to begin their relationship in this way' (Ben-Ze'ev, 2004, p. 34). Rejection is less likely to cause distress when you can disconnect from this cyber-world at any time, and the chances are remarkably decreased as to the likelihood of ever having a chance meeting with your cyber-playmate. Moreover, there are more opportunities for an individual to be creative and experiment with identity and sexuality and love. While offline flirtation undeniably could be also seen as type of play (e.g., the married man or woman who flirts at a party in order to be reassured they are still attractive, but with no intention of taking things further), we would contend that cyberspace creates more opportunities for the type of play that Winnicott describes. This type of play requires that one sustains an illusion, and we propose that this is easier to maintain in an online environment.

We are not the first to argue that cyberspace is a playful space. The well-known academic Howard Rheingold (1993) has talked about the internet as being a virtual playground, a space where co-operative play can take place. Danet, Ruendenberg, and Rosenbaum-Tamari (1998) have also written about the playful qualities of CMC. To quote from Danet et al. (1998):

> Computer-mediated communication (CMC) is strikingly playful. Millions of people are playing with their computer keyboards in ways they probably never anticipated, even performing feats of virtuosity – with such humble materials as commas, colons, and backslashes. Not only hackers, computer "addicts," adolescents and children, but even ostensibly serious adults are learning to play in new ways. (p. 41)

Danet et al. (1998) considered the flow experience inherent in synchronous communication (see, for example, Voiskounsky, Mitina, & Avetisova, 2004; Voiskounsky & Smyslova, 2003). Voiskounsky et al. (2004) explain that the major characteristics of flow include: a temporary loss of self-consciousness and time, high levels of concentration and control, clear objectives, intrinsic motivation, and immediate feedback. Danet et al. (1998) argue that this flow effect invites playfulness. These researchers, in particular, focused on play in IRC (Internet Relay Chat). They identified three inter-rated, but nonetheless distinct, forms of play in this space, which include: playing with identity; playing with frames of interaction; and playing with typographic symbols. We have already talked about playing with identity and typographic symbols in respect to cyber-flirting; however, we have omitted a consideration of playing with frames. Danet et al. (1998) parallel the idea of playing with frames with multitasking. When it comes to multitasking online, one can have a number of frames open at the same time, but only one is typically in the foreground. While these researchers refer specifically to IRC, we could extend the frames to include other spaces online. For example, one might have email and IM going at the same time. Moreover, when it comes to Chat and IM one can have more than one window open and so be talking to numerous individuals almost simultaneously (depending on how well co-ordinated the individual is). Of course, one can also be involved in multitasking activities both online and offline at the same time (e.g., writing email while talking to someone and listening to music online simultaneously). When an individual flirts face-to-face they typically focus their attention on one individual at a time; however, with the allowances of a variety of frames online one can flirt simultaneously in numerous places in one session.

Cyberspace as a potential space for psychological growth and 'liberation'?

Much of the emphasis in Winnicott's discussion of play was about the manner in which play was liberating, conducive to the development of self, and facilitated psychological growth, at one point he makes the general observation that:

> In other words, *it is play that is the universal*, and that belongs to health: playing facilitates growth and therefore health; playing leads into group relationships; playing can be a form of communication in psychotherapy; and lastly, psychoanalysis has been developed as a highly specialised form of playing in the service of communication with oneself and others. (Winnicott, 1971d, p. 41, italics is original emphasis)

The emphasis upon the creative and healthy nature of play did not, however, obscure his appreciation that play could lead to unhealthy outcomes. Often in the same breath as he was describing the merits of the transitional realm, he was inferring or describing the manner in which a 'good enough' environment was required to facilitate the maintenance of the potential space such that the boundaries, and dialectic interplay, of pure fantasy and pure reality do not collapse. While earlier in this chapter we raised Winnicott's appraisal of those who live predominantly in either realm, the question arises as to the consequences of those who stray too close to the borders of reality or fantasy? Ogden (1985a) notes four different 'ideal'-types, or cases, that result in different psychopathologies: where *reality subsumes fantasy* the consequence is an inability to 'entertain' ideas and feelings, illusions are replaced with delusion; in cases where *reality forms a defence against fantasy* the result is a foreclosure on imagination; in the case *where reality and fantasy are dissociated* the consequences are fetishism and perversions; and where there is a *foreclosure of reality and fantasy*, that is, a failure to create the potential space, the consequence is a state of non-experience where perception does not lead to an attributed meaning and results, therefore, in a failure to generate appropriate emotional responses.

It is demonstrably the case that cyberspace can be a place that is not necessarily conducive to psychological growth, the development of self or in any way a liberating experience. Indeed, cyberspace can be an unsafe place to inhabit which is a matter that we will discuss in greater depth in Chapters 5 and 6. At this stage we would like to draw attention to some other object-relations theories useful in examining aspects of the behaviour of those who play at love in cyberspace.

Object-relations theories: Regressive behaviour and splitting

Psychodynamic theories of human behaviour emphasise the importance of the unconscious. Like the proverbial iceberg, the unconscious is viewed as the domain of mental activity that resides below the 'surface' – the subterranean strata of the psyche that consists of previous experiences, memories, feelings and urges, of which the individual is not actively aware due to defensive mechanisms or other active psychodynamic processes. Freud, when describing the unconscious, actually often used the metaphor of the cauldron. Freud actually referred to that part of the unconscious he called the 'id' as 'a cauldron full of seething excitations' (Freud, 1933/1988, p. 106). This metaphor underscores how active he viewed that part of the mind called the 'unconscious'.

In Freud's now familiar, topographical, and dynamic model of the mind, he referred to three regions, realm of provinces that he dubbed the id, ego, and superego. The id was that province of where various urges, drives, or instincts resided and operated entirely unconsciously. The ego was the province that was responsible for engaging logic, memory, and judgement in an endeavour to satisfy the demands of the id within parameters set by external reality. The superego was the province of the mind whose concern is for obeying society's 'rules of conduct', that is, morality and social norms, and reminds the ego of these social realities. Part of the ego and superego reside in the area of the unconscious and the relationship between the three provinces and the outside world was interactive – Freud (1933/1988) described the relationship as follows:

> the ego, driven by the id, confined by the super-ego, repulsed by reality, struggles to master its economic task... If the ego is obliged to admit its weakness, it breaks out in anxiety – anxiety [fear] regarding the external world, moral anxiety

regarding the super-ego and neurotic anxiety regarding the strength of the passions in the id. (pp. 110–111)

Indeed, excessive and unresolved conflict between the ego and the other agencies leads to different pathologies, ranging from phobias to hysterias and from manic-depression to paranoia.

In an attempt to avoid acute psychopathologies, and the anxiety that goes with them, a variety of mechanisms are engaged to defend the psyche against painful and threatening ideas, desires, and emotions. These defence mechanisms are now part of the layperson's language and include: repression [the omnipresent mainstay of defences that usually accompanies all other defence]; regression; rationalisation; denial; sublimation; identification; projection; displacement; and reaction formation. While these defence mechanisms are engaged with an aim to distort or deny the source of anxiety from the conscious mind, these repressed 'memories' remain active in the unconscious and influence the individual's behaviour without the individual being aware of what prompted their response to specific situations (see Carr, 2002; Carr & Gabriel, 2001).

The psychodynamics described above occur in normal face-to-face circumstances, but they can also be noted in the interpersonal exchanges that occur on the internet. However, if one examines the email exchanges that occur one-to-one, or in the chat rooms and various other internet forums, it becomes clear that the 'talk' appears to be much less 'restrained' than that in normal face-to-face situations (see, for example, Joinson, 2001). Some topics are discussed in a much more open and frank manner on the internet than would appear to be in the case in offline discussion. The lack of inhibition is evident in a high level of self-disclosure and the phenomenon of *flaming*, while at the same time we are often witness to greater levels of sincerity. By way of example, the following is a much-cited email that was sent to a journalist who had written a somewhat complimentary article about the head of Microsoft, Bill Gates. The email is from a fellow-journalist:

Crave THIS, asshole: Listen, you toadying dipshit scumbag... remove your head from your rectum long enough to look around and notice that real reporters don't fawn over their subjects, pretend that their subjects are making some sort of special contact with them, or worse, curry favor by TELLING their subjects how great the ass-licking profile is going to turn out and then brag in print about doing it. Forward this to Mom.

Copy to Tina [the publisher of The New Yorker] *and tell her the mag is fast turning to compost. One good worm deserves another.* (Seabrook, 1994, p. 70; see also Holland, 1995, p. 1)

The 'worm' referred to in the email message is, of course, a computer virus and thus there is an implied threat.

In terms of a psychodynamic explanation of such behaviour, it could be argued that the passions of the id get expressed in a most primitive type of relating to the world – *regressive* behaviour. As Norman Holland (1995) observes: 'Talking on the Internet, people regress. It's that simple. . . . People regress, expressing sex and aggression as they never would face to face' (p. 1). Anonymity seems to 'suspend' or ignore the normal engagement of the prohibitive aspect of the superego in a reversion to an earlier state of mental functioning. It is assumed in this understanding of human behaviour that earlier stages of development are not 'entirely outgrown, so that the earlier patterns of behaviour remain available as alternative modes of functioning' (Rycroft, 1995, p. 154; see also Freud, 1915/1985, p. 73). A detailed description of the concept of regression was provided by Freud in the following paragraph that he added to the 1914 reprint of his work *The Interpretation of Dreams*:

> Three kinds of regression are thus to be distinguished: (a) *topographical* regression, in the sense of the schematic picture of the [psychical apparatus] . . .; (b) *temporal* regression, in so far as what is in question is a harking back to older psychical structures; and (c) *formal* regression, where primitive methods of expression and representation take the place of the usual ones. All these three kinds of regression are, however, one at bottom and occur together as a rule; for what is older in time is also more primitive in form and in psychical topography lies nearer to the perceptual end. (Freud, 1900/1986, p. 699, italics is original emphasis)

Regression is most notably observed under conditions of anxiety particularly in a context of a perceived threat, under conditions of frustration, and, more generally, in the face of unpleasant situations. The reverting to an earlier stage of 'relating' has also been noted to be associated with an enactment of resistance (Balint, 1968). In the clinical situation, Winnicott (1958, p. 280) similarly notes regression as being a defensive 'shield' and a form of 'self holding'. In the face of frustrating or threatening circumstances, the child at play may seek to withdraw from the situation and/or what is colloquially called 'throwing a temper tantrum'. Some of the flaming, and flaming wars that occur on the internet seem akin to a temper tantrum. The aggressive, sexual, and less restrained content of internet messages can be 'read' as being a regression to a more primitive way of relating, but some subscriber lists and forums have appointed 'moderators' who may block certain emails and may remove the offending party from the list or forum. In the case of the latter action the moderator could be construed as seeking to make cyberspace a safer place to play.

In addition to regressive reactions we have described above, we can note in the content of some communications a regressive behaviour of *splitting* the 'world' into idealised 'good' and demonised 'bad' parts; such that aggressive communication is generated in an effort to avoid the anxiety posed by potential persecutory 'bad objects'. It is in the work of the object-relations theorist Melanie Klein (1944, 1975a–d) that we find a coherent description of this primitive way of relating. Klein argued that primal interpersonal relationships are based in paradox or mutual causalities. In a kind of Manichaean world in the first years of life, Klein argues an important initial process for the infant is to resolve an ambiguity and conflict posed by the mother's breast. The breast is a good object and a bad object at the same time. The infant *idealises* the 'good' breast and projects love onto it because through the transfer of milk (Suttie, 1935) it triggers feelings of contentment that are absorbed or introjected by the infant: these feelings represent the mother's reassurance, which is life sustaining. This 'good' object also confounds the infant because it inspires a degree of *envy* from the emphasis of the infant's need and dependence upon it. During unwanted disruptions of milk or separations from the breast, the infant experiences the good object as being outside its control, because the infant cannot have what it wants, when it wants it. Because of the undeveloped ability to understand the paradox, in the child's mind, the breast becomes simultaneously, a frustrating, terrifying, and omnipotent 'bad' object that is perceived to have the persecutorial power to destroy both the infant and the 'good' object, causing separation anxiety or the feeling of isolation from the life force. This anxiety becomes acute; it threatens to transform isolation into total dissolution, which becomes synonymous with the fear of 'death' (Carr, 2003a, 2003b).

As early as the third month of life, the infant usually comes to this realisation that it both loves and hates the same breast, a 'condition' that Klein refers to as the *depressive position*. The infant may, as another defence mechanism for this less developed ego, seek to deny [or as Freud (1940/1986) terms 'disavowal'] the reality of the persecutory object. It is the good breast that becomes the core around which the ego seeks to develop as if it were the grain of sand that yields the pearl (see Klein, 1975c, pp. 178–180). The experience of envy of the good breast is, however, a potential source of interference in that process. It is in this psychodynamic process called *splitting*, the child minimises conflict by attempting to maximise clarity. There is an exaggeration of differences between good and bad objects in order to eliminate 'gray' areas and to create a 'black and white picture', so part of the object becomes either all 'good' or reassuring and the other part, all 'bad' and persecutorial. Klein termed this as a *paranoid-schizoid position*, highlighting 'the persecutory character of the anxiety and ... the schizoid nature of the mechanisms at work' (Laplanche & Pontalis, 1967/1988, p. 298). Some writers in psychodynamic theory regard splitting as the precursor to or rudimentary context of the superego (see Laplanche & Pontalis, 1967/1988, pp. 430, 436–438). While in normal development we pass through this phase, this primitive defence against anxiety is a regressive reaction that, in the sense of always being available to us, is never transcended. The 'good' objects in the developed superego come to represent the fantasised ego-ideal.

In terms of cyberspace, we can readily point to 'flaming wars' in which individuals and whole classes of people and groups become demonised while others are idealised and the hallmarks of a world that is perceived to be composed of 'us' and 'them'. This form of regressive behaviour distorts the manner in which communication is transacted. In respect to developing relationships online, this notion of splitting is also worthy to consider. When interacting with others in cyberspace individuals might split this relationship off from the rest of the world. Moreover, as Walther et al. (2001) have suggested in some situations individuals idealise their virtual partners. This is most probably partly down to the strategic attention individuals pay to presentation of self online. In addition, it might be a consequence of splitting off these relationships from the rest of one's world. We will revisit this concept of splitting in Chapter 5 when we examine internet infidelity.

Object-relations theories and the circulation of quasi-objects: A 'ball' in play

The work of Winnicott and his notion of transitional objects, in particular, is very instructive in terms of how an *individual* engages in play and their motivation for doing so. Recently (see Carr & Downs, 2004a, 2004b; Whitty & Carr, 2006) it has been noted that this notion of transitional objects has a parallel in the work of the French philosopher, Michel Serres' (1993/1995) notion of *quasi-objects*. While Winnicott was interested in an individual's relationship with an object, Serres has focused upon how 'objects pass through a social group and, in so doing, forms relations among the members of that group' (Carr & Downs, 2004a, p. 357). In *Angels*, Serres' (1993/1995) character Pia says:

> *Look at those children out there, playing ball. The clumsy ones are playing with the ball as if it was an object, while the more skillful ones handle it as if it were playing with them: they move and change position according to how the ball moves and bounces. As we see it, the ball is being manipulated by human subjects; this is a mistake – the ball is creating the relationships between them. It is in following its trajectory that their team is created, knows itself and represents itself. Yes, the ball is active. It is the ball that is playing.* (pp. 47–48)

According to Serres, objects lie at the origins of sociality. The collective arises with the circulation of quasi-objects. The quasi-object, like a token or the joker in a deck of cards, is blank; it is a 'general equivalent' (Serres, 1982, p. 229) passed or thrown to whomever and defined by the exchange among subjects. Serres' theory of the quasi-object extends object-relations theory in important ways, just as object-relations extends Freudian theories. Freud's primarily one-person model of inner conflict becomes a two-person model in object-relations theory; and Serres' theory of the quasi-object is a three-person model, or more accurately, a model of quasi-subjects and a quasi-object. Most importantly, Serres' theory connects the micro-level world of object-relations to macro-level social relations.

Serres' notion of quasi-objects potentially has great significance to understanding the creation of some social dynamics in cyberspace. The manner in which 'topics' and email content is moved around the internet, in chat rooms, newsgroups, and so forth, as though it were a ball in play, can be instructive as the dynamics may reveal the nature of the group itself and developing social networks as well as some of the motivations for individual's seeking to play in the first place.

Some sociologists and communication theorists, in particular, not only have studied similar social dynamics in respect to cyberspace, but have also done so with a firmer connection with offline relationships and in terms of the 'utility' of the social networks that are formed. For example, the prolific writer, Barry Wellman, has written extensively on social networks in cyberspace. Wellman (1997) aptly remarks:

> When a computer network connects people, it is a social network. Just as a computer network is a set of machines connected by a set of cables, a social network is a set of people (or organizations or other social entities) connected by a set of socially meaningful relationships. (p. 179)

Wellman, amongst others, has considered the strong and weak ties developed online. Wellman and Gulia (1999) have found that many online relationships exhibit strong ties similar to offline relationships. They contend that many online relationships are considerably supportive. Importantly, researchers are not limiting their research to exclusively consider online relationships in a vacuum. Although we argue in this book that individuals sometimes split the cyber-world off from the offline world, in the main, communication on the internet is not separate to the rest of one's life. To quote again from Barry Wellman (2004):

> The Internet has burrowed into my life, but is not separate from the rest of it. I integrate offline and online activities. To connect with my friends and relatives, I email, chat, web search and instant message – but I also walk, drive, bike, bus, fly, phone, and send an occasional greeting card. I am not unique. Both the exoticness of the Internet in the 1990s and the fears that it would undermine 'community' have faded. The reality is that using the Internet both expands community and changes it in subtle ways. (p. 23)

In other research, Cummings, Sproull, and Kiesler (2002) have looked at the effectiveness of online social support for deaf people. They found that integrating online and real support was more beneficial than online support online. Clearly the manner in which social networks are formed is an important dynamic for us to understand. The insight that comes from

Serre's theory of quasi-objects provides a valuable tool in tracing the development and dynamics of these social networks.

Identity

When children play they may seek to 'dress-up' and pretend to be someone they are not. They may seek to create a completely new character for themselves, or simply, embroider upon reality such that part of what is being said is based upon 'facts' about themselves. Similarly, in cyberspace, it has been widely noted that 'people try out new ways of being, often in very playful ways: Different professions, the opposite gender, altered self-descriptions. There is a sense that "it doesn't matter", a feeling of invulnerability' (Holland, 1995, p. 2).

The construction of new identities, or variations of their current self, that are presented on the internet truly allows for the engagement of the *imagination* of all parties concerned. In respect to online relationships, the ability to create a presentation of self that may seek to resonate with the fantasy of another person can produce relationships that are intensely more passionate than offline relationships (see Ben-Ze'ev, 2004, pp. 83–88). Of course, as we noted earlier, straying too close to the boundary of fantasy and away from reality can, potentially, have undesirable psychopathological outcomes.

The internet provides a forum in which an individual may seek to act out not their current identity, but one that they are seeking to attain – *an ego-ideal*. To understand the significance of this psychodynamic, and the consequences for the individuals concerned, we need to first have a deeper understanding of where that ego-ideal comes from and the potency of it as a seductive force.

It was Erik Erikson who suggested that 'linguistically as well as psychologically, identity and identification have common roots' (Erikson, 1959, p. 112). Identity is generally considered as a relational psychodynamic of self and other(s). We 'acquire' an identity-set derived from a variety of social interactions and situations, such as family, work, and social groups. The psychodynamics in which the largely unconscious processes of 'identification' result in identity were described by Sigmund Freud. Laplanche and Pontalis (1967/1988) thoughtfully note: 'In Freud's work the concept of identification comes little by little to have the central importance which makes it, not simply one psychical mechanism among others, but the operation itself whereby the human subject is constituted' (p. 206).

Freud, in his initial theory of the 'mind', or psyche, argued that the primitive ego (the self) was dominated by the pleasure principle, seeking to satisfy wishes, desires, and drives (libido) by, initially, taking itself as its own love-object (ego-libido) – a process referred to as *primary narcissism*. Subsequently, it discovers the 'external' world of the other and seeks to attach itself and derive pleasure through 'good' objects, for example the mother's breast (object-libido) – a process referred to as *secondary narcissism*. The infant may make itself, to some degree, independent of the other by, in this case, sucking his/her own finger. In putting forward his second theory of the 'mind', Freud posited the now familiar realms of id, ego, and superego, revising his original theory to retain the concept of narcissism, but to include the concept of the *ego-ideal*.

In introducing the concept of the ego-ideal, Freud (1914/1984) initially argued that the individual

> is not willing to forgo the narcissistic perfection of his childhood [and] . . . seeks to recover it in the new form of an ego ideal. What he projects before him as his ideal is the substitute for the lost narcissism of his childhood *in which he was his own ideal.* (p. 88, italics is added emphasis)

The ego-ideal was clearly that desire for the wholeness and perfection that was enjoyed before experiencing alien others. This ego-ideal, as we noted earlier, represented the idealised and positive sense of the superego, while simultaneously acknowledging that the superego also had a negative aspect – performing the role of censoring the ego's wishes and punishing the ego for any failures by creating feelings of moral anxiety. The superego, with its prohibitive and ideal aspects, was established, according to Freud (1921/ 1985), through three different forms of identification:

> First, identification . . . in the original form of [an] emotional tie with an object; second, in a regressive way . . . [as] a substitute for a libidinal object-tie, as it were by means of introjection of the object into the ego; and thirdly . . . [as] a new perception of a common quality shared with some other person who is not an object of the sexual instinct. (p. 137)

Laplanche and Pontalis (1967/1988) capture the importance of the notion of identification when they define it as a

> psychological process whereby the subject assimilates an aspect, property or attribute of the other and is transformed, wholly or partially, after the model the other provides. *It is by means of a series of identifications that the personality is constituted and specified.* (p. 205, italics is added emphasis)

Thus, for Freud, identification is the mechanism through which the ego-ideal is established and re-established, with narcissistic gratification being the driving force in the quest for wholeness. At this point it needs to be appreciated that narcissism, like any other trait, is part of the human condition that is neither sick nor healthy, but has exaggerated forms, or the potential for a Janus-like nature. Through identification, narcissism is transformed into a 'dependence', not necessarily centred upon self, but on an ego-ideal, satisfaction of which may come from alternative objects. In the context of these psychodynamics, identity can be understood in terms of 'fluctuations of projective and introjective identifications... [in which] the latter must be predominant' (Bassols, Bea, & Coderch, 1985, p. 173; Carr, 1994a). That is, the individual absorbs, largely unknowingly, aspects of his or her external world, and seeks to integrate these aspects with previous identifications and self/mutual recognition experiences. It is in such a context that identity can be seen to be in a state of continual flux or, alternatively expressed, 'in a state of being continually *made* in the developmental struggle of self-growth and mastery' (Dunn, 1998, p. 31).

In relation to the internet, it can be readily appreciated that at least some aspects of the ego-ideal that the individual has constructed can be presented and acted out as though it had been attained. The success in being able to act out such an ideal yields narcissistic pleasure that could be seen as unobtainable, or less easily obtainable in offline relationships. The offline situation may place significant constraint on an alternative presence in the world. The current reality of one's physical appearance (e.g., age, race, gender, weight, hair colour, and height) and the social assumptions and stereotyping that may follow the actual presence in the world can be held in check. Similarly, the present social circles and peer group that affirm the current identity and may hamper new identifications can, to a large extent – remembering that past identifications remind one of an existing identity – be bypassed as new relations are formed online which are more akin to considering the person as a 'blank' canvass. In 'trying-out' aspects of one's ideal identity, as empathetic voices are drawn from co-internet inhabitants, a heightened degree of self-disclosure occurs and co-sympathetic friendships established (see Bargh et al., 2002; Coleman, Paternite, & Sherman, 1999).

Research has clearly revealed that interacting with others online can improve self-esteem and facilitate some changes in self-concept (see McKenna & Bargh, 1998, 2000; Stryker & Statham, 1985; Turkle, 1995). Those who find it difficult to relate to others in face-to-face situations, due to social anxiety or lack of 'normal' social skills, generally appear to find the internet a better place to relate and they emerge with better a self-concept and ability to relate face-to-face.

Danet (1998) has previously noted a gender-related 'liberating' potential of the internet. Danet (1998) argues:

> many people who have never before been interested in cross-dressing as a member of the opposite gender are experimenting with gender identity in typed encounters on the Internet. . . . In cyberspace, *the typed text provides the mask.* Motivations for doing so are varied. Men are curious about what it is like to be a woman or seek attention that female-presenting individuals typically receive. Women want to avoid being harassed sexually or to feel free to be more assertive. For still others, women and men, textual masquerade may be a source of titillation or a way to experiment with their sexuality. . . . I believe that masquerading in this fashion promotes consciousness-raising about gender issues and might contribute to the long-term destabilization of the way we currently construct gender (pp. 129–130). . . .
>
> Although there are social and cultural constraints on individuals' behavior, for women in particular, this medium is potentially very liberating. (pp. 129–130, 136, italics is original emphasis)

The notion that cyberspace is conducive to gender-related liberation for individuals and the broader social construction of gender is something that potentially could reframe the manner in which socio-sexual patterns of behaviour occur. In saying this, we still acknowledge that empirical research (see, for example, Whitty, 2004a) has found that many individuals are not taking up the opportunities to play with gender roles as much as they possibly could.

Danet's argument that cyberspace is potentially particularly liberating for women if gender is masked or neutralised is an argument that causes us to reflect, perhaps more deeply, on issues such as being 'permitted' to have similar 'air-time' and space to be heard without the overlay of being subordinated in the competition for such time-space by males. The issue of physical appearance and its effect upon being heard, in a similar manner, is also rendered less problematic. Suler (1999a) notes in a case study description an instance of a female switching to male persona and in so doing allowed her 'to freely express certain aggressive and powerful actions that I don't seem able to project when perceived as a female'. The stereotypes that are intervening factors in social discourse offline, arguably, become less inhibiting and controlling. While the manner in which gender experimentation and gender is masked or neutralised in cyberspace is an important arena for future research, the degree to which such experimentation and masking is liberating is worthy of our continuing attention as is tracking of the social-psychological effects of such experimentation on social discourse offline. This said, some individual's have been devising and suggesting strategies in order to unmask those who are being deceptive about their gender (see Suler, 1999a) and thus the extent of online gender-switching may become less than it has in the past.

It cannot be ignored that some research reveals there are potentially negative outcomes for the individuals who experiment with their identity in cyberspace. For example, it has been shown that if aspects of these new identities do not become integrated within in the current self, a fragmentation can occur such that it undermines confidence in the current sense of self, and in more extreme cases can result in schizoid or multiple personality (see Donahue, Robins, Roberts, & John, 1993; Glass, 1993). Suler (1999a) offers a sobering note that rare cases of gender-switching on the internet could be a symptom of a clinical condition of gender-confusion in which there has been a failure to develop a gender identity. An inability to differentiate between the two (or more) identities may also lead to delusional-types of behaviour, akin to some of the experiences under psychotropic drugs. In extreme cases, allured by increasing narcissistic gratification,[4] the individual may seek to develop even more elaborate presentation identities. In this context the computer becomes an object of even greater allurement – a seductive object that excites for its potential to yield narcissistic pleasure not always as easily obtained offline.

This chapter has primarily attempted to offer a theoretical framework to help in the understanding of human relationships in cyberspace. The work of object-relations theorists has been the major source for such a conceptual framework. There is, however, further insight to be gained from object-relations theorists in relation to the significance we place upon the transitional objects that we encounter in our efforts to play at love in cyberspace. The next chapter continues this contextual discussion of object-relations.

CHAPTER 4

Object Engagement and Dysfunctional Aspects of Relating Online

In the last chapter we explored how object-relations theory was extremely useful in trying to understand relationships in cyberspace. In the discussion of Winnicott's work, we noted that transitional objects are fundamental to negotiating our way between inner and outer worlds. Our relationship with these transitional objects is not, however, simply a benign and instrumental relationship, but instead is part of an emotional and embodied experience that is intimately connected with unconscious processes and affective states. This chapter briefly discusses these embodied responses to technology and how they are related to the manner on which we engage cyberspace. The work of Christopher Bollas (1987, 1992) is particularly instructive in this regard and it is to his work that we would like to initially turn our attention.

Psychodynamics of object engagement: The work of Christopher Bollas

Those readers that have seen the popular film *You've got mail* (Donner & Ephron, 1998) may recall that the film opens with a background musical track that has lyrics about a 'wish of making friends ... and a wish is just a dream'. While this song is playing, we see and hear a journalist named

Frank Navasky (played by Greg Kinnear) reading the morning paper to his awakening girlfriend, Kathleen Kelly (Meg Ryan):

> *This is amazing. The entire workforce of Virginia had to have solitaire removed from their computer because they hadn't done any work in six weeks. . . . Do you know what this is? What we are seeing here is the end of Western civilization as we know it. . . .* (looking at the portable computer, he continues talking to the world in general) *You think this machine is your friend, but it isn't.*

Frank then quietly proceeds to go off to work as per normal, leaving Kathleen behind who is still in her pajamas. Kathleen after assuring herself that Frank has actually gone to work, immediately checks her email. The film director then cuts to a character named Joe Fox (Tom Hanks) who, in a similar morning 'departure' scene with his girlfriend Patricia Eden (Parker Posey), checks his email having assured himself that Patricia has left for work. We then have Joe reading an email, with a voice-over from Kathleen as though she were speaking to him directly:

To: NY152
From: Shop girl
Subject: Dear Friend

> *I turn on my computer. I wait patiently as it boots up. I go online and my breath catches in my chest until I hear three little words. You've got mail. I hear nothing, not even the sound on the streets of New York, just the beat of my own heart. I have mail. From you.*

Having read their emails, Joe and Kathleen then both set off for work passing each other in the street, oblivious to their 'intimate' connection that occurred only minutes earlier, courtesy of the internet. The director then follows Kathleen into her small 'Shop Around the Corner' bookshop and we are then to overhear a conversation between her and a female friend/employee in which the female friend/employee asks about the reasons for Kathleen's good mood and thinks she must be in love. Kathleen subsequently asks: 'Is it infidelity if you are involved with someone on email?' Unbeknown to their respective boyfriend and girlfriend, Kathleen and Joe continue to send emails to each other as though they were entering a 'dear diary' note about their workday and their philosophical pondering about life in general. In subsequent scenes, we see the two stars of the film glance and 'dance' around their computer as though the object itself was alive, or was about to spring to life. In one scene, in particular, Joe is shown walking back and forth past an open doorway stopping to look at his computer. It is as though he was waiting for the computer to say or do something, or for him to make up his mind about going online. Both Joe and Kathleen are shown talking to their computer and, at times, 'hitting' the keys as though they were projecting their emotions through the hardware itself.

The scenes from *You've got mail* are very much in keeping with aspects of the behaviour we have described in the previous chapters. Indeed, it might be recalled that in the last chapter we made the observation, in passing, that we invest emotion towards objects such that, in the case of cyberspace, the mere thought of going online or touching the computer (and other transitional objects) may trigger emotional responses. It was in such a context it is worth recalling that we noted the effect of turning on the computer had on one person. This description bears repeating:

> When I turn on my computer . . . it makes a little sound. This sound I sometimes playfully interpret as a cheerful 'Good morning' greeting, for the action of bringing my computer to life usually happens first thing in the morning . . . In conjunction with my cup of tea, the sound helps to prepare me emotionally and physically for the working day ahead, a day that will involve much tapping on the computer keyboard and staring into the pale blue face of the display monitor. (Lupton, 1995, p. 97)

Both Lupton's reaction to her computer and the similar behaviour described above from *You've got mail* would seem to be a good glimpse of some dimensions of *object engagement*. In the psychodynamic literature, the work of Christopher Bollas (1987, 1992) cogently describes the dynamics of such object engagement. In an extension of Winnicott's work, Christopher Bollas aptly argues that transitional objects, like all objects, leave a trace within us. Bollas (1992) maintains that:

> as we encounter the object world we are substantially metamorphosed by the structure of objects; internally transformed by objects that leave their traces within us, whether it be the effect of a musical structure, a novel, or a person. In play the subject releases the idiom of himself to the field of objects, where he is then transformed by the structure of that experience, and will bear the history of that encounter in the unconscious. (p. 59)

Some objects do appear to have much more meaning for us and seem to unlock unconscious thought processes and affective states (Bollas, 1992). In a sense, these objects are 'transformational' and may act like 'psychic keys' (Carr, 2003a; Whitty & Carr, 2003). The objects themselves, in acting as psychic keys, appear to enable past unconscious experiences to be released to inform present behaviour.[1] Bollas conceives the psyche as very much influenced by early life experiences, particularly those with the mother and before the acquisition of language. It is as though these early experiences form the core ('idiom') of the self, and through which we engage and interpret the object-world with a subjectivity that is akin to, what psychoanalysts previously called, 'dream-work' that is, symbolic, latent, and manifest meaning and condensed. This process of object engagement, Bollas (1992) describes in the following way:

> The processional integrity of any object – that which is inherent to any object when brought to life by an engaging subject – is used by the individual according to the laws of the dream work. When we use an object it is as if we know the terms of engagement; we know we shall 'enter into' an intermediate space, and at this point of entry we change the nature of perception, as we are now released to dream work, in which subjectivity is scattered and disseminated in to the object world, transformed by that encounter, then returned to itself after the dialectic, changed in its inner contents by the history of that moment. (p. 60)

The manner in which we engage and interpret the object-world, including our relationship with transitional objects, can be both a healthy and an unhealthy process. While we have described much of the normal healthy engagement we need to be alert to the manner in which the engagement can be dysfunctional and unhealthy to our 'normal' functioning in our offline world.

Object engagement and attachment: Dysfunctional and unhealthy outcomes

Fetish and sexual disorder

The process of object engagement and attachment, and specifically to transitional objects, is a normal part of growing up and crucial in developmental behaviour. However, like the dangers we noted in the last chapter in relation to play, there are dangers to investing 'too much' emotion towards objects. Winnicott (1953) argued that normally the transitional object provides a healthy experience, which loses its meaning after a while. As we noted in the previous chapter, he believed that the first transitional object stood for the breast in an illusory way. Later on in a child's life, he suggests, objects such as toys represent body parts. Problems can arise, however, if attachment to a transitional object persists for too long. Winnicott (1951/1971b) proposed that the 'transitional object may eventually develop into a fetish object and so persist as a characteristic of the adult sexual life' (p. 9).

Winnicott's linking of fetishism with aspects of sexuality is a matter that can be noted in the very early work of Sigmund Freud and his colleagues. In 1914, Sándor Ferenczi wrote to Sigmund Freud about a masochistic patient with 'foot fetishism' (Brabant, Falzeder, & Giampieri-Deutsch, 1993, p. 534). Ferenczi was to link this foot fetishism with sexual arousal (see Ferenczi, 1916/1994, pp. 16, 22). In an early comment upon foot fetishism, Freud (1906/1990, p. 71) suggested more generally that 'ever since Binet [1888] we have in fact tried to trace fetishism back to erotic impressions in childhood'. Elsewhere, Freud (1905/1977, p. 67) expresses his view slightly differently when he says that Alfred 'Binet [1888] was the first to maintain that the choice of fetish is an after-effect of some sexual impression, received as a rule in early childhood.' 'Sexual impression' and 'erotic impression' are not precisely the same thing, but in his earliest works, Freud commented on fetish in a context that was linked to early childhood and sexuality.

From these early observations, Freud was later to revise his opinion on the adequacy of fetishism being viewed as simply in the realm of the erotic and the sexual. It needs to be clearly understood that these initial observations were made in a context in which Freud had conceived psychodynamics in terms of a *libido theory*. Freud argued that one's innate instincts create 'psychic energy' – a biological force produced in a manner akin to the way a dynamo produces electrical power. Freud viewed thoughts, feelings, and behaviour, as powered by libido. While libido needed expression, a number of influences caused its repression – that is relegation of the ungratified impulses to the unconscious where they still sought expression. Much of this early formulation simply conceived libido as specifically related to sexual instincts and bodily pleasures. This initial conception of the psyche was evident in Freud's work in the first two decades of the last century. It was in the early part of the 1920s that Freud started to put forward a significantly revised view of the psyche that, in turn, caused him to reconsider a range of explanations he had previously advanced for various behaviours.

In an unfinished paper of some four pages entitled 'Splitting of the ego in the process of defence' (1940/1985), Freud moved beyond his initial notion of fetishism as an instance of sexual perversion or erotic/sexual impression. His initial idea was that fetishism was almost always a male 'perversion', narrowly related to the castration complex – that is, fetish as a non-sexual part of the body (or, another object) becomes a substitute for the mother's penis, that the son once believed in (Freud, 1927/1977). The fetish object becomes simultaneously both a means of denying sexual difference as well as a defence against the fear of castration. In this unfinished paper, Freud (1940/1985) began to link fetish with the broader psychological processes of the ego's function and with the psychodynamics of defence – particularly those of displacement. This glimpse of Freud's intended revision of how fetish should be considered has led some within the psychoanalytic community to include a rendering of the term as being, 'metaphori-cally, an extravagant devotion to an object' (English & English, 1958/1966, p. 205).

Part of the prompt for Freud to reconsider the notion of fetish was related to the revised view of the dynamics of the psyche – in what we earlier noted as his second model of the psyche. We are left to speculate upon the exact manner in which fetish would be explained in terms that related to the psychodynamic processes of the ego and, specifically, those related to defence. Notwithstanding, we can readily envisage fetish as part of a constellation of psychodynamic processes that deals with the threat and idealisation of 'other'. Indeed, in keeping with the ideas of some within the psychoanalytic community, a meta-psychology of fetish may simply insist that fetish is an exaggerated response in the psychodynamics of 'devotion to an object'.

The complex manner in which fetishism is linked to displacement and the psychodynamics of defence and, indeed, how the object chosen as a fetish is symbolically sexual in nature is complicated all the more when we talk about transitional objects and the internet. Transitional objects, such as the computer itself, are the means through which one may get to relate to others in both the realm of the sexual and fantasy. It is not uncommon to hear some computer owners talking about: the size of their hard drive;

the size of their RAM; the speed of their processor, and alike. The owner-ship of the object itself has become a source of 'prestige' as well as fetish that has sexual symbolism. Indeed, in relation to the internet, the capacity of transitional objects to become fetish objects is something both under-theorised and under-researched. The manner in which these transitional objects are used for cyberspace contact carries a symbolically sexual meaning. This is something that would appear worthy of investigation. Moreover, under-researched is the degree of transference reactions occur in relation to the computer (see Suler, 1998) and how such transference is intertwined with development of a fetish.

Cybersex: Object engagement of the (overt) sexual kind

It was noted in Chapters 1 and 2 of this book that cyberspace provides a place where individuals can be more sexually liberated than is the case in their offline situation. The range in the nature of the sexual activity online was noted to be variable. The term 'cybersex' is most often used to denote synchronous communication in cyberspace in which typically two individuals engage in discourses about sexual fantasies and is accompanied by mastur-bation. Some studies have found those who engage in cybersex may find such an activity is a healthy and emotionally satisfying experience (see, for example, studies by Cooper & Sportolari, 1997; Cooper et al., 2002; Turkle, 1995). Sometimes cybersex might even galvanise one's offline sex life (Whitty, 2003b). However, as demonstrated in Chapter 5, in the main, cybersex is seen as an act of infidelity if one is already in an offline relation-ship. Hence, for some individuals, online sexual activity may have a range of destructive and unhealthy consequences, especially if one is already in an offline relationship. Jennifer Schneider (2003), for instance, reported adverse effects of their partner's cybersex involvement including feelings of 'hurt, betrayal, rejection, abandonment, devastation, loneliness, shame, isolation, humiliation, jealousy, and anger, as well as loss of self-esteem. Being lied to repeatedly was a major cause of distress' (p. 329). In Schneider's study that comprised 91 women and 3 men, almost one quarter were now separated or divorced as a result of their partner's cybersex involve-ment and several others within the group were seriously contemplating leaving their partner. Other detrimental effects were also noted in respect to the children and family life in general. Some would argue that cybersex involvement can become an addiction (see Cooper, Delmonico, & Burg, 2000; Cooper, Putnam, Planchon, & Boies, 1999; Schneider, 2003).

In Chapter 1 we noted that Cooper (1998) put forward a 'Triple A engine' to explain how the internet is a potent medium for sexual activity – the Triple A engine being that the internet is easy to *Access*, it is *Affordable* and one can be *Anonymous*. Certainly psychodynamic explanations of cybersex involvement would highlight the more regressive and primitive nature of this behaviour in the absence of an inhibitive social environment. The essence of such a reading of cybersex was noted in Chapter 3, where it was argued that anonymity seems to 'suspend' or ignore the normal engagement of the prohibitive aspect of the superego in a reversion to an earlier state of mental functioning. This would appear to be a formula for compensatory narcissistic pleasure of the more aberrant kind and may include issues related to fetish as we have described previously in this chapter. Object-relations theories would additionally suggest the engagement with others for sexual gratification could arise from a number of early in life experiences. In one of his earlier works, Christopher Bollas (1978) introduces the notion of a 'transformational object' to distinguish the first maternal object as a process rather than a thing in itself. In a slight variation of Winnicott, Bollas (1978) argues:

> I have termed the first object the transformational object, as I want to identify it with the object as process, thus linking our notion of the object with the infant's subjective knowing of it. Before the mother is personalized to the infant as a whole object she has functioned as a source of transformation, and as the infant's own nascent subjectivity is almost completely the experience of the ego's integrations (cognitive, libidinal, effective) the first object is identified with the alterations of the ego's state. The ego experience remains as an unconscious memory in the adult who relives it through his adamant quest for a transformational object: a new partner, a different form of work, a new material acquisition, an ideology or a belief. (pp. 105–106)

Cyberspace represents not just a place to play, but a place where one can regress. The increased use of the internet would appear to increase the chances of sexual partners online being a 'quest for a transformational object'. This clinicians' perspective has started to make its mark in the literature on cyberspace, but further research through such a conceptual lens would seem to commend itself.

The generational character of objects

Before we leave the discussion in relation to embodied responses to technology and object engagement, it is interesting to reflect upon the idea that the objects of technology that are engaged may themselves be generational in character. Bollas (1992) makes this point clearly when he argued that:

> Were we to study this psychology of generations closely, it would be of interest to contrast the nature of generational potential spaces, to note those objects selected as signature of a generations consciousness, and to analyse the field of such objects as unconscious ideas that may be generative or pathological. (p. 266)

He further argues that generational objects weave into historic time and specifically that 'Generations form objects that signify the history of childhoods, that speak to the collective march through time of a vast group expecting and expected to shape history' (Bollas, 1992, p. 267). Although it is too early to tell, in decades to come we might look back over the objects, such as computers, modems, keyboards, and so forth, and, in retrospective, see these items are signifying meaning for a particular generation in history.

In raising the argument about the generational character of the objects we are also reminded of the work of Serres raised in the previous chapter. Examination of the generational character of objects may need to include an appreciation of the manner in which these objects play through us. Such an appreciation has yet to make an appearance in the research literature. It is anticipated that by understanding the manner in which objects play through us we also appreciate the manner in which we are 'taken up' or drawn in by the nature of the play (see Friedman, 1989). Our object engagement is mediated through language yet the manner in which language services such engagement has largely gone unexamined in the research literature. These avenues for future research potentially will deepen our understanding of the unconscious and taken-for-granted assumptions about the embodied responses to technology and object engagement.

CHAPTER 5

Cyber-Cheating

Can We Really be Liberated in Cyberspace?

My husband of two and a half years has done something weird. I have found emails from a girl that is in the same line of work as him. He says that it was all just fun and games but he would ask her if she had a webcam and IM so they could chat later. She says that she will be coming to visit his area in about three weeks. I confronted him about this and he says that its just a computer he has not even touched anyone and it was all a big game. Can emails with sexual undertones be considered a form of adultery?

(Anonymous, Cheating wife stories – cheating husband stories)

In the previous chapter we touched upon problems that might arise when engaging in sexual activities in cyberspace. In this chapter we examine the dark side of online relationships further – more specifically by considering internet infidelity. We consider Michael Civin's (2000) apt point that 'just as cyberspace may potentiate, it may also thwart and debilitate' (p. 40). While of course successful relationships are indeed formed online (as demonstrated in Chapters 1 and 2), there are many tales of online relationships going horribly wrong. Sometimes one's playful activities online are not always liberating.

Not all teddy bears are transitional

As discussed in earlier chapters of this book, the well-known writer Sherry Turkle presented a utopian view of cyberspace in her in-depth discussion of MUDders. While we too believe that cyberspace provides unique liberating opportunities, we also take on Civin's (2000) view that this is not the case for everyone (Whitty & Carr, 2003). Civin (2000) has emphatically argued that 'the transitional and facilitative nature of the use of cyberspace as potential space is much less of a given than Turkle might be suggesting' (p. 38). Instead, he states, 'that no object or process, the cyber system included is essentially transitional' (p. 39). Civin suggests that some people might be drawn to the internet because they see it as a place of isolation – a safe haven. However, in the end this might not be what they achieve. He has written that:

> Faced with the prospect of persecution, whether aimed at us from without or ricocheting about from more internal origins, we tend to seek psychological relief by retreating to safer psychic dwellings. These dwelling-retreats are often likened to a fortress buttressed against the invasive threats of outside assault. But an alternative metaphor seems even more powerful and useful when applied to the Internet. Instead of a fortress, imagine the Internet users confined in isolated cells, locked away so that they may neither do harmful things nor have harmful things done to them....
>
> But many people, however, threatened and in retreat they may be, and however many times they may have incarcerated themselves in the relative safety of their isolated cells, crave more than partial and limited relationships....
>
> Eventually, the study of Internet relations leads us to the conclusion that many people confined in cells away from connection with others may choose to seek the best illusion of something that seems like a complete relationship, even when they have volunteered for that confinement to seek protection from actual contact with others. (pp. 41–42)

Civin reminds us that Winnicott was not suggesting that all teddy bears and blankets are essentially transitional! Likewise, not all cyber systems will act as transitional objects. Civin adds that in stark contrast, cyber systems are potentially invasive, so much so that they can foster *persecutory anxiety*. Civin (2000) argued that for some, 'the computer system seems a far cry (in all meanings) from the teddy bear or favorite blanket, and the breach between the cyber system and the transitional or potential looms unnegotiably vast' (p. 51).

To illustrate his point, Civin (2000) cited a case study in which a married woman, Jeanette, started to feel alone in her marriage. To counteract her loneliness she immersed herself in her studies and since much of her studies required her to use her computer, she found herself becoming interested in chat. She befriended a man online, and at first very much enjoyed his attention. However, this friendship went sour when Jeannette told her other online friends about a program, which this man had suggested her to install. This program would notify her instantly when he wanted to chat to her. Jeannette was eventually forced off the net after this man become enraged after he found out she had been sharing their program. The man's rage became transformed into jealousy and the woman found herself the target of an emailing frenzy in which she was being sent email at a rate beyond her capacity to respond. This increase in email activity served to increase her anxiety that her husband would eventually discover her online relationships. Jeannette finished up having to discontinue using the computer and, as a consequence, had to give up her studies. This was doubly difficult for her given that she had immersed herself in these activities as a way of dealing with her unhappy marriage.

The above example clearly demonstrates that not all relationships developed online are conducive to psychological growth. We would like to develop this argument further by considering the new phenomenon of cyber-infidelity.

Internet infidelity

Arguably, online affairs can in some ways be more seductive than offline affairs (Whitty & Carr, 2005a). This critical point will be addressed later in this chapter; however, first this chapter defines offline infidelity and compares this with internet infidelity. This chapter also highlights some of the differences between the sexes when it comes to views on betrayal.

Offline infidelity: More than just sex

Most researchers would agree that we need to consider other acts of infidelity in addition to sexual intercourse. For example, Roscoe, Cavanaugh, and Kennedy (1988) focused on undergraduates' views on acts of infidelity and found that participants indicated three principle behaviours: dating or spending time with a different partner; having sexual intercourse with someone else; and engaging in other sexual interactions with someone else, such as kissing, flirting, and petting. To supplement work such as Roscoe et al.'s study, Yarab, Sensibaugh, and Allgeier (1998) investigated which extradyadic behaviours individuals identify as unfaithful acts in the context of committed romantic relationships. Yarab et al.'s (1998) study yielded an array of unfaithful behaviours in addition to sexual intercourse, including passionately kissing, sexual fantasies, non-sexual fantasies about falling in love, sexual attraction, romantic attraction, flirting, and behaviour in dyads, such as studying, having lunch with, and going to a movie with someone other than one's partner. These researchers claim that '*mental exclusivity*' might be considered as important as '*sexual exclusivity*'. Interestingly, Yarab and Allgeier (1998) found that when considering sexual fantasies the greater the threat of the sexual fantasy to the current relationship, the higher the fantasy was rated as unfaithful. For instance, fantasising about a partner's best friend (a great potential to disrupting the current relationship) was considered by most to be more of a threat, and therefore more unfaithful, than fantasising about a movie star. In addition, these researchers found that participants were more jealous about the idea of their partner fantasising about their best friend than fantasising about a movie star.

Offline infidelity: Men and women's views

The general consensus has been that men and women hold different viewpoints on offline monogamous relationships. For instance, Sheppard, Nelson, and Andreoli-Mathie (1995) have argued that men tend to view commitment and monogamy as less attractive options than women do. It also seems that men and women enter into extramarital relationships for different reasons; women more because they are seeking a friendship or emotional relationship, while men tend to be more interested in sexual relationships (Glass & Wright, 1985). Satisfaction within a marriage is also often marked by these gender differences, with men more likely to report sexual problems, and women more likely to indicate problems with affection as the cause of discord within the marriage (DeBurgher, 1972).

Noticeably, men are more likely to at least own up to having some type of extradyadic sexual experience compared to women (Hansen, 1987; Townsend & Levy, 1990). Yarab et al. (1998) found that men admitted more than women did to fantasising about having sexual intercourse and giving and receiving oral sex with someone else other than their partner.

Moreover, men in their study were more likely to state that they had 'hit on' someone else.

Research has also considered gender differences in attitudes towards infidelity. For instance, Taylor (1986) found that men tend to judge a husband's affair as more justifiable than a wife's affair. Furthermore, Sheppard et al. (1995) found that male college students were more likely to rate infidelity as more acceptable than women rated infidelity. Paul and Galloway (1994) found in their sample of undergraduate students, that women (52%) were much more likely than men (30%) to say they would end the relationship if their partner was unfaithful to them. However, such gender differences are not always supported. For instance, it has been established that men and women tend to assess their own extradyadic behaviour as more acceptable than that of their partner (Yarab et al., 1998). Furthermore, researchers have revealed that individuals are more forgiving of extradyadic behaviours committed by members of their own gender compared to individuals of the opposite gender (Yarab, Allgeier, & Sensibaugh, 1999). One of the reasons for these discrepancies could possibly be the variations in samples being used, including people who are experienced in relationships who are asked to reflect on their current relationship, compared to non-experienced participants who are asked to imagine a hypothetical cheating partner.

In respect to which extradyadic behaviours cause more upset for each gender, women are more prone to focus on emotional implications of infidelity and men are more sensitive to the sexual aspects of infidelity. However, it is also noteworthy that both men and women report extradyadic sexual behaviour to be more unacceptable and a greater betrayal than extradyadic emotional behaviour (Buss, Larsen, Westen, & Semmelroth, 1992; Shackelford & Buss, 1996). Roscoe et al. (1988) also identified gender differences in what participants considered as violations of infidelity. In their study, they asked participants to list what behaviours they believed constituted being unfaithful to a dating partner who is involved in a serious dating relationship. They found that men were more likely to state that a sexual encounter with a different partner was an exemplar of infidelity. In contrast, women were more likely to state that spending time with another and keeping secrets from a partner were acts of infidelity. Buss et al. (1992) argue, from an evolutionary point of view, that men should be more likely than women to react with greater jealousy to sexual infidelity due to paternal uncertainty. In contrast, women should be more likely to react with greater jealousy than men to emotional infidelity because they would perceive this as a greater threat to paternal investment.

There are a number of shortcomings of the above research. First, that most of these studies have focused on how upset people might feel about these varying infidelities. More current research is starting to uncover varying results when considering other emotions, such as anger and hurt (Becker, Sagarin, Guadagno, Millevoi, & Nicastle, 2004). Another limitation of most of the research in this area is the heavy reliance on college students as participants. This is clearly problematic given that these are younger people who are often not married or in cohabiting relationships. Hence, their lack of experience in long-term relationships could dramatically influence how these individuals perceive acts of infidelity.

Internet addiction and online infidelity

The pioneering theorists in field of cyber-affairs were researchers, such as Kimberly Young, Al Cooper, and Marlene Maheu (see, for example, Cooper, 2002; Maheu & Subotnik, 2001; Young, 1998a). Young, Griffin-Shelley, Cooper, O'Mara, and Buchanan (2000) defined a cyber-affair as 'a romantic and/or sexual relationship that is initiated via online contact and maintained predominantly through electronic conversations that occur through e-mail and in virtual communities such as, chat rooms, interactive games, or newsgroups' (p. 60). The problem with Young and other such researchers' work is that they concentrate on the link between 'online sexual compulsivity' and internet affairs (more on internet addiction in the following chapter). Moreover, many of their claims are not supported with convincing empirical evidence. The assumption seems to be that individuals with psychological disorders have online affairs and that an online affair is the only act that constitutes infidelity. Other acts of betrayal, which are not affairs, might be behaviours, such as cyber-flirting or sharing intimate secrets with someone an individual is attracted to. Shaw (1997), at least, argues that 'Internet infidelity is, of course, behaviorally different from other kinds of infidelity; however, the contributing factors and results are similar when we consider how it affects the way partners relate' (p. 29). Shaw, however, did not qualify how online and offline infidelities are behaviourally different. The first study, to our knowledge, to attempt to do so is Whitty's (2003b) study.

Pushing the wrong buttons

Monica Whitty (2003b) surveyed 1117 participants about their attitudes towards online and offline infidelity. The sample consisted of 42 per cent men and 58 per cent women and ages ranged from 17 to 70 years of age. Online and offline samples were obtained. The survey considered acts, such as sexual intercourse, cybersex, hotchatting, emotional disclosure, and various types of pornography. Interestingly, the research revealed that individuals do believe that some interactions that occur online are acts of betrayal. Some of these behaviours, such as cybersex, posed a greater threat than other behaviours, such as downloading pornography. Of further importance, the study found that there are separate components of infidelity that we need to consider, including sexual infidelity, emotional infidelity, and pornography. This is consistent with previous research (described earlier in this chapter) on offline infidelity which has purported that infidelity should not be reduced to sexual infidelity, but that mental exclusivity is also an important component of fidelity (Yarab & Allgeier, 1998). However, what is unique to Whitty's (2003b) study is that the factor analysis she performed revealed that online acts of betrayal do not fall into a discrete category of their own. For example, sexual intercourse, hotchatting, and cybersex all combined to make one factor. Therefore, we might conclude from such a study that people hold similar attitudes towards online and offline infidelities.

Some other interesting results emerged from Whitty's (2003b) study that are worthy of note. It was found that those with no internet sexual experience were more likely to rate the factors 'sexual' and 'pornography' as forms of betrayal than those with internet sexual experience. Whitty argues that those with internet sexual experience might have perceived these acts as less threatening, given that they are more aware of what these acts entail. Alternatively, perhaps these individuals are more sexually liberated and less prudish than the rest of the population. It was also found that there was an interaction between gender and age in relation to the factor sexual infidelity. Women overall were more likely to believe that sexual acts were an act of betrayal. Overall, the younger group (17–22 years) believed that these sexual acts were acts of betrayal more than the older groups. Men in the age range of 23–44 were also more likely to rate sexual infidelity higher than the oldest group of men (45–70 years). However, the interaction effect occurred for the older women (45–70 years) who rated this factor higher than the women in the age range of 23–44. Finally, there was an interaction between age and relationship status on the factor sexual infidelity. The younger individuals (17–22 years), who were currently in a relationship, believed that these sexual acts were acts of betrayal more than the 17–22 year-olds not in a relationship. Moreover, the 17–22 year-olds in a relationship rated this factor higher than any other individuals. Interestingly, this pattern is reversed for the 23–44 year-olds, where those who were not in a relationship were more inclined to rate the factor sexual infidelity as an act of betrayal, compared to the 23–44 year-olds in a relationship. Again, contrasting results occur for the 45–70 year-olds, where those individuals not in a relationship rate this factor the lowest compared to other individuals; however, the drop in scores was not as dramatic for the 45–70 year-olds in a relationship. Whitty (2003b) believed there is a plausible explanation for why younger people in a relationship rate sexual acts of infidelity higher than other individuals. Courtship has been described as 'a "trying-out" period that individuals use to assess the qualifications of each as a more permanent mate' (Paul, Foss, & Galloway, 1993, p. 403). These younger individuals, who are more likely to be in a trying-out phase in a relationship, are perhaps less tolerable of any sexual form of betrayal. Interestingly, the result is reversed for the older adults (23–44 years) with those not in a relationship more likely to rate the factor sexual as an act of betrayal than those in a relationship. Moreover, the oldest individuals not in a relationship (presumably some of which are widows) rated sexual acts of infidelity lower than any other group.

Whitty (2003b) warns us that the age effect yielded in her study might not be a developmental difference, but rather a cohort effect. Although, it is difficult to tell from a cross-sectional design, we might want to consider that the different age groups have experienced different social changes in their lives. For instance, the 23–44-year-old group had experienced the women's movement and the sexual revolution, whereas, the younger group in their formative years experienced a sexual counter-revolution that took place in the 1990s because of the emergence of sexual diseases in the 1980s, such as HIV.

The results from Whitty's (2003b) study demonstrate that individuals do perceive that some interactions that occur online are indeed acts of betrayal. It is perhaps not the amount of physical contact or the idea that one's partner is masturbating, but rather that their partner *desires* another and is seeking out a sexual encounter with another individual other than themselves. Whitty argued that therefore cybersex is *'real sex'* and could have the same impact on an offline relationship as one's partner having sexual intercourse with someone else. So while there are no bodies physically touching this does not mean that the action is unauthentic or unreal. Moreover, we might again consider Yarab and Allgeier's (1998) view that when considering sexual fantasies, the greater the threat of the sexual fantasy to the relationship, the more likely the fantasy is considered unfaithful. It is probable that participants perceived that sexual acts, such as cybersex and hot chat were more of a threat than pornography, since individuals were more likely to meet face-to-face with their cyber-lovers than with porn stars. As outlined in Chapter 1, whilst many sexual encounters do initiate online, it has been found that a large proportion of individuals continue these relationships offline.

Cyber-cheating stories

In a follow-up study, instead of asking participants directly about what they believed were acts of internet betrayal, Whitty (2005) employed a qualitative method to investigate people's representations of internet infidelity. Drawing from a study conducted by Kitzinger and Powell (1995) on offline infidelity, Whitty devised a story completion method where participants were asked to write a story in response to a cue relating to internet infidelity. In this study, 234 participants ranging in age from 17 to 57 years were given one of two versions of a story-completion task, as shown below:

> *Version A*: Mark and Jennifer have been going out for over a year. Then Mark realises that Jennifer has developed a relationship with someone else over the Internet...
> *Version B*: Jennifer and Mark have been going out for over a year. Then Jennifer realises that Mark has developed a relationship with someone else over the Internet...

This type of 'projective test' was chosen for a number of reasons.

> Projective techniques are advocated when the researcher suspects the existence of barriers to direct self-report: these might include the 'barrier of awareness' (people's lack of awareness of their own motives and attitudes) and the 'barrier

of admissibility' (people's difficulty in admitting certain feelings). Projective techniques, by providing ambiguous stimulus material are supposed to create conditions under which the needs of the perceiver influence what is perceived, and people ascribe their own motivations, feelings and behaviours to other persons in the stimulus material, externalizing their own anxieties, concerns and actions through fantasy responses. (Kitzinger & Powell, 1995, p. 348)

Both of these especially apply to cyber-cheating, given that individuals might not be completely aware of their attitudes towards this behaviour and that admission of such feelings or motives might be deemed as socially undesirable.

A content analysis was performed on the data. The data were analysed considering whether forming a relationship on the internet with someone other than one's offline partner is an act of betrayal, and if so why is this believed to be infidelity. Next, the data were examined for how this internet interaction impacts on the offline relationship.

While Kitzinger and Powell (1995) found that 90 per cent of their sample interpreted their cue story, which was developed in respect to offline infidelity, to be an act of sexual involvement, this was not the case in this particular study. While all of the participants understood this to be a dilemma about infidelity, some were divided as to whether the betrayer believed they were committing an act of infidelity, while others wrote that the partner was not certain that they had been betrayed. Moreover, unlike Kitzinger and Powell's study, when participants interpreted the cue story as a story about sexual involvement, this was not necessarily about a sexual relationship, but in many cases was exclusively an emotional involvement.

Although the majority of the participants (86%) wrote in their stories that the aggrieved felt that they had been betrayed, and 51 per cent wrote that the betrayer believed that they had been unfaithful, a small number of participants were uncertain that this was a scenario about infidelity. Explanations given as to why the scenario should not be considered as infidelity were that (these are followed by some extracts to illustrate some of these themes – note these extracts are written up exactly as the participants wrote them, keeping true to their spelling and grammar):

- the interaction was 'just a friendship'
- the interaction was merely flirtation or fun
- the relationship was with an object (computer) in virtual space, rather than with a real human being

- the interaction was with two people who had never met and did not ever intend to meet
- it could not be infidelity as there was no physical sex taking place.

The most common explanation given for why the scenario should not be considered an act of infidelity was that the interaction was 'just a friendship', as illustrated in the following extracts:

> *Jennifer explains to Mark that the relationship is not romantic & that they are only friends.*

> *He did not think he had done anything wrong, after all this girl was only a friend who existed in text.*

Another explanation was that the interaction was 'merely flirtation or just a bit of fun', as illustrated below:

> *Jennifer on the other hand thinks she's doing nothing wrong. So what if she flirts a bit with someone who lives far away.*

> *Mark at first brushes it off thinking that its "only the Internet, no harm in having fun."*

Interestingly, there were others who pointed out that this was not infidelity, as the relationship was with an object (computer) in virtual space, rather than with a real human being.

> *She tried to explain, that he was just a faithful companion and the only feeling she had were not real as this man was just words on a screen. . . .*

> *When she confronts him about it one night over dinner, he denies everything saying that they were just friends. And that she should not take it so seriously and worry about it because it was not a real relationship, but a net relationship. That net relationships mean nothing because everyone lives in a virtual reality.*

There were others who emphasised that the interaction could not be considered an act of betrayal as the two had never met, nor did they intend to meet. Moreover, often the stories had the two cyber-lovers interacting from different countries, making it unlikely that they could potentially ever meet.

Jennifer retaliates and says how can I be having an affair, without even meeting this guy.

Mark tells her to calm down, & says that although he chats to her regularly he has never offered to meet her, & she hasn't suggested it either.

There was a significant effect of perpetuator's gender on the use of the explanation that 'it cannot be infidelity if there is not any physical sex occurring'. Both men and women were more likely to write this when Mark was the betrayer.

"No I'm not cheating. It's not like I'm bonking her anyway".
Although Mark believes that because there was no physical contact, he has not cheated, Jen disagrees.
However, Mark said that it is not cheating at all. He said he just enjoyed an imaginative relationship which is only made through computers. He said he never met the girl he had been seeing on the net and his point is that he doesn't think it is cheating unless he has a sexual relationship with someone else.

Finally, there were three participants who explained that this was not an act of infidelity, but more sexual experimentation, as the cyber-affair was between two people of the same sex.

Finally he asks, "So how serious is it?" Jennifer replies, "Well its just really a bit of fun, you have nothing to worry about!" In fact, she goes on to say, "It's actually a female!!" (ARRGHH Shock Horror!!)

Although some of the stories (as demonstrated above) focused on explaining away why the online act was not an act of betrayal, many more took it for granted that this was a scenario about infidelity. Quite a number of the stories provided reasons for why this was an act of infidelity, either by admissions of guilt from the perpetrator or as justifications for why the aggrieved felt they had been betrayed (these are summarised below, followed by some quotes to illustrate these themes):

• cannot have a relationship with more than one person
• emotional infidelity
• sexual infidelity
• relationship kept a secret

The most frequently stated reason for why this was an act of infidelity was that participants reasoned that one should not have a romantic relationship with more than one person. Sometimes this was because the online relationship was considered to be as real as the offline relationship, or that it had the same effect as being in another face-to-face relationship, or because the individual intended to meet up with the cyber-lover, as demonstrated in the exemplars below:

> *Jennifer can't live with Mark's betrayal and gives him an ultimatum – she is not prepared to 'share' him with someone else.*

One of the more interesting results obtained in the analysis was that emotional infidelity was stressed as much as sexual infidelity. Consistent with previous research on offline infidelity, women stressed the problems they had with emotional infidelity more than the men did. Emotional infidelity is perhaps best illustrated in the following extract:

> *"It is cheating". She said rather calmly.*
> *"No I'm not cheating. It's not like I'm bonking her anyway. You're the one I'm with and like I said I have <u>NO</u> intentions of meeting her." He hopped into bed.*
> *"It's 'emotional' cheating." She said getting annoyed.*
> *"How so?" He asked, amusement showing in his eyes.*
> *"Cheating isn't necessarily physical. That's one side of it . . ." He pulled the sheets over him and rolled over.*
> *"Well . . . I know you have not met her <u>yet</u> that's why, but I'm still a little annoyed, Mark." She sat on the edge of the bed.*
> *"Don't be mad. You're the one I love. So <u>how is it</u> emotional cheating". He sat up.*
> *"You're keeping stuff from me. Relationships are about trust! How can I trust you if you keep stuff from me about the 'Internet' girl'?"*

When participants discussed sexual infidelity, sometimes they referred to cybersex, and on other occasions they wrote about flirting online or hotchatting. Rarely did they refer to these participants having offline sex with their cyber-lovers. Examples of erotic encounters online that were believed to be acts of betrayal are provided below:

> *He sneaks behind her and sees that his girlfriend is in fact flirting with a man by the name of Buzzy. He screams at her and tells her that their relationship is over. She begs*

him to stay, but he tells her that all this time he feels like she has been cheating on him and she can never gain his trust again.

Mark's obsession with the Internet is sure to cause a break-up in the relationship. Jennifer discovered, late one night after Mark had left his computer that he was partaking in "cyber-sex" with a woman by the name of "Buxan Blonde bombshell" Jennifer confronted Mark who admitted that he was having an online relationship with this woman and that she was satisfying his sexual fantasies. This caused a relationship breakdown between Jennifer and Mark.

A further explanation given for why this cyber-act was an act of betrayal is because it was kept a secret. Had the perpetrator been an innocent player he/she would not have concealed their internet activities from their partner, as shown in the extracts below:

Mark follows this statement with why was he not informed of this relationship, and had to find out for himself.

Stories were also analysed considering the kind of impact the cyber-cheating had on the offline relationship. Sixty-five per cent of the stories mentioned that the aggrieved had indeed been hurt or upset by this virtual encounter. The results clearly highlight that the online infidelity did have a real impact on the aggrieved offline relationship, including in many cases leading to a break-up of the relationship. These are summarised below followed by some extracts of the stories to illustrate some of these themes:

- aggrieved feels hurt/depressed/upset/anger
- break-up
- loss of trust
- revenge
- betrayer feels hurt/depressed/upset/anger
- less time together
- shock
- sexually inadequate
- self-esteem

The most frequently reported impact on the offline relationship was that the aggrieved felt upset by the incident. Women were significantly more likely than men to write about the aggrieved being upset. Sometimes the aggrieved expressed deep hurt, while others were considerably angry about the betrayal, as demonstrated below:

> *Mark is shocked, upset & hurt. He feels betrayed by Jennifer that she does not view him as being important enough to confide in him. Marks' hurt quickly turns to anger. He becomes defensive to cover his hurt. He doesn't understand why he feels this way.*

> *Mark is not happy with Jen. He says "Not happy Jen."*

Forty-six per cent of the sample wrote that the offline couple broke up as a consequence of this internet affair. In some cases, the offline relationship was already on rocky grounds and the internet affair was sought out because of the dissatisfaction with the relationship, and in other instances it was simply the cyber-affair which was the cause of the break-up. Women wrote about the couple breaking up more than the men did in their stories.

> *Next day, Jenni told him everything about the affair. She thought that coming clean will be the best option but she was wrong. Mark just ask her to leave the house and never coming back. She couldn't do anything and unable to say anything she packs her bags and left.*

> *She breaks up with him, giving him no explanation, stalks him until he develops signs of paranoia then marries his best friend, who is a doctor and earns easily $500,000 p.a. at minimum, and looks like a god.*

Forty-two per cent of the sample wrote that the cyber-cheating lead to a loss of trust in the offline relationship. Women wrote this more than men and individuals wrote this more when Mark was the perpetrator.

> *From that day forth she began to question who was on the phone, who he stays out for drinks with, and who the girls are who he works with, Jennifer tried to guess his email password and checked his voicemail messages. Eventually it was mistrust, the belief of deceit and the obsession that ended the relationship.*

There were some interesting and often rather cruel ways that the aggrieved sought revenge. For example, some participants wrote that the aggrieved logged on and pretended to be their partner online in order to destroy the cyber-relationship. Sometimes participants wrote that the aggrieved sought revenge by having their own affairs, while others wrote about psychologically or physically harming their partner or the cyber-lover.

Jennifer then decides to play a little game... through a little bit of deception and assumed identity, she manages to assume the identity of Mark's lover when he is chatting and assumes the identity of Mark when his lover is online. Jennifer then convinces them to meet each other, assuming they both love each other. Mark and his Internet lover agree... When Jennifer met the Internet lover she bludgeoned her to death with a keyboard, shoved a mouse up her arse and then replaced her head with a monitor. Transporting her body to the meeting with Mark was next. Mark walks in to find the defaced body, due to his shock Jennifer was able to capture him. Keeping him as a human punching bag, whenever she returned home after a bad day she would kick the shit out of him. She would never forget or allow herself to be betrayed, and Mark had no choice but to remember what he had done.

The results of this study suggest that when individuals are presented with a hypothetical scenario of cyber-cheating they do, in the main, consider this to be a real form of betrayal that can seriously affect the offline relationship. Similar to Kitzinger and Powell's (1995) study, and other studies on offline infidelity (e.g., Feldman & Cauffman, 1999) the participants wrote that the aggrieved expressed upset and anger over the affair. Also, akin to Kitzinger and Powell's study were the revenge stories that were elicited. Importantly, this study demonstrated that people wrote about 'real' feelings being hurt and that, although it was an online affair, that nonetheless, trust was broken as a consequence of the affair. What is perhaps the most significant indication that this was a real affair was the amount of participants who wrote that the couple broke up as a result of the affair.

Another interesting finding was that, as with previous studies on offline betrayal (e.g., Cramer, Manning-Ryan, Johnson, & Barbo, 2000; Shackelford & Buss, 1996), women in this study focused more on emotional betrayal more than the men did. Kitzinger and Powell (1995) also found that women emphasised the emotional components of the relationships and betrayal more than the men did. These researchers purported that women used emotional words in their stories more than men did. This result was also obtained in Whitty's study, where women were more likely than men were to write that the aggrieved had been hurt or upset by the cyber-affair.

Splitting the good from the bad in cyberspace

While the above section points out some of the similarities between online and offline infidelity, there are also some differences that we also need to consider. We have previously argued (see Whitty & Carr, 2005a) that online affairs might appear in some ways to be more *seductive* than offline affairs. To explain why we believe online affairs are potentially more seductive, we have drawn from Melanie Klein's work on splitting. Splitting, she believed, was one of the most primitive or basic defence mechanisms against anxiety. As we noted in Chapter 3, according to Klein (1986) the ego prevents the 'bad' part of the object from contaminating the 'good' part of the object by splitting it off and disowning a part of itself. An infant in its relationship with the mother's breast conceives it as both a good and a bad object. The breast gratifies and frustrates and the infant will simultaneously project both love and hate on to it. On the one hand, the infant idealises this 'good' object, but on the other hand, the 'bad' object is seen as terrifying, frustrating, and a persecutor threatening to destroy both the infant and the 'good' object. The infant projects love and idealises the good object but goes beyond mere projection in trying to induce in the mother feelings towards the bad object for which she must take responsibility (that is, a process of projective identification). This stage of development Klein termed the *paranoid-schizoid position*. The infant may, as another defence mechanism for this less developed ego, seek to deny the reality of the persecutory object. While in the normal development we pass through this phase, this primitive defence against anxiety is a regressive reaction that, in a sense of always being available to us, is never transcended. The 'good' objects in the developed superego come to represent the fantasised ego-ideal and thus 'the possibility of a return to narcissism' (Schwartz, 1990, p. 18).

In line with Klein's object-relations theory it might be useful to understand the individual one is having an online affair to be the 'good object'. Given that the interactions that take place in cyberspace can be seen as separate to the outside world, it is potentially easier to split an online affair off from the rest of the individuals' world. Online relationships can potentially cater to an unfettered, impotent fantasy that is difficult to measure up to in reality. Hence, the online affair can potentially lead to a narcissistic withdrawal.

It has been argued that offline infidelity occurs because there are problems in the relationship, or because of certain personality characteristics (see Fitness, 2001). Buss and Shackelford (1997) have identified some key reasons why people betray their partners, including: complaints that one's partner sexualises others; exhibits of high levels of jealousy and possessiveness; condescension; sexual withholding; and drinks alcohol to excess. These are perhaps the same reasons why individuals are motivated to initiate online affairs. However, drawing from Klein's theory, we would like to suggest that these relationships are perhaps easier to maintain than an offline affair. We contend that the online relationship can become idealised through the process of splitting, while simultaneously, denying the 'bad' aspects of the person they are having the affair with and at the same time the bad aspects in themselves. It is possibly easier to idealise an individual online (the 'good' object) when you can more easily filter out the potential negative aspects of the relationship (the 'bad' object). The relationship can be turned on or off at one's leisure and the communication content, to some extent, can be more easily controlled. Moreover, the internet does provide an environment where it is easier to construct a more positive view of the self and avoid presenting the negative aspects of the self. In contrast, it is not so easy to indulge in one's fantasies of perfection in an offline affair as one has to still deal with the 'real' person.

The idealised online lover

We are not the only theorists to make the claim that internet relationships can be potentially more idealised than offline relationships. Civin (2000), mentioned earlier in this chapter, has also considered Klein's notion of *paranoid-schizoid position*, and presents case studies of some individuals who have seen him in therapy who have immersed themselves into communication online – so much so, that he contends they deny much of their own psychic reality. Levine (2000) also provides a warning to those wanting to develop online relationships. She believes that it is easy for individuals online to idealise one another by developing the picture of the perfect lover in one's head. She states that:

> Because the proximity is virtual and not real, there is much room for idealizing your potential partner and the relationship that could ensue. . . . My suggestion to individuals who are looking for love online is to use the Internet to explore an

intimate attraction, then take it offline within 1 month in order to get a concrete idea of the other person's attitudes, behaviors, and movement in the world. People who let attractions build online for long periods of time often have falsely raised expectations, leading to proportional disappointments. (Levine, 2000, p. 570)

Walther et al. (2001), mentioned earlier in this book, have also argued that under certain conditions, individuals idealise their virtual partners. They observed interactions between people with and without photographs online. These researchers believed that their results suggest that idealisation and selective self-presentation is more likely to occur online when there is no photograph present. Walther and his colleagues' research highlight the importance of not treating cyberspace as one generic space. Hence, perhaps our assumption that idealisation is more likely to occur online than offline is correct, but that this only happens under certain conditions – perhaps the conditions where one is better able to play with identity.

Relationship scripts

We have also suggested that with the advent of the internet, couples are now having to re-negotiate the rules in their relationships (Whitty & Carr, 2005a). Whitty's research summarised earlier in this chapter highlighted that not all participants were convinced that a cyber-affair was 'real' betrayal. Fitness (2001) has pointed out that the key to defining betrayal lies in 'relationship knowledge structures'; for example, individuals' theories, beliefs, and expectations about how relationships should normally work and how their own relationships should work. Given that the types of interactions that take place online are somewhat different and perhaps in some ways feel less real than offline relationships, it might be that virtual sex and developing close emotional bonds with someone online might be perceived by some as not breaking the rules of the offline relationship (we would also like to state here that it does not have to be understood as betrayal).

The rules when it comes to what are acceptable face-to-face behaviours in a relationship are perhaps more clear-cut. If you consider again cyberspace as being potential space – somewhere between fantasy and reality – then the boundaries could be perceived as a little fuzzy. Given that the research is suggesting that the rules for couples on what is acceptable online behaviour is not always so obvious – our advice to couples is to make the rules clear in their relationships and to not keep online activities a secret.

Sticking to the rules

It is also noteworthy that individuals' behaviour is not monitored in the same manner that it is face-to-face. If one was to be flirtatious around the photocopier with a colleague then that behaviour is likely to be witnessed by others – if deemed inappropriate, that person is likely to receive feedback, either directly or indirectly via the office gossip. Cyberspace can be perceived as a more private space – but in turn, this might mean individuals could become carried away with their online interactions without others to keep them in check. It is perhaps not surprising then, that software has been developed to keep check of individuals' online activities. For example, this Spyware package has advertised how to put a stop to infidelity by using their software:

> Spector automatically takes hundreds of snapshots every hour, very much like a surveillance camera. With Spector, you will be able to see exactly what your spouse, kids and employees have been doing online and offline.

Another software package, 'NetAccountability' assists one to be a good 'Christian'. The way this software works, is as described:

> The NetAccountability service offers a different approach than filtering – real-world accountability. Instead of software telling you what you can and can't look at (as a filter does), the NetAccountability software simply allows a friend or family member to see what sites you surf.

There is an instructive quote on the site, written presumably a Christian: 'Every Christian using the Internet should be Net Accountable and personally accountable. We must be part of the solution – not part of the problem' (Chuck Swindoll, NetAccountability). Still, one wonders how this software makes one a '*good*' Christian.

Other problematic online relationships

A cyber-affair is not the only type of problematic online relationships. As mentioned earlier in this book, researchers have noted that in some spaces aggressive communication abound in the form of flaming. In the following chapter we explore in-depth how playing around in cyberspace can have negative repercussions. We do so by considering such deviant behaviours as cyber-addiction, paedophilia, cyber-harassment, cyber-stalking, and misrepresentation of self online.

CHAPTER 6

Deviance and Cyberspace

Although anonymity may provide optimal conditions for less powerful individuals and groups (e.g., women) to resist or challenge powerful others, it also makes it easier for the more powerful to manipulate others and facilitates the "darker side of relationships".

(Lea & Spears, 1995, p. 224)

As demonstrated in the last chapter, playing around in cyberspace is not a positive experience for everyone. This chapter continues to explore the dark side of online relating. Individuals, for instance, can be harassed online, and this harassment often has repercussions offline. Shy individuals looking for a safe space to explore their identity might find that their apparent private activities become very public, as illustrated in the following story.

The Numa Numa dance

The following story is reported by Alan Feuer and Jason George in the New York Times (2005). They tell us about the embarrassment and humiliation a 19-year-old guy, Gary Brolsma, felt from uploading a video file of himself performing, what he named, the Numa Numa dance online. Feuer and George (2005) write:

> Here, then, is the cautionary tale of Gary Brolsma, 19, amateur videographer and guy from New Jersey, who made the grave mistake of placing on the Internet a brief clip of himself dancing along to a Romanian pop song. Even in the bathroom mirror, Mr. Brolsma's performance could only be described as earnest but painful.

109

His story suggests that the quaint days when cultural trinkets, like celebrity sex tapes, were passed around like novels in Soviet Russia are over. It says a little something of the lightning speed at which fame is made these days.

To begin at the beginning:

Mr. Brolsma, a pudgy guy from Saddle Brook, made a video of himself this fall performing a lip-synced version of "Dragostea Din Tei," a Romanian pop tune, which roughly translates to "Love From the Linden Trees." He not only mouthed the words, he bounced along in what he called the "Numa Numa Dance" – an arm-flailing, eyebrow-cocked performance executed without ever once leaving the chair.

In December, the Web site newgrounds.com, a clearinghouse for online videos and animation, placed a link to Mr. Brolsma on its home page and, soon, there was a river of attention. "Good Morning America" came calling and he appeared. CNN and VH1 broadcast the clip. Parodists tried their own Numa Numa dances online. By yesterday, the Brolsma rendition of "Love From the Linden Trees" had attracted nearly two million hits on the original Web site alone.

However, Feuer and George (2005) have written about the consequences this unexpected fame has had on poor George's life.

He has now sought refuge from his fame in his family's small house on a gritty street in Saddle Brook. He has stopped taking phone calls from the news media, including The New York Times. He canceled an appearance on NBC's "Today." According to his relatives, he mopes around the house.

What's worse is that no one seems to understand.

"I said, 'Gary this is your one chance to be famous – embrace it,'" said Corey Dzielinski, who has known Mr. Brolsma since the fifth grade. . . . The question remains why two million people would want to watch a doughy guy in glasses wave his arms around online to a Romanian pop song. . . .

The teacher, Susan Sommer, remembered Mr. Brolsma. He was a quiet kid, she said, with a good sense of humor and a flair for technology.

This story nicely illustrates the point that while cyberspace might provide a space for the 'quiet ones' to have a voice and perhaps even display their 'true' selves, this is not always beneficial or transformative for a person's life. One would have to follow George's life to know the long-term effects of this ordeal, but at least in the short term, playing in cyberspace was not liberating for him. Had the potential number of viewers of George's website been obvious to him from the outset, he might not have felt cyberspace was such as safe space to play in. If the link is still active, his video is well worth a look: http://www.newgrounds.com/portal/view/206373.

Internet addiction

In the previous chapter we discussed the seductive appeal of online relationships. Here we would like to extend upon this notion by examining internet addiction in more detail. Ivan Goldberg in the mid-1990s is responsible for coining the phrase 'Internet addiction disorder' (IAD); however, he did not originally treat the notion seriously. His message detailed symptoms, such as fantasising about the internet and giving up important social or occupational activities because of excessive internet use. He intended his posting to be a joke – a parody of addiction disorders; however, to his surprise, people took this very seriously. He started to receive numerous emails from individuals claiming to suffer from IAD. Since this time, other researchers, such as Kimberly Young and Mark Griffiths have also considered internet addiction in their research.

Kimberly Young (1998a) published a book titled 'Caught in the net: How to recognise the signs of internet addiction and a winning strategy for recovery', which considered in detail the problem of internet addiction. She reports numerous case studies of what she believed to be internet addiction. To give an example:

> Tony, a recently married construction worker, rushes home every night to go on-line to slay monsters and dragons and beat up opponents in the interaction gave DOOM_II. "By day, I am a mild-mannered husband and a dedicated worker." Tony told me, "but by night, with a click of the button, I turn into the most aggressive bastard you can imagine. And no one knows it's me doing this. I think it keeps me from actually hurting people – like beating my wife. It's scary to me. I need help with this". (Young, 1998a, p. 15)

The instrument designed by Young (1998a, 1998b, 1999) for a diagnosis of internet addiction was an adapted version of the criteria used in the 'Diagnostic and statistical manual of mental disorders-IV' for pathological gambling. Staying online for an average of 38 hours per week for recreational activity was deemed *prima facie* evidence of an internet addiction. Young identified 5 types of internet addiction, namely: (1) cyber-sexual addiction to adult chat rooms; (2) cyber-relationship addiction to online friendships or affairs; (3) compulsions to online gambling, auctions or forms of trading; (4) compulsive web surfing; and (5) addiction to online game playing or computer programming.

Young developed the ACE model to explain how *'accessibility'*, *'control'*, and *'escape'* play a significant role in the development of internet addiction (see, for example, Young, Pistner, O'Mara, & Buchanan, 1999). According to the ACE model, it is possible that a person looking for sexual kicks, or searching out a place to gamble or play games, would be attracted to the internet to seek out such activities because of the unique qualities of the internet. The internet, she argues, allows some degree of escape from everyday life.

There are a number of problems with Young's work. First, the ACE model implies that the problem lies with the internet, rather than the individuals who are becoming addicted to it. Secondly, Mark Griffiths (1999, 2000) has argued that many excessive users are not necessarily 'Internet addicts' as such. He states that, in many instances, a gambling addict, sex addict, and so forth are simply using the internet as a place to engage in their addictive behaviours. Another, perhaps more serious, criticism that can be made about Young's work is the way she has operationalised addiction. For example, she has classified internet addicts as individuals who use the internet for an average of 38.5 hours or more. Participants had to reply in the affirmative to any three of Young's (1996) criteria. The problem with this is that many people were probably diagnosed that ought not to be.

As an alternative to Young's diagnostic criteria, Mark Griffiths (1998, 2000) argues that when it comes to internet addiction, we should consider the six traditional core components of addition: salience, mood modification, tolerance, withdrawal symptoms, conflict, and relapse. Grohol (1999) has, however, criticised Griffith's suggestion for diagnosing internet addiction saying that 'any behavior can be viewed as addictive given such criteria, whether is be watching television, listening to the radio, ironing, going online, reading, sewing, or exercising' (p. 396). Janet Morahan-Martin (2005) adds a completely different viewpoint. She maintains that internet abuse is a symptom of other problems, such as depression, sexual disorders, or loneliness. Instead, she believes, it is the psychological problems, such as, depression that ought to be treated, rather than the addiction.

The types of cyber-addictions this book is most interested in are more the cyber-relationship and cyber-sexual addictions online. Very little empirical research has been carried out in this area. One researcher that has examined cyber-sex addicts is Al Cooper. Cooper et al. (2000) examined a group of 'cyber-sexually compulsive' internet users. They came to the conclusion that there is a small proportion of individuals whose online sexual behaviour is clearly compulsive behaviour. They also identified some demographic variables, which they believe put an individual at greater risk for cybersex compulsivity. Both women and gay men were more highly represented in the cybersex compulsive group. The propensity to be a risk taker in both sexual and non-sexual behavioural domains was also more common in cybersex compulsives. Finally, the use of chat rooms as well as spending more time online was more indicative of the cybersex compulsives. While we believe, it is important for researchers to examine who might be more at risk at becoming addicted to online sexual activities, we believe that Cooper et al.'s (2000) work does not shed much light on this question. For instance, many more women, gay men, and chat room users are not addicted to cybersex than those that are. What this research does show, however, is that not all cyber-sexual activities are liberating and that we do need to learn more about these problematic behaviours so that counsellors can better assist individuals with such addictions.

Drawing again from object-relations theory, 'addiction' is understood as representing a form of primitive maternal transference and that the internet poses the possibility for an individual to create an internal object family. This explanation is largely derived from the work of Thomas Ogden (1985b, 1991). In Chapter 3, through the work of Winnicott, it was noted that the infant in its relationship with the mother comes to discover what is 'me' and what is 'not me' and in the engagement with as-if objects the infant learns to detach itself from a continuing reliance on the mother. As the infant plays and engages the object world it does so in a space that it creates inter-subjectively with the mother – a space, it might be recalled, that Winnicott (1967/1971f, p. 100) referred to as 'potential space... between the subjective object and the object objectively perceived'. The mother must foster the environment in which the infant may play while not allowing the infant to engage the mother as an object, otherwise the infant becomes dependent upon the presence of the mother.

Ogden (1985b) has noted that in situations where potential space is not created, the infant appears to become addicted to the mother as an object. As an example to support of this contention, Ogden cites a number of research studies in relation to infantile insomnia where the infant will not go to sleep unless the mother is physically holding them. 'These infants were unable to provide themselves an internal environment for sleep... mothers of many of these infants interfered with the attempts of their infants to provide themselves substitutes for her physical presence (e.g., in auto-erotic activities such as thumb sucking), thus rendering the infant fully dependent upon the actual mother as object' (Ogden, 1985b, p. 359). Ogden provides further evidence of this phenomenon citing situations in which therapists working with patients fail to create a therapeutic environment – an analytic space – but instead the therapists succeeds in inserting themselves 'into the patient's life as an omnipotent object' (Ogden, 1985b, p. 360). This equivalent primitive maternal transference fosters addiction to the therapist.

In terms of the general developmental significance of what has just been described, Ogden (1985b) captures it well when he argues:

> The crucial psychological-interpersonal phenomenon that makes possible the weaning of the infant from the maternally provided psychological matrix is the maintenance of a series of paradoxes: the infant and mother are one, and the infant and mother are two; the infant has created an object and the object was there to be discovered; the infant must learn to be alone in the presence of the mother, and so on. It is essential that the infant or child never be asked which is the truth (Winnicott, 1951/1971b). Both are true. The simultaneous maintenance of the emotional truth of oneness with the mother and the separateness from her makes it possible for the infant to play in the potential space between the mother and infant. (pp. 360–361)

This capacity to generate potential space between the individual and the environment (originally the object) was seen by Winnicott as having an ongoing significance to creativity and personal development.

In relation to the internet, the internet itself can be experienced as both a space in which to 'play' and as an 'object'. It is in this context, that chat rooms and other online forums pose a possibility for the individual to create their own online 'object family' and that the primitive maternal transference (see Suler, 1998 for a discussion of different forms of transference reactions to computers) may occur such that the individual becomes addicted to the internet as an object. The individual's engaging the internet in this way may do so simply because the online 'family' provides a relationship matrix that enhances the individual's capacity for self-definition. The internet provides the holding environment that is absent offline.

Whilst this working theory, from object-relations, has proved useful in the clinical situation, to date, we are unaware of any research that has examined internet 'addiction' from this perspective. Indeed, as others have noted (see, for example, Walker, Harper, Lloyd, & Caputi, 2003, p. 524), research studies that have addressed the issue of internet addiction appear to be devoid of any coherent theoretical trajectory that explains how this phenomenon comes into being and how prevalent it really is.

Cyber-harassment

Other online deviant behaviours include cyber-harassment and cyberstalking (a more severe form of online harassment). Electronic communication can be used to harass in both similar and new ways to offline traditional harassment. Cyber-harassment can occur between known individuals or between strangers. Cyber-harassment might occur as a consequence of a romantic relationship gone wrong, or from unwanted romantic and/or sexual attention.

In a thoughtful review of the literature to date, Azy Barak (2005) points out three types of sexual harassment that can take place in cyberspace: gender harassment, unwanted sexual attention, and sexual coercion. He argues that gender harassment and unwanted sexual attention are the more common types of online sexual harassment. To give an example:

David Cruz, in 1993, was given a prison sentence of five months for cyberstalking Chloe Easton. Cruz met Easton through friends and he quickly became infatuated with her. Chloe Easton was going through a messy divorce and she found that Cruz was very supportive throughout the process. When David Cruz made romantic advances towards Easton she made it clear that she wanted the relationship to remain platonic. This angered Cruz who proceeded to launch a campaign of harassment over six months against Chloe and her family. Throughout most of the harassment, David Cruz pretended to be a concerned friend and tried to help Chloe find her stalker. Some of the harassment included sending a pornographic video in an email attachment to Chloe's father – the video showed a woman who looked very similar to Chloe, engaged in group sex. Chloe was also sent up to 30 sexually explicit text messages a day with 'disgusting sexual connotations' (Wilkins, 2003).

Although, currently, there is no universal definition for cyberstalking, a fairly comprehensive definition has been offered by Bocij (2004):

> A group of behaviors in which an individual, group of individuals, or organiza-
> tion uses information and communications technology to harasses another indi-
> vidual, group of individuals, or organization. Such behaviors may include, but
> are not limited to, the transmission of threats and false accusations, identity
> theft, damage to data or equipment, computer monitoring, solicitation of
> minors for sexual purposes, and any form of aggression. Harassment is defined
> as a course of actions that a reasonable person, in possession of the same
> information, would think causes another reasonable person to suffer emotional
> distress. (p. 14)

Importantly, Bocij points out that cyberstalking is not just between individuals but can also involve both individuals and organisations, as illustrated in the following example: A classic case which occurred between Woodside Literacy Agency's dealings with Jayne Hitchcock (Bocij, 2004; Deirmenjian, 1999). When Jayne Hitchcock sent her book proposal to the Woodside Literacy Agency, she received a reply compli-menting her on her proposal and a request for a reading fee. A few months later, post emerged on Usenet groups warning writers of this company, which prompted writers to test the company's credibility by sending their worst manuscripts. They too were complimented on their work and were requested to pay a reading fee. When Woodside discov-ered what was happening, the owner Leonard retaliated by spamming individuals. He then impersonated Hitchcock in various newsgroups and sent messages containing inflammatory comments. In one such message, it claimed that Hitchcock was into sadomasochistic practices and provided her phone number. This lead to a barrage of phone calls to Hitchcock, which she obviously found harassing. Leonard was arrested in 2000 on charges of conspiracy to commit mail fraud.

Cyber-obsessive relational intrusion

While the literature on devising a typology of a cyberstalker is scant, a few authors have attempted to outline the characteristics of a cyberstalker. In one of the few empirical studies conducted on cyberstalking, Spitzberg and Hoobler (2002) have explored what constitutes '*Cyber-Obsessive Relational Intrusion*' (Cyber-ORI). Brian Spitzberg and his colleagues have preferred to focus on '*Obsessive Relational Intrusion*' (ORI), rather than stalking, in their research and understand this term to mean 'repeated and unwanted pursuit and invasion of one's sense of physical or symbolic privacy by another person, either stranger or acquaintance, who desires and/or presumes an intimate relationship' (Cupach & Spitzberg, 1998, pp. 234–235). Cupach, Spitzberg, and Carson (2000) have argued that ORI is closely related to the legal concept of stalking, except that ORI is broader in meaning. Stalking, they have claimed, is an 'extreme and severe manifestation of ORI. Stalking involves a pattern of intrusion that a reasonable person would find threatening. Although ORI can be threatening, sometimes it is merely harassing or annoying' (p. 132). They have also argued that the motivations for stalking and ORI can be different in that ORI is motivated by a relational connection and stalking does not have to be.

In Spitzberg and Hoobler's (2002) seminal study, they identified three types of cyber-obsessional relational pursuit, including '*hyperintimacy*', '*RL-transference*' (Real-Life-transference), and '*threat*'. 'Hyperintimacy' included sending excessively disclosive messages, tokens of affection, exaggerated messages of affection, and sending pornographic/obscene messages or images (interestingly, hyperintimacy cuts both ways – in other sections of this book we have discussed the positive aspects of hyperintimacy, in particular drawing from Walther's work). Examples of 'RL-transference' included meeting first online and then threatening the person, meeting the person online and then following them offline, and attempting to disable the person's computer. Finally, examples of 'threat' included sending threatening written messages, sending threatening pictures or images, and sabotaging the individual's private reputation.

There are many examples of case studies of cyber-harassment and/or cyberstalking that have taken place after an online relationship went wrong. To give another example, one of the earliest and more extreme cases of cyberstalking occurred in the late 1990s, when a security guard was rejected by a woman he met in church. His vengeful act included placing adverts on the internet in her name claiming that she was into 'rape fantasy and gang-bang fantasy . . . the adverts included a detailed physical description, her address and phone number and even instructions on how to bypass her burglar alarm' (Gumbel, 1999). This woman was woken up at night by men pounding on her door yelling they were going to rape her.

Cyber-harassment in the workplace

Cyber-harassment is not always a consequence of a romantic relationship gone wrong. Empirical research has also revealed that cyber-harassment takes place in the workplace. In 2001, Elron reported that one out of three participants stated that they received sexist material at work via email and one out of eight participants stated that they received racist material at work via email. In Whitty's (2004b) recent research, similar concerns arose. In her Australia-wide study, which was conducted for Surf Control, 17 per cent of participants stated that they had been harassed in emails in their workplace, while 49 per cent said they had received offensive emails. In response to what type of material should be banned in the workplace, a significant proportion of women (67%) compared to men (55%) stated that offensive material, such as porn, should be banned. Furthermore, women disagreed more strongly than men did in their responses to whether workers should be permitted to access sexual material from the web at work.

While individuals are overall concerned about the material available at work on the internet and the types of annoying emails they receive, they nevertheless approve of using the internet and email for personal usage. What appears to be a stark contradiction is that some of this personal usage could, in turn, annoy, offend, or potentially harass others. For example, in Whitty's research it was surprising to find that one-third of the sample of 524 participants believed it was acceptable for workers to discuss sexual matters online at work (Whitty, 2004b).

Managing cyber-interactions in the workplace

When we consider that cyberspace is a new place to play in the workplace, we also need to consider the rules that accompany this new activity

(Whitty & Carr, 2006, 2005b). Winnicott contends that we need to consider the rules of the game, as while play is separated from the ordinary world, it is still constrained by the rules. As discussed earlier on in this chapter, in respect to cyber-infidelity, the rules on how to play in cyberspace are still currently being devised. Legislators and psychologists are still grappling with how to define cyber-harassment and cyberstalking. Despite the lack of consistency in these professionals' definitions (or understanding of the 'rules') workplaces have managed to develop clear policies in respect to cyber-harassing and discriminatory behaviour. However, these rules are not consistently applied by workers in respect to how they conduct their electronic communications. One reason we would like to offer for this is because cyberspace is considered to be a different kind of space in the workplace, a place where the rules are still being negotiated and defined. It would be reasonable to assume that this space is perceived by workers to be a more private space and quite separate to the 'real' world. An employee might see this as a space that is, in a sense, more one's own space where an employer has no right to intrude upon and effectively spy on an individual.

This illusion of privacy is perhaps sustained given that work colleagues are not necessarily privy to all the conversations that take place online and the information that is downloaded. This is quite different to the conversations that take place in the workplace either face-to-face or over telephone, where one is more obviously accountable for one's actions given that others can witness them. Of course, the reality is that while workers might be sustaining an illusion in respect to cyberspace being a more private space, this is not the case. Others can see colleagues' computer monitors, the computer keeps a trace of where the individual has been surfing on the internet, those who have access to the server have access to emails being sent back and forth, and commonly emails are accidentally sent to people they were not intended for. Nonetheless people often separate themselves from this reality when they log on into cyberspace. Hence, given the separateness of this space to other spaces, this might explain why individuals are not applying old rules to this new form of communication.

Again, we could apply Klein's theory on splitting the world into 'good' and 'bad' objects. If we consider, as argued earlier in this book, that one of the objects that occupy cyberspace is the text, we can identify some interesting splitting behaviour that appears to take place here. We pointed out above the contradictions in people's attitudes towards internet and email behaviour in the workplace. It appears that for some, double standards are being applied, where it is acceptable for an individual to talk about sexual matters or to send chain or joke emails (which often contain sexual material), while at that same time disapproving of sexual content on the web, offensive emails, and being sent chain emails (Whitty, 2004b).

Rape in cyberspace

There are perhaps even more serious crimes that could take place in cyberspace. The supposedly first rape in cyberspace is commonly known as the 'Mr Bungle affair' that occurred in 1992 in Lambda MOO (see Turkle, 1995). In cyberspace a player masqueraded as another player's character by using a MUD programming technique often referred to as a voodoo doll. The Mr Bungle character used the voodoo doll to force another character to perform sexual acts on him. Given that cyberspace is not complete fantasy – and as we have witnessed in the case studies throughout this chapter, serious and non-trivial crimes can take place in this space – we should perhaps not dismiss this case. If one identifies strongly with their online character in MOOs and MUDs, then an incident, such as the Mr Bungle affair, might have a serious psychological impact on an individual.

Paedophilia

Adults are not the only people to be affected by sexual abuse online. This is exemplified in a 13-year-old women's experience of a cyber-affair, described below (see Tarbox, 2000).

Initially, Katie embraced the attention she received from a much older man online; however, this later became a source of fear and regret. According to Katie, a lack of understanding from others motivated her to go online to seek like-minded people. Although she was unimpressed by many of the men she encountered online, she still persisted in seeking out someone whom she could connect with. To quote from Katie:

And they all want to know what you look like, especially your body. You can be sure that every time you go on-line someone is going to ask you your breast size. I don't really see why anyone bothers to ask. Everyone lies when they answer.

It didn't take me long to figure out that a lot of the guys in the teen chat rooms were not normal guys. They were animals that wanted to be excited by someone they thought looked like Cindy Crawford with a breast size of 36F.

Despite all of this – despite all of the weirdos and the creepy feeling of being detached from reality – a small part of me believed that there was someone out there on the Web like me. (Tarbox, 2000, pp. 25–26)

Eventually Katie did meet someone she felt resonated with her sense of self. He claimed to be a 23 year-old called Mark, and the two discussed in detail favourite fashions. What she did not know was that he was older, his name was not Mark and he was a paedophile. Mark remained an online friend, and Katie purported that they both became so close that she eventually replaced her best girlfriend with Mark as her closest confidant. About a year from when they first met online Katie relented to Mark's constant requests to meet her (she had been cautious not to give out her address or last name). She organised to meet him while she was away in another city with her swimming team and their parents. They met in the hotel where she was staying, and Mark managed to persuade Katie to go back to his hotel room. Indeed, he did attempt to assault her; however, fortunately for Katie one of her friends had followed her (without her knowing) and called her mother for assistance. Whilst Katie avoided being assaulted, as one might imagine, the ramifications of this event for Katie were psychologically damaging.

While paedophilia is not a new crime, with the advent of the internet, there are now new ways that paedophiles can access children. We also need to find new ways to ensure children are protected. The Pew Internet and Life Project found that 60 per cent of the 12–17 year-olds they surveyed received an instant message and/or an email from strangers (Lenhart, Rainie, & Lewis, 2001). Livingstone (2001) has provided a descriptive summary of other individuals' research on safety on children. She writes that a survey found that one in five of American youths (aged 10–17 years) reported receiving some kind of sexual solicitation in a chat room. Livingstone (2001) believes that while information is available for parents to help them protect their children online, many parents do not know where to find this information. She also argues that 'of the various safety strategies proposed, most are more appropriate for younger children rather than for teenagers'. Needless to say, there is much more work needed into understanding paedophiles activities online, how children are communicating and developing relationships online, and how to best protect children from paedophiles online.

Misrepresentation of self online

As we have already remarked, having the freedom to play with identity in cyberspace can be a psychologically healthy experience. It can allow one to explore and learn about new aspects of themselves. In fact, white lies can probably provide people with a safety net to disclose more about themselves – to reveal more important truths. However, is misrepresentation of one's identity online always a good thing and are we more likely to lie online than offline?

The media relish in telling us how much people enjoy gender-bending online. This is partly supported in the literature, but perhaps not to the degree they would have us believe. Whitty (2002) found that men (28%) were more likely in chat rooms to pretend to be women than women (18%) pretend to be men. Lea and Spears (1995) argued that gender switching often occurs in MUDs. In contrast, Whitty's study suggests it happens, but not to as large an extent in chat rooms. In Whitty's (2002) study on lying in chat rooms, she found that men were more likely to admit to lying about a variety of aspects about themselves compared to women. Men were more likely to lie about gender, occupation, education, and income. Whitty also found that people who spend the least amount of time in chat rooms per week were more likely to tell lies. Perhaps these individuals are not treating the space as seriously as regular users.

Lying can, in fact, be detrimental to the social fabric of an online group. For example, Feldman (2000) reports a case where a woman, named Barbara, joined an online cystic fibrosis group. This woman pretended to the group that she was at home waiting to die and was being cared for by her elder sister, Amy. The group were very supportive of Barbara, and were distraught to learn from Amy that Barbara had died a few days later. The group eventually worked it out that Barbara was lying when they noticed that Amy shared Barbara's spelling errors. Barbara/Amy or whatever she was really called admitted to the group that it was a hoax, and taunted the group for their gullibility. Feldman (2000) noted that when such incidences occur in online support groups, a typical reaction was for the group is to split into believers and doubters of the claims. Moreover, the group typically breaks up after members start to lose trust with one another.

With all this concentration in the academic literature as well as in the media on lying online – one is left feeling that a great deal of lying takes place online more than it does in face-to-face situations. However, recent research does not support this assumption. Hancock et al. (2004) in a diary study asked participants to record all their lies and social interactions for a seven-day period. They considered lies told in face-to-face settings, phone, IM, and email. The rate of deception in each medium was worked out by dividing the number of lies in a given medium by the number of social interactions in that specific medium. Interestingly, they found that more lies were told in telephone conversations when compared to face-to-face settings, and that people lied in email significantly less than in face-to-face. There was no significant difference between IM and face-to-face. Hancock et al. (2004) explain these results saying that the more synchronous and distributed, but the less recordable a medium is, the more frequently lying should occur.

As discussed earlier in this book, lying or misrepresenting oneself in cyberspace does not necessarily have negative consequences. The following chapter looks in detail at how individuals present themselves on an internet dating site. Sometimes these presentations of self were outrageous lies, while at other times they were more ideal representations of themselves. The chapter examines the repercussions of misrepresenting oneself on an online dating site and focuses on how these relationships develop from online to offline.

CHAPTER 7

Online Dating

Shopping for Love on the internet

This chapter draws from Monica Whitty's recent research on an Australian internet dating site. It presents some new insights into online dating and clearly demonstrates that the way relationships are initiated and developed online vary depending on where individuals in cyberspace meet. What the space looks like, the rules developed to interact in such a space, and the purpose of using a particular space online can all affect the dynamics of online relationships.

Online dating sites are set up for individuals to meet online and possibly develop a social, romantic, or sexual relationship. Such services allow individuals to set up a profile where they provide personal information, such as age, gender, personality, hobbies, and so forth. Some sites require individuals to conduct a personality test so that individuals can be matched on compatibility. Most sites encourage individuals to include a photograph on their profile. Some sites have large membership, including over a hundred thousand members, others are more specialised (e.g., for special interest groups, such as vegans or goths). Most sites also require their users to pay for this service.

The research reported in this chapter examined Australia's largest online dating site. This site is set up where individuals typically present a photograph of themselves on their profiles. Individuals are also required to present general as well as more in-depth details about themselves (e.g., gender, location, physical description, interests, and what they are looking for in a partner).

In 2003/2004, Whitty and her research assistants interviewed 60 participants (30 men and 30 women) who were using an Australian online dating site. In recruiting the sample, the dating site manager randomly selected 300 individuals using the site and contacted them via email inviting them

124

to contact Monica Whitty to line up a telephone interview. The response rate was 20 per cent, which was considered fairly reasonable (this was especially good, given many of the emails could have been 'dead' emails). Participants were enthusiastic individuals who were very willing to share their online dating experiences. Some told of wonderful romantic experiences, sometimes even leading to marriage; others expressed hope of finding their true loves online; while others had some horror stories to report. In order to protect these individuals' privacy, pseudonyms are used here instead of their real names.

Motivations for using an online dating site

The participants in this research gave accounts of a variety of reasons for signing up to an online dating company. Fifty-seven per cent of the sample spoke about using online dating as an alternative to the pubs and clubs scene, either because they had exhausted their options in these spaces; they did not drink; or did not enjoy this way of meeting people. Some talked about using online dating to find a short-term relationship, although the majority hoped to find a long-term relationship (91%). Others did say they were just using the site for fun or to find casual sex (12%). Some were attracted to this way of dating as they admitted to being quite shy and reserved individuals (10%). Almost half stated that the number of choices on the site appealed to them (47%), while more than half (67%) felt they had no other option (because of their work situations, family commitments, dislike for other venues to find partners). Thirty-five per cent of the sample talked about liking the convenience of online dating; that is, they could date in the privacy of their own home without having to go out or get dressed up (a bit like doing the grocery shopping online). Moreover, this was a much more convenient option for the shift workers in the sample. The extracts below provide some accounts of why individuals opted to use an online dating site to find a partner.

I   *What motivated you to use online dating site?*
G   *Just a new way of meeting people. I'm changing from pubs, you get too old for pubs and it's really convenient.*

(Grant)

D   *Well I was looking for an alternative to the clubs and pubs and all that sort of stuff.*

I   *Are you using online dating site to make new friends, develop short-term romances or develop long-term romances?*

D   *Long-term, that's my intention, yeah.*

(David)

S   *Well I had my heart smashed. I have got a pretty good idea about what I want from my life and what direction I am going in and . . . I don't want to spend my life on my own and I am sure that there is that someone special out there for me. And working shift work and stuff it is not always the easiest way to meet people. And the hospital I work in . . . the doctors are all female too (laugh) so I had to find an alternative way to meet men . . .*

(Suszi)

J   *I'm still tied up with the kid activities. I suppose because I've been out of circulation for a while if you like, I just thought well it was a way of actually meeting people, particularly coming to a middle age period of life.*

(Jeff)

N   *Yeah and also, where do you meet people? I mean all my friends are married. I mean there are two girlfriends that are not anymore, but my real close friends, they are all married. I am in that group and I still go out, we are all going out tonight for dinner, and I will be by myself because the other guy hasn't rung me, but you know that is the people that I see. I don't mix in single groups and I don't go to bars to meet guys.*

(Noleen)

S   *Well I mean I used to be almost pathologically shy, and I went into the internet dating at the end of a 10 year de facto. I had always heard about house parties but I was desperately shy. And I came out of this relationship about 50 and I am single now and what is life out there like at 50.*

(Shane)

G   *Whatever it was though, single, whatever . . . All of a sudden I was back in Australia and I didn't know what the hell I was going to do next and I just thought . . . It was like being a kid in a lolly shop, all these choices.*

(Greg)

Different paces for different spaces: Progression from online to offline

As mentioned earlier in this book, previous researchers have found that relationships typically move *gradually* from online to offline (e.g., Baker, 2002; Whitty & Gavin, 2001). To reiterate, individuals develop trust first by giving out one's email (these days often accompanied by IM), then phone number (often this is a mobile number), and then possibly moving to face-to-face. As we presented in this book, many individuals find cyberspace to be a safe space to relate and to self-disclose sensitive aspects about themselves. While the empirical evidence does seem to support this notion when people meet for the first time in a chat room or newsgroup, a different process takes place when individuals get to know someone from an online dating site.

Whitty's research suggests that online daters do not want to waste time getting to know one another online. In fact, 65 per cent of the sample stated that they typically met their date within a week of first making contact online, and 11 per cent said they typically met within a month of initial contact. Therefore, while these individuals might exchange emails, phone numbers, and chat for a short period of time using the sites' IM, the objective is typically to move offline as quickly as possible. The explanations given for meeting people so quickly included a need to establish if there is any *'physical chemistry'*, a desire to not waste time and to move to consider new profiles if the date did not work out, a lack of trust in people's profiles, and a desire to get to know the *'real'* person behind the profile as quickly as possible. The process and the reasons given are illustrated in the following extracts:

R   *First of all it was the kiss* [an automatic statement that one can select that is delivered through the site to indicate they are interested in someone], *she sent a kiss reply saying she was interested, and would like to receive an email from me, to which I sent an email, and told her a little bit more about myself. And then she emailed back and told me a little bit more about her and then we arranged to meet. I asked if she would like to have coffee somewhere and meet in town. She agreed and we met and it went quite well.*

I   *How long did all that take and in what stages? How long were you doing email?*

R   *Just a week.*

(Robbie)

A   *We exchanged at least two emails to each after the first contact email I guess,*
     and then probably phoned up to organise a time to meet and get together. Not
     so much as getting on the phone and speaking for three hours or anything like
     that, cause once again it's a bit of a case of an unknown quantity.
I   *So how long did it take between email and phone, a week, a few days?*
A   *Probably closer to between one and three weeks.*

     (Andrew)

J   *I had learnt from a few very early test runs that too many emails and phone*
     calls before actually meeting over coffee or whatever can be a big mistake. Well
     at least for me, because although you start to develop a sort of friendship and a
     certain intimacy if there is no chemistry and you don't want to retain them as
     a friend it feels very awkward. So I make it a rule that...I don't sort of
     become emotionally close to someone I don't actually, I haven't seen in the
     flesh, because it is disappointing for both parties and it can feel quite strange.

     (Jenny)

I   *So did you email each other?*
A   *Not for very long. I don't use email for very long because I don't think it works*
     very well. Some people like it, I just find you can email someone for weeks and
     then find that they are quite a different person in real life. Email gives you time
     to respond and compose your responses and I don't have that sort of time. I don't
     want to sit there typing, I do it all day. I get on the PC all day for work so
     I don't want to do it all night. So, I basically say to people that unless they are
     prepared to meet quickly then don't worry about it.

     (Ann)

Based on Whitty's research, it is apparent that developing a romantic relationship via an online dating site is very different to establishing a romantic
relationship in other online spaces, such as MUDs, chat rooms, and
discussion boards. Rather than initially communicating with individuals or
witnessing individuals' conversations (as in a chat room or newsgroup), on
an online dating site one is first presented with a profile. The profile
presents a gamut of information, carefully selected by the online dater. In
addition, the profile typically has a photograph of the individual. Hence, it
is little wonder that individuals are unmotivated to get to know one
another gradually in cyberspace, given they are already equipped with
enough knowledge of their potential mate to decide whether they want to

meet offline. Furthermore, as Ann points out above, participants are aware that people can be strategic in email as well as in their profiles. Armed with this knowledge, individuals want to move to face-to-face where they can see how well people match up to their online self.

Social penetration theory, initially proposed by Altman and Taylor (1973), and modified by others (e.g., Morton, Alexander, & Altman, 1976), argues that relationships move from less intimate to more intimate involvement over time. The process has been described using the '*onion analogy*', arguing that people self-disclose deeper and deeper aspects about themselves as the relationship progresses. This theory discusses depth and breadth. Depth represents dimensions starting from the surface and moving to the central core aspects of personality. Breadth refers to information about a broad range of topics, such as one's family, career, and so forth. According to social penetration theory, in the early phases of relationship development one moves with caution, discussing less intimate topics and checking in the conversations for signs of reciprocity. Gradually one feels safer to admit to other aspects of themselves. This process arguably happens in chat rooms, discussion boards, IM, and the like. Moreover, as mentioned earlier, researchers have found that this process often takes place quicker, since people are potentially in a safer environment to reveal core aspects of themselves.

If you consider the process of online dating there is far less opportunity for relationships to develop in this way. The profiles are set up in such a way as to reveal both depth and breadth. For instance, when writing up a profile an individual typically has to provide information about surface level aspects about themselves, such as eye colour, drinking and smoking habits, relationship status, number and types of pets, and occupation. In addition, profiles are set up with spaces to write more in-depth aspects about oneself, such as a description of their personality, interests (what they read, music they listen to, and so forth), their ideal date, and their political persuasion. They are encouraged on these sites to open up about all aspects of themselves so that they will attract the most appropriate person.

Thus, online dating is arguably even more removed from what people are used to when it comes to developing a relationship. There is no real opportunity to test the waters gradually and check for reciprocity. Rather, attraction and decisions about whether someone might be a good match is determined prior to communication with the individual. Interestingly, one way individuals try to find a way around this problem is by developing multiple profiles. For example, if they are interested in someone and they make initial contact with no response, they might develop a second profile and test the waters to see if the auxiliary profile is a better fit.

Online and offline attraction: Is it all that different?

As has been highlighted in this book, researchers have discussed in detail the benefits of the absence of the physical body online, which they believe provides a space for a meeting of minds. For example, Lea and Spears (1995) have argued that:

> Instead of being at the forefront of face-to-face interactions, one's physical appearance recedes into the background in CMC, and its disclosure to others is under the control of the subject, who can choose when and how to reveal it. As a consequence, stage models of relationship development, or indeed our cultural expectations about how relationships develop that assume first and foremost an attraction between physical bodies, no longer work for us in this medium. (p. 208)

While cyberspace might provide an opportunity to de-emphasise physical attractiveness in order to allow people to self-disclose more as well as to explore other dimensions of their personalities, in this book we have argued that the body still plays an important role. This is especially the case when it comes to presentation of the self in online dating sites. As explained in Chapter 2, participants using the Australian online dating site talked about the importance of selecting a photograph to represent themselves as well as choosing their dates by taking account of what the person's photo looked like. As is well documented, physical attractiveness plays an important role in offline dating. For example, Cloyd (1976) found in bar settings that the most important variable in determining whether an individual will be able to initiate communication with someone of the opposite sex was physical attractiveness. Woll and Cozby (1987) found this was also the case with video dating.

Considering again Whitty's online dating data, it was found that men (97%) placed slightly more importance on looks than women (83%) did. This is consistent with research on gender differences and offline dating (e.g., Davis, 1990). Moreover, men (47%) were much more likely to place importance on body size compared to women (27%). As exemplified by the following quote:

S   *But in terms of their actual profile it would include, I have got a thing about slender women so I like slim sometimes I wouldn't contact somebody who would describe themselves as being overweight.*

(Shane)

Savvy shoppers

I   *What are some of the differences and similarities you have found in meeting people through this online site and meeting people with other methods?*

D   *Really, I have found that, I suppose the online dating site women are really out there searching for, they are shopping. They have a person in mind and they are really looking to see what takes their eye or what stinks, but still looks ok. But they really are shopping. I use the VCR for example in this one in my own mind, while it has got a play and record, it's got to look good in the stereo cabinet.*

(Danny)

The participants in this study were often quite particular in what they hoped for in a partner. Generally, they viewed the profiles as if they had a '*shopping list*' where they would tick off which '*products*' met the specifications they were looking for. While the most important qualities were physical attributes, other important features included sharing similar interests and values, socio-economic status (SES), and personality (see Table 7.1 for a full list of the attractive qualities people were seeking for in a partner).

Hence, when it comes to online dating sites, people are placing much importance on 'good looks'. The importance placed on physical characteristics may be greater for online daters than for individuals developing relationships in other places online. This is for two reasons: (a) when individuals first 'meet' the person on the internet dating site, they are presented with a photo and not simply text; and (b) there are so many choices (and unlike places where hundreds of people are interacting online, such as MOOs, these individuals 'know' that everyone on the site is seeking romance), and so they can bypass the less attractive profiles and make a play for the more attractive ones.

Table 7.1   Aspects participants were looking for in a partner

Attractive qualities	Men	Women	Total
Looks	29 (96.7%)	25 (83.3%)	54 (90.0%)
Similar interests/values	25 (83.3%)	26 (86.7%)	51 (85.0%)
SES: Education, intelligence, occupation, income, being professional (sometimes demonstrated by good grammar/spelling)	22 (73.3%)	22 (73.3%)	44 (73.3%)
Personality	19 (63.3%)	24 (80.0%)	43 (71.1%)
Honest/genuine/real people	17 (56.7%)	15 (50.0%)	32 (53.3%)
Attracted to a certain age group	11 (36.7%)	17 (56.7%)	28 (46.7%)
Height	9 (30.0%)	16 (53.3%)	25 (41.7%)
Proximity	11 (36.7%)	13 (43.3%)	24 (40.0%)
Size/weight	14 (46.7%)	8 (26.7%)	22 (36.7%)
Non-smokers	11 (36.7%)	6 (20.0%)	17 (28.3%)
Different/unique people/ people with different interests to their own	7 (23.3%)	10 (33.3%)	17 (28.3%)
Humour	6 (20.0%)	8 (26.7%)	14 (23.3%)
Someone with no children/off their hands	5 (16.7%)	7 (23.3%)	12 (20.0%)
Someone who has children	5 (16.7%)	5 (16.7%)	10 (16.7%)
Opening line	5 (16.7%)	2 (6.7%)	7 (11.7%)
Star sign	1 (3.3%)	5 (16.7%)	6 (10.0%)
Someone who wants children	1 (3.3%)	3 (10.0%)	4 (6.7%)

Physical characteristics play a critical role in attraction offline, for both men and women. As stated above, when it comes to offline dating, physical attractiveness ranks as the most important attribute when it comes to initial attraction. However, some distinct gender differences are also worthy of mention. Men are typically more readily aroused sexually than women by visual stimuli (e.g., Ellis & Symons, 1990; Townsend, 1993). Given this, it is no surprise, as reported in Chapter 2, that more women than men included photos in their profiles, and more women than men choose to have 'glamour' photos of themselves. Offline, women in contrast are typically more attracted to earning potential, social dominance, prowess, personality, and men who are willing to invest in them (Buss & Barnes, 1986; Kenrick, Sadalla, Groth, & Trost, 1990; Townsend & Wasserman, 1997). This result is only partly supported by these results. Women did focus more on looking for a man with specific personality characteristics more than men did; however, there were no significant differences in wanting a partner with higher social economic status. Rather than this being downplayed by women, it appears that men are also considering SES to be an important attribute to seek in a woman. With this gamut of available information about someone, perhaps one's dating preferences will change – if immediately armed with the knowledge about one's wealth and status this might now become a more important attractive quality for men to seek out in a woman.

Examples of what participants considered to be attractive qualities are illustrated below:

B   *Yes, it's a matter of finding common interests, people with creativity, intelligence, intellectual pursuit, you find the description that has those sort of attributes I tend to be generally attracted to that*

      (Bill)

I   *And what is it that you're looking for?*
M   *Someone who's well groomed. . . Model, or teacher, something*

      (Morton)

A   *Characteristics that I'm looking for in a person. They have to have a photo and they have to be attractive, they have to be into fitness, reasonably intelligent, show that they were independent, just the qualities I'm looking for.*

      (Andrew)

P   *Their height, I think that is every girls' dream, that is my first priority and then if they want children, and then if they are a smoker or a non-smoker.*

      (Patricia)

I   *So, that was appealing to you?*
S   *Yes she was to me and she sounded very interesting. She said she was attractive and slim.*

      (Shane)

P   *Yes and if you get to talk to somebody first up you can get an idea. I like to know that I have got an educated person. I don't mind if they are dyslexic and I don't mind if they have got a speech impediment from a car accident, cause I did actually talk to a guy like that for awhile, but I just want a certain level of education*

      (Patricia)

I   *Ok, if you have sent a kiss or an email to another person from the site, what actually attracted you to an individual and what made you decide to contact them?*

K   *Usually if they sounded really down to earth and family orientated. You know somebody with standards and values. Somebody who didn't seem to be playing the game, somebody that seems to be totally genuine. Probably if someone was shorter than me.*

(Kevin)

Interestingly, Whitty's study did find that individuals emphasised similar interests and values as an attractive quality (85% stated that this was an attractive quality). Most of the literature on attractiveness focuses upon physical attractiveness versus socio-economic status. This is possibly because many of the researchers in this field take a socio-evolutionary approach. Whatever the reason, when it comes to initial attraction there is little empirical evidence to support the view that similar beliefs and values are initial attractors. This is perhaps because, as social penetration theory suggests, in face-to-face courting one typically does not learn about someone's inner beliefs and values until later on in the courting process. Online dating sites, however, provide this information about a person prior to any interaction between individuals. This result provides more evidence to suggest that the way people go about online dating is considerably different to other forms of dating both online and offline.

It is also noteworthy that proximity was important when it came to selecting a partner (with 40% of participants mentioning this). Some researchers have contended that 'in the online world, proximity is not defined by physical location, but instead by a particular chat room, message board (Internet forum), listserv, or type of Internet software that users have in common' (Levine, 2000, p. 566). However, the results revealed in Whitty's research highlight, at least, when it comes to online dating, physical location is an important determinant of whether the relationships will develop successfully. Instead, many of these participants expressed a desire to find someone in the same area that they lived in. Often this was not simply the same city, but also the same suburb. The importance of proximity is highlighted in the following quote:

I   *Do you want to tell me a little bit about how that worked?*

M   *Basically when you say communicate, this is via email, I didn't speak to anybody on the telephone. I just found out where they lived and that was, if they lived too far away then I wouldn't consider it.*

(Margaret)

All based on the first meeting

As highlighted above, participants in Whitty's online dating study mostly all wanted to meet their date within a week or so of first contact on the site. Many also emphatically agreed that the first date determined if they were going to move further into a serious relationship or end the building of the relationship immediately. The first meeting was not only important as a means to get to know the person, but also to determine if there was any *physical chemistry*. In fact, if there was no physical attraction the online daters typically did not move the relationship beyond the first date. The importance of the first face-to-face meeting is illustrated in the following extracts:

Well I got sick of meeting girls and everything's based on this, even though it's not supposed to be looks, everything's based on the first meeting, that's the big shock compared to meeting someone in a pub or someone introducing you.

(Phil)

Most of them do nowadays. I can't speak for anybody else, but basically all of the ones that I've had, there's very little writing goes on, just get on the phone, have a couple of chats and then you meet. There's no point in wasting time because if the chemistry's not there then there's no point in mucking around so people that have been on these programs for a short time will tell you that. If they've been on there for about three or four months and had a few meetings, they'll tell you there's no point in wasting time because as soon as you open that door or as soon as you walk into that coffee lounge and you see the person, you know. Sure, you can go out with them for another few times and you may then decide one way or another or you might even change your mind. Most times that first meeting is the one that will tell you where you go from there.

(Martin)

One of the reasons why the participants thought the first meeting determined a continuation of the relationship is nicely expressed by Lisa (see below). Like many of the other participants, Lisa tells us that being equipped with a fair amount of knowledge about the person saves time. Unlike meeting someone in a pub for the first time, individuals do not have to spend time on the preliminaries.

> *I have found it more beneficial because say if you meet someone in a bar or a coffee shop or whatever, you meet them, to get all the information you already have about a person out of the profile, you have to see this person at least four times, so there goes four weekends you have wasted on a person that you don't know much about. But, if you have the information in front of you, you are already ahead because you already know their likes or their dislikes, and you already know their background a little bit. So a little bit, if they put the truth there, is very beneficial because it is not time wasting. You wouldn't, in a bar if you meet somebody, you have got to find out all this information, you have got to see them at least four or five times before you find out all the information you know when you read a profile, can you understand what I am saying?*

(Lisa)

Participants mostly saw the first date with someone from an online dating site as more of a *screening out process* and far less as a romantic occasion. Going to coffee was usually the favourite place for a first date, since it was both a safe and an easy place to make a quick getaway if they were unimpressed by their date. Examples are presented below:

I   *Where do you arrange your meetings?*

J   *Generally a public place like cafes, we try and pick a significant spot that's easy to meet, like on the corner of something or outside a particular store. We just go there and head off for coffee. It's usually coffee, I don't think I've ever actually met anybody first other than coffee, it's always been coffee.*

(Jeff)

L   *I meet him at a shopping centre. I always meet them in a very open place during the day.*

I   *And why do you do that?*

L   *I wouldn't meet a stranger in a dark alley. I have this image of meeting strangers in dark alleys or whatever so I thought in a coffee shop or a restaurant if it is a nice place.*

I   *And this is for safety reasons?*

L   *Yes.*

(Lisa)

If the coffee date finished up working well individuals often extended the date to include food or sometimes a film. This is described by Crystal below:

I   *And how did that date take place?*

C   *We had coffee, or we met, we met for coffee at a café type situation, sort of a busy type café, we ended up getting on really well and, so we actually stayed for lunch and that was really good.*

(Crystal)

A numbers game

This Australian online dating site was set up in such a way that individuals contact one another first by sending someone a '*kiss*'. The 'kiss' is a sentence sent through the site to an undisclosed email with a statement indicating that the individual was interested in the person they contacted. The contacted person could then respond to three options; they could state that they were interested and requested that the other person spend money on sending an email through the site, or that they were interested and they themselves would spend money on emailing the person through the site, or that they were flattered, but uninterested. Next, individuals would pay for '*stamps*' which would enable them to send emails through the site or wait for the other to pay to contact them. This is how the company makes their money. They could write anything in these emails. It is within this email that individuals can disclose their personal email so that contact can be made off the dating site.

In Chapter 3 we discussed the notion that cyberspace can be a liberating space where gender roles can be transgressed. However, these results suggest that despite the opportunities that cyberspace has to offer, as with offline, men were typically the ones who contacted the women and paid for the email to communicate with them. More than this, as expressed by Patricia and Patrick, the women expected them to behave as stated below:

P   *I prefer the old fashioned way, the guy makes the first move and then I know he is at least interested and I am not wasting my time.*

         (Patricia)

P   *Being a male I think you would be waiting until you're grey and old for someone to pay to email you.*

         (Patrick)

When it came to contacting others, about half of the sample saw online dating as a '*numbers game*', that is, sending out more expressions of interest than they expected to receive. More men (60%) than women (43%) perceived online dating to be a numbers game. Given the number of choices available, individuals could keep trying until they managed to get a response, as Alan told us:

I   *Do you contact many people and just hope that one will respond?*
A   *Yes, it's a numbers game. Between you, me, and the gatepost mate, life is a numbers game and you win some and you lose some and unless you are in their pitching you ain't going to get nothing.*
I   *Ok*
A   *You select those that obviously there is some interest and some similarity, commonality, and pass the rest by, but still it's a numbers game.*
I   *Right*
A   *You look at the picture and you read the words, and if it is better than 50 per cent you send them a kiss.*

         (Alan)

I   *Do you contact many people and just hope that one will respond?*
B   *I don't just want anyone to respond, no, but often I'll send out a virtual kiss where I'm in a 50/50 situation, I'm 50 per cent interested, and I've done that on quite a few occasions.*
I   *So you'll send out a number and see how many respond?*
B   *Let them have a look at me, if they want to go on they go on, if they don't they don't. I have done that quite a bit, I'd send out a 50/50 so if a woman gets a virtual kiss from me she shouldn't assume that I'm besotted with her.*

         (Bob)

Does anyone really read the profiles?

Given the numbers game the men, in particular, admitted to playing, it should come as no surprise that quite a number of the women (30%) compared to men (3%) spoke about concerns that those who contacted them were not actually reading the profile. This concern is nicely expressed in the following extracts:

I   *So you get the impression that they are not even reading your profile?*

J   *No that they are not reading it, but just that they are just mass kissing everyone, it's like an orgy of kisses (laugh). It's just stupid, whoever thought that up, I just think that it is really dumb.*

I   *So it really doesn't work for you.*

(Joan)

I   *Were there any changes you did in order to attract different types of men or was it more just an updating type of thing?*

A   *I re-wrote it to try and make it briefer. On the assumption, I think, that men don't like to read lots and lots of words. I wanted to make it more concise because it was a bit wordy and I tried to make it briefer*

(Ann)

Filtering through the lies

As mentioned above, one of the reasons why individuals were keen to meet their online dates in the flesh was because they wanted to see if the 'real' person matched up to the profile. Individuals became acutely aware after a few dates that this was not always the case. In Whitty's study, they talked about some of the exaggerations as well as the blatant lies online daters had included on their profiles.

The most common way that individuals misrepresented themselves was in regards to their physical appearance. Sixty-eight per cent of the participants stated they had met up with someone face-to-face from the site who had lied about their looks (e.g., describing themselves as more attractive than they were, using out-dated photos, or using a photo of a different person than themselves). Forty-two per cent of the participants said they had met up with someone who lied about their weight or size (women were more likely to do this compared to men). Seventeen per cent of the sample stated they met people who lied about their height (men were more likely to do this compared to women). Some of the exaggerations and lies about how one physically looked were quite extreme, as in the following examples:

I   *Any examples?*

A   *Yes, I've met people who had, in fact there was a girl who I was talking to the other day who said oh, I've had my hair cut since I submitted that photo, here's my latest photo and that was a completely different person. A few of the people that I've dated off the site have said the same thing, that they've actually turned up and it's a completely different person that they've turned up to meet. That was one that I nipped in the bud right there but I have had two where I actually turned up for the date and they looked nothing like their photos or descriptions.*

(Andrew)

R   *Oh yes. One lady I meet once described herself as slim and she had to be a size 18 at least. I didn't even recognise her and she came over to me and she said 'are you Rob' and I said 'yes' and she said 'I am such and such' and I just went white.*

(Rob)

K   *Yeah. And another guy told me he was six foot tall and he did this, and he did that, and when he showed up he was nearly bald, and he was shorter than I was, and I was like going, I mean you can't tell that from a photograph granted, but I sort of said to him 'this isn't right'. I pulled him up on it and he said 'oh no I think I am six foot and I said "I"m telling you right now there is no way you are over five foot seven' (laugh).*

(Kath)

S   *Another gentlemen, his profile looked good, we spoke on several occasions, we met and what I saw in the profile was different to what I saw face-to-face.*

I   *So his photo was different?*

S   *Yes . . . he was ten years older than what his photo was and I am thinking in my head, hang on a minute, you look like this yet your photo shows me that you are a younger man, not that I am after a younger man but the photo, I could see the similarities in the face-to-face person, but I was totally disappointed. Why can't people just be honest?*

(Sophia)

C   *It was just for a drink down in a club in the area.*

I   *And you say that it was unsuccessful, so why was it unsuccessful, how did that date go?*

C   *Because he was nothing like his photo, he was nothing like what he sounded in his emails or on the phone. He just named dropped the whole time, and I don't know whether he was nervous and he was just trying to impress me or what, but, I wasn't comfortable with him.*

I   *So his photo was really different, in what way was it different?*

C   *It was his brother.*

I   *Oh it was the brother. And so did he give an explanation as to why he was a different person.*

C   *No, he just said he put his brother's on because they looked similar.*

I   *And so he also didn't click well with you either you are saying?*

C   *Well he was short and fat and bald.*

I   *And his brother is not?*

C   *No*

     (Christine)

Other people's misrepresentations of their physical looks were only slight exaggerations. Nonetheless, the online daters were rarely forgiving of any lies told. For example, Melissa became very frustrated when one of her dates lied about his height:

M   *Some guys might say they are five foot eleven which is kind of border line for me and they turn out to be five foot ten or something*

     (Melissa)

Given the heavy emphasis on looks, as described earlier in this chapter, it is not so surprising that participants often expressed great disappointment when the person did not live up to their photograph. Interestingly, about half (53.3%) of the sample emphasised that they were looking for honest, genuine people. There were other ways that individuals lied about themselves on the site, including:

- personality
- interests/hobbies
- age

- their intentions (e.g., lied about wanting a relationship when they just wanted sex)
- socio-economic status
- their relationship status (e.g., lied about being single when they were married)
- having children
- being a non-smoker

To give some further examples of lies or exaggerations:

I   *In what way do they lie about their profession?*

L   *Most guys make you understand on their thing [profile] that they are in management, but when you talk to them they are not really in management, they are not even middle management some of them.*

I   *So they kind of exaggerate their role considerably?*

L   *Yes definitely.*

    (Lisa)

C   *A lot of people say they are looking for a long-term relationship or a friend-ship, and what I think they are after is a one night stand.*

    (Christine)

I   *Do you think was there any information that people exaggerated or distorted in any way?*

J   *Sometimes people do, yes.*

I   *Can you give any examples off-hand that you can think of?*

J   *Well, the one I said before that if somebody says I like bushwalking, but what they understand by bushwalking and what I understand can be a totally different thing, and then that you haven't really done any anyway. It's just something that you might think you'd like to do.*

    (James)

Clichéd self: Too many people strolling on the beach sipping red wine

In addition to sorting through the lies presented on profiles, online daters were often weary of profiles that contained 'cheesy' clichés. They mostly avoided these types of individuals, as they seemed to be more appeasing and far less 'real' than other profiles. To some, such as Grace (see quote below), clichés became a 'turn off', rather than the 'turn on' that the person writing the profile had hoped. Some examples of clichéd profiles that the participants stated were unappealing include:

I love walking on the beach and all this stuff that says bugger all.

(Phil)

if you run through the profiles every girl wants to sit by an open fire with a glass of red wine or walk along a beach. I mean it just repeats itself. If you find someone who's put a bit of thought into, more particular about what they're all about and they vary it a bit you think well there's someone a bit different there. They tend to all be run of the mill in what they say they want. They put in the obvious, good sense of humour, well you wouldn't put in you had a bad sense of humour.

(Grant)

T   *I tend to stay away from those people with sort of cliché stuff. I think it appears in a lot of profiles...*

I   *What would be some of the clichés that you would be turned off by?*

T   *With some, on some profiles it has a very sexual overtone, which puts me off totally. Sometimes it is like a passage of clichés, walks on the beach, romantic evenings, romantic getaways, a bottle of wine, and nice crackling fire. It just doesn't ring true, it just sounds like a, it doesn't seem very real.*

    (Teresa)

G   *and everyone says that they like walking on the beach, and anyone will tell you that it is so god damn boring (laugh). And when they say that I think 'oh my God, not another one, it is almost a turn off'.*

I   *They are all on that beach walking (laughing).*

G   *Oh my God, if there are so many on that beach walking, why don't they run into each other.*

I   *So a bit cliché that one?*

G   *Terrible, it is almost a turn off now.*

    (Grace)

Seeking out the 'true' self online

Before moving to consider how individuals talked about constructing their own profiles the chapter considers previous research by Bargh and McKenna and their colleagues, outlined earlier in this book, that argues that cyberspace allows one to reveal one's 'true' self (e.g., Bargh et al., 2002; McKenna et al., 2002). The 'true' self being the traits or characteristics that individuals' possess and would like to but are not typically able to express. To reiterate, these theorists have suggested that given the lack of physical presence online, individuals are able to feel more comfortable to self-disclose and reveal their true self or 'Real Me'. They believe that those individuals who reveal their true selves online are more likely to develop romantic relationships online that move successfully offline.

This theory does not seem to hold true when it comes to online daters. It does appear, as highlighted above, that online daters are attracted to genuine and honest people, and that they would hope that an individual's profile presents something about who the individual 'really' is – rather than a stereotypical, clichéd self or a self that the individual would like to possess but typically do not express in their day-to-day settings. In fact, over half of the participants said that an attractive person was one who was genuine and real. It seems, however, that the 'real' self these participants were referring to was more what Higgins meant by an 'actual' self. That is, online daters perceived honest and genuine people to be those who included in their profiles the traits or characteristics that they typically express in everyday offline social settings.

These online daters were most concerned with what their date looked like and how they behaved in their first face-to-face meeting. If the individual did not match up to the profile, as described earlier, the online dater was highly disappointed. The online daters were savvy enough to know the possibility that people might present a different self online than they do offline. Therefore, unlike McKenna et al.'s (2002) sample, individuals who used the online dating site did not want to spend time getting to know one another in cyberspace. In fact, they were quite the opposite, expressing a desire to meet the person face-to-face as soon as possible. Hence, there was little opportunity or desire for people to get to know individuals' 'true' selves or for individuals to gradually express their true selves. Rather than an unravelling of the self online – as seems to happen in other online spaces – individuals in online dating sites acquire a '*snap shot*' of the person. That is not simply a photo, but a 'snap shot' of the entire person. This is quite different to gradually getting to know a person, where contradictions can become evident and the complexity of an individual becomes more apparent.

Finding chemistry

A   *Well I think, there is no question that everybody has a different personality. And I could use the word chemistry and I think is more apparent and longer lasting and of a greater foundation when it is a person face-to-face, than it is when it is telephone or email. There is the ground work, but it is obviously cemented when you met personally and if there is chemistry from the word go, then you are going to get further quicker.*

(Alan)

It is also noteworthy that 'physical beauty' slightly outweighed 'inner beauty' in importance for selecting a date. Given the priority attributed to physical qualities, one can understand the online daters' motivation for wanting to meet face-to-face the potential romantic partner rather than getting to know someone online, only to find that they are not physically attracted to them. Furthermore, these online daters expressed a desire to find chemistry with another, which seemed to be something beyond physical attractiveness. While 'physical chemistry' is a common term in our everyday speech, it is nonetheless an abstract phrase. The taken-for-granted meaning by these participants, as far as Whitty could deduce, was that physical chemistry is a mutual physical and mental attraction. The strong, unanimous belief was that this could only be determined face-to-face.

The difference in the results obtained in Whitty's study to that in McKenna et al.'s (2002) study highlights the importance of accepting that the internet consists of many different spaces. It is noteworthy that McKenna et al. investigated people using newsgroups. Moreover, they deliberately chose newsgroups as they believed that people using such sites were not motivated to do so to find a romantic relationship. This is very different to online daters, who are obviously there to develop a romantic relationship of some form. Moreover, as described above, the online dating sites are set up very differently to a newsgroup. A newsgroup is set up in a way to encourage and facilitate conversations. On an online dating site one can get to know some aspects about the other person prior to any interaction. Of course, there is the opportunity to get to know one another further in cyberspace; however, as illustrated in the extracts earlier on in this chapter, the online daters expressed an emphatic desire to meet their date as soon as possible, rather than 'wasting time' communicating in cyberspace.

Did they get what they paid for?

Beyond the desire to get a better idea of what their online mate looked like, the online daters were keen to meet their online mate face-to-face as they did not trust all the information detailed in people's profiles. Meeting a person face-to-face allowed them to check out the facts and determine if the profile matched up to the 'real' offline person. The scepticism displayed by these online daters was not a paranoid concern, as most individuals had met at least one person who had misrepresented himself or herself on the site. Individuals were very aware of not wasting too much time on a person online in case they were not the person they believed them to be. This allowed them to get on with the task of finding other potential dates.

Another noteworthy difference between the set up of a newsgroup and an online dating site is that one typically has to pay to use an online dating service. Hence, people do not want to waste their money or time buying a product they do not really want. One of the online daters nicely expresses this:

C   *I don't think people can be expected to be more forthright than they are. You know it is like, you are buying, you are out there shopping and when you shop for something you never quite know what you get.*

      (Colin)

Strategies used to compose one's own profile: Which 'self' to present?

Self-presentation is more fluid and under one's control online; people make decisions in each situation about when, how, and if they will disclose aspects of their physical appearance to the other. In a setting such as the Internet, where presentation is carefully chosen and consciously manufactured, control over one's self-presentation is greater than in face-to-face interactions. (Levine, 2000, p. 567)

Participants also admitted to the trials and tribulations of developing their own profiles. They were consciously aware of trying to attract people, but at the same time wanting to present themselves as 'real' people. Writing a profile was a *dynamic process*. Online daters would monitor who responded to their profile and accordingly alter their profile to either attract more people, attract a different type of person, or to filter out too many people from responding. Many would also have a few profiles at the same time to see which ones attracted what types of people. For example, Jessica started using the site by having a number of profiles, one in which she stated she was more interested in sex:

I *You have put together more than one profile?*

J *Yes, I have got four.*

I *Do you have more than one profile on at the moment?*

J *I find that different photos attract different men and it all depends on how they see, like, I have got four different photos there. I have got one without a photo and I have to say the one without the photo, some days I used to get a lot of response, just because I haven't got a photo there. It is probably what I was saying on the actual profile details.*

I *That one was more successful than the ones with the photos?*

J *Yeah, but I wasn't getting much replies back on that.*

I *How did the photos vary and what type of responses did you get according to each photo?*

J *According to what you say on your profile details, look there is just one thing that men, there are men who just, who think that there are women on the website just to have sex and no relationship and I have gathered that with one profile, I just tested it. I had to do that.*

I *So, what did you do in that particular profile, what did you write?*

J *I automatically said that I want a friend lover. You know you actually go straight to the point and I find that it attracts a lot of men and I even said that I want short and long relationships. But the problem with that is, I got a lot of guys and I did communicate with one who actually, well it didn't end up very nicely, so I had to change all my profile details to longer relationships.*

(Jessica)

Table 7.2 How people misrepresented themselves on the online dating site

Misrepresentations	Men	Women	Total
Looks: photo over a year out of date	2 (6.7%)	14 (46.7%)	16 (26.7%)
Details about their own relationship/children (e.g., having them, who they live with etc.)	4 (13.3%)	2 (6.7%)	6 (10.0%)
Age	3 (10.0%)	1 (3.3%)	4 (6.7%)
Weight (e.g., said average when a bit overweight)	2 (6.7%)	2 (6.7%)	4 (6.7%)
SES (occupation, being employed, professional, income)	2 (6.7%)	1 (3.3%)	3 (5.0%)
Interests	3 (10.0%)	0 (0.0%)	3 (5.0%)

Although the participants interviewed in Whitty's study (as shown earlier in this chapter) were rather annoyed and unforgiving with anyone who deviated from the precise truth about themselves in their profiles, they nonetheless admitted to telling lies themselves in their own profiles. As shown in Table 7.2 below, some admitted to lying about their looks, weight, height, personality, age, intentions, having children, as well as being a smoker.

The main motivation for lying was to attract others. Interestingly, the women lied about looks or used outdated photos more than men did. As we outlined earlier in this chapter men place more importance on physical attributes compared to women; hence, women had more reason to exaggerate their looks. Most participants rationalised that these were not out-and-out lies, but rather mere exaggerations, and often exaggerations that they thought others were probably also doing in their profiles. To give some examples:

I   *How did you decide what type of photograph to put up of yourself?*

A   *Well obviously you want something decent and I didn't have a lot of things around so the photograph that I have got was a studio glamour photograph, where they did your makeup and your hair and made you look gorgeous. But that is the only decent photograph I had.*

I   *You used that one. And you have used that the whole four years?*

A   *Yeah I haven't actually changed it, which I should because it doesn't look like me anymore but still close enough.*

(Ann-Maree)

S   *Actually, it's quite funny that there is, you can pick, there is a thing for body type and you can pick 'slim, average, athletic, a bit overweight'. Do you know any chick that is going to tell you that they are a bit over-weight?*

I   *I wouldn't know, I guess not?*

S   *That is right, so I just say average.*

I   *It's like the idea of perception of what is 'average', and average is you know probably a bit overweight anyway.*

(Suszi)

P   *One, I said I'm 46, I put it down by a year. I think because I was 46 and I put the 45 because I think a lot of girls in their profiles say they're looking to 45 so that's why I thought well if they do a search, they want to do to 45 so now it's 46. I haven't changed it because I think so many guys lie.*

(Phil)

M   *Well it's all perception of reality isn't it. Everyone's view of the world is different, my view of myself may be very different to what someone else thinks it is. But you know, my view is that you had to sell yourself without being. I mean the last thing you want is reality shock, when people get there and go 'that is not what he said he was about', so you have got to make the most of what you have got without exaggerating it so much that they never see you again. So, I would say it was probably 90 per cent accurate with a few little embellishments you know.*

I   *Tell us about the embellishments.*

M   *Oh gosh . . . you know things like portraying things in the most positive light. You know things like interests. I don't think I really have definite music inter-ests or anything, but I just said, 'I am on a first name basis with people at HMV' but I am not really but it doesn't matter. You know that sort of thing.*

(Matthew)

As some of the extracts above illustrate, the participants seemed to be trying to create a balance between keeping their profiles real (actual self) as well as selling themselves (or describing how they would like to be). The motivation for this was based on not wanting to disappoint the date once they met them face-to-face, but at the same time trying to attract a decent number of individuals to choose from. Wayne explains well how writing his profile was a way to sell himself.

W   *The other thing for me personally is I'm great at writing trade manuals for someone, but when it comes to writing about yourself and trying to sell yourself it's a very different story. I don't know whether that's more of a male trait than a female trait. It depends how good you want to try selling yourself too isn't it?*

(Wayne)

Participants also admitted that writing profiles was a considerably arduous task. What is perhaps more interesting is that they recruited friends and family to assist them in constructing their profiles. Some were self-aware enough to know that their own view of who they are is not necessarily how others view them. Therefore, friends and family were helpful in constructing a profile that reflected how the individual is typically in everyday situations, as Danny explains:

D   *The accuracy of the information is something I put ahead of everything else. I took forever to put up that profile, I didn't just stick up a photo and put up a profile. Have you seen my profile?*

I   *No, No, I haven't mate.*

D   *Ok that is fine. I laboured and drafted and sent across to a friend for clarification, I then re-drafted.*

(Danny)

Online dating strategies: How to play the game

In Chapter 1, Joe Walther and his colleagues' work on internet interactions was outlined. They have found that individuals are strategic in their self-presentations. Whitty's study shows very clear evidence that online daters are very strategic in the way they devise their online profiles. In considering the structuring of a profile participants are mindful of two things: (a) to attract others; and (b) that others will not be disappointed when they meet up face-to-face.

We have argued throughout this book, that cyberspace is akin to Winnicott's notion of potential space; that is, a safe place to play with identities and to play at love. It does seem that individuals using online dating sites do play and experiment with identity. Some do present a 'True Self' or 'Real Me' in the way that Bargh and McKenna discuss. However, these individuals tend not to be too successful at moving past the first date. Many also present a clichéd self – the stereotype of a romantic lover who likes to go for walks on the beach have candlelight dinners and sip red wine. These individuals tended to not even be chosen for a face-to-face meeting. The individuals most liked and respected and more likely to win a second date were the ones that matched up to their profiles – presenting a more 'actual' self.

We mentioned in Chapter 3 that play is a serious activity – where rules are devised. Although online dating is relatively new, the individuals interviewed in Whitty's study already had some expectations on how individuals ought to play this online dating game. One rule already mentioned in this chapter was the expectation that men ought to pay to contact the women. Another important rule is that once contacted people ought to respond back (this response did not cost the person any money) out of politeness, even if the response is a rejection. As Tony expresses:

I   *What have been your experiences in respect to sending out kisses and or emails and what's your feeling about those?*

T   *I think I mentioned that 60 per cent of the people that I've contacted either by kiss or email didn't even have the courtesy of responding. Even if you're not interested, the least you can do is, particularly the kiss system, it does give you a number of options and I think at least it's common courtesy to say I'm flattered that you're interested, but no I don't want to make any contact, at least you know . . . I think it's really a lack of courtesy, it's almost like somebody coming up to you in the street and you just look at them and ignore them. That's part of what the net is like now, it gives you that anonymity and you don't have to be face-to-face with somebody, so you can get away with probably a lot more than you normally would in a face-to-face conversation.*

(Tony)

Given that respondents can monitor each other's activity on the site – that is, they can tell what day and time they last logged in – another interesting rule was established by many of the participants. They believed that if they started seeing someone on the site, even if a relationship was not yet established, that person should take themselves off until it has been established that the relationship is not in the cards. As Melissa expresses:

M   *I am only interested in dating one person at a time I take myself off straight away. I notice men don't do that*

I   *That is interesting.*

M   *It is.*

I   *So, you have looked at their profile when you have met them and they are still there?*

M   *They are still very active and I have actually confronted a few people with that and they have said 'it doesn't really mean anything, it doesn't mean anything'. I have never been able to work that out, that guys don't take their profiles off unless you ask them to.*

(Melissa)

Conclusions about online dating

It seems apparent that online dating is here to stay and will continue to increase in popularity as a means of dating (see Chapter 9 for a more in-depth discussion of the future of online dating). The data in Whitty's study suggests that the way people go about establishing these types of online relationships vary considerably to the way relationships initiate and develop in other online spaces. This confirms the view that we should not treat the internet as one generic space. As summarised in Chapter 1, researchers, such as Katelyn McKenna and Andrea Baker, have discussed how they believe successful relationships can be established online and move offline. Whitty's research suggests that different rules apply to online dating sites. For successful relationships to be established one needs to 'live up to their profile', and not be clichéd in their presentations. However, another important suggestion for online daters to consider is just because there are seemingly more choices available online this does not mean they will score a supermodel or a Brad Pitt look alike. Instead, individuals still need to be realistic as to what types of individuals, in turn, will find them attractive. The art of compatibility is discussed in more detail in Chapter 9.

In continuing with our view that different types of interactions take place in different spaces online we now turn to consider personalities in cyberspace. In the following chapter we make the argument that different personalities could potentially be attracted to different aspects of the web.

CHAPTER 8

Characters and Archetypes in Cyberspace

This chapter focuses on what the research literature reveals about character type and relationship formation. Specifically, we are drawn to consider the question of whether or not the various places (spaces) that comprise cyberspace seem to attract or to be inhabited by some character types more than others. Drawing from the heuristic value of the psychodynamic literature we are also compelled to consider whether some places in cyberspace might be somewhat '*transformational*' of aspects of character and how this may or may not relate to success in forming relationships. Consistent with much of the precepts of psychodynamic theory, throughout this book we have championed the view that individuals are 'active' players in cyberspace rather than merely 'passive' receivers who are 'acted upon'. Thus, we agree with others that unlike television, radio, and print media that can be conceived largely as one-way communication, cyberspace is potentially much more interactive with the individual. In cyberspace, it is this interactivity that yields a variety of research questions that have yet to be investigated. From the standpoint of a psychodynamic understanding of behaviour in cyberspace, it is the potentially predictive nature of character that commends its investigation to the field to deepen our comprehension of human relationships.

Character type: The psychodynamic entrée

A psychodynamic appreciation of the term *character* 'refers to a person's typical or habitual pattern of responding to instinctual or interpersonal forces' (Gibson, Malerstein, Ahern, & Jones, 1989, p. 1139). Most broadly, character can be thought of as 'the pattern of traits, motives, attitudes, values, and behavior shared by members of a group, class, organization, society, or culture' (La Bier, 1986, p. 135).

Freud on character

Sigmund Freud (1905/1977) first argued that character could be traced to an individual's fixation to a particular stage of psychosexual development or to regression to the fundamental experiences that are related to such stages. These character types (e.g., oral-sadistic, anal-retentive) were associated with Freud's early work on libido theory. Freud in the founding of his second theory of the psyche (1923/1984, 1926/1983, 1933/1988, 1940/ 1986), identified character types that were in addition to those associated with psychosexual development and reflected that part of the psyche (i.e., id, ego, or superego) that was dominant in the person's life. These character types were dubbed as 'pure' types, but Freud was also of the view that we encounter these character types more frequently as part of a 'mixed type' (i.e., erotic–obsessional, erotic–narcissistic, and narcissistic–obsessional).

Neo-Freudians and character

Some within the psychodynamic community have refined the pioneering work on character type by Freud in a manner that has a very important heuristic value in reviewing the research on relationships in cyberspace and character. While generally *agreeing with Freud's clinical description* of character types, some have also suggested that the character, while it might be related to 'biological' and developmental stages, is firmly related to the socio-economic context of childhood. Prominent in this latter group of theorists are Karen Horney, Erich Fromm, Erik Erikson, and Harry Stack Sullivan who are often described as *neo-Freudians*. One commentator argues, accurately in our view, that the neo-Freudians' 'deviations from the orthodoxy of Freudian psychoanalysis may be viewed as merely a matter of different emphasis, but they have resulted in elaboration of points barely touched upon by Freud' (Levitt, 1980, p. 21). Fromm captures the slightly different emphasis when he argues that it is 'attitude' that is the key issue, and reference to infantile erogenous regions is simply 'the expression of an attitude toward the world of language of the body' (Fromm, 1941/1994, p. 290). For example, the term 'anal-retentive character' is used to particularly denote a combination of three traits – orderliness, thrift, and obstinacy. For Fromm, these characteristics of this anal character had much to do with the ethic of Protestantism.

Fromm (1932/1970, p. 268) noted that 'since the character traits are rooted in the libidinal structure, they also show relative stability'. Indeed, Maccoby (1976) was to comment: 'Fromm and I believe character traits are *relatively* fixed in childhood, formed by influences of culture, modes of work, environment as mediated through the family, and the child's constitution (p. 42). In contrast, Freudian theory considers character as set in childhood and unlikely to change without psychoanalytic intervention' (italics is original emphasis). The term 'relatively' is important here in as much as Maccoby and Fromm believe the same socio-economic influences that were influential earlier in life could still hold the potential for some change later in life. Fromm and Maccoby (1970) argue:

> The character of the child, as we believe with Freud, develops as a result of dynamic adaptation to the family constellation. Since the family represents the spirit of the society into which the child enters, the same influences which have been the main determining influences from the beginning continue to mold the adolescent's and adult's character structure. Institutions of schooling, work, and leisure do not differ essentially from the way of life transmitted to the child in his family. Thus the character structure acquired in childhood is constantly reinforced in later life, provided the social circumstances do not change drastically. (pp. 21–22; see also Maccoby, 1976, pp. 42–43)

Maccoby (1976) notes the citation above in his book *The gamesman* and adds: 'This addition to Freud does not contradict the expectation that unconscious and deeply irrational attitudes formed in childhood resist change, even if social conditions are different' (p. 43).

Character type, change, and cyberspace

The possibility that character type might be susceptible to some 'change' in a changed environment, as was highlighted particularly by neo-Freudians, has important consequences in terms of the cyberspace. Is it possible that in entering and playing in the different spaces in cyberspace the character type may be 'changed', albeit temporarily, by the nature of the space itself? For instance, in this area, an aspect of character that is much mentioned in the literature is that of shyness. In such an example, the question then becomes not just whether more people who are normally shy are attracted to particular spaces of cyberspace, but also whether, as a result of experiencing those ever-changing spaces on the internet, the degree of shyness changes online and/or offline. In this context, the psychodynamic heuristic naturally leads to the question of whether or not the research literature, thus far, supports the notion that cyberspace itself serves as a *transitional object* in respect to producing a *'transformational effect'* on aspects of character. Further consideration would also pose the query that different interacting character types may be dialectically linked or at least act as mutually causal transitional objects.

This question is prompted, particularly, by a group of psychodynamic studies conducted by Maccoby (1976), La Bier (1983, 1986), and Carr (1993, 1994b, 2001; Degeling & Carr, 2004) who collectively provide powerful evidence that immersing oneself into different spaces may stimulate specific traits and attitudes that represent a different character for the individuals involved. The different space, in these studies, was that of the work environment but the issue of a possible transformational effect can be similarly raised in respect to that space called cyberspace (see, for example, Whitty, 2003a).

Character type and cyberspace: Research findings

In earlier times and in a somewhat *generic* conception of cyberspace, the media appeared to suggest that this 'place' was largely inhabited by the shy, socially inept, socially isolated, and depressed. Indeed, much of the research that has considered, or could have a bearing upon, the matter of character types in cyberspace has mostly looked at 'personality' characteristics. In reviewing this existing research, we have considered it helpful to discuss and group the various studies in terms of perceived clusters of related 'personality' characteristics. We say 'related', as the researchers themselves viewed them as related or overlapping.

The shy, socially inept, socially isolated, and depressed

The somewhat antiquated popular tabloid press speculation that cyber-space is a generic place inhabited by the shy, socially inept, socially isolated, and depressed has been a conception that has attracted a good deal of attention by researchers in the field. The veracity of such posits has been investigated, and now recognises that cyberspace is not one generic place, but is comprised of many places – some of which may have a differential 'appeal'.

In a pilot study of 30 self-selected undergraduate University students in America who were regular users of the internet, McCown, Fischer, Page, and Homant (2001) used a 'Personality Mosaic inventory' to ascertain whether particular personality characteristics were more highly represented in internet users. These researchers' findings were that 'cyberfriends tend to be socially skilled, have strong verbal skills and demonstrate empathy for others' (McCown et al., 2001, p. 593). Of course, the question that remains to be answered is whether the majority of these internet users were like this before using the internet or whether they became this way as a result of using the internet. Birnie and Horvath (2002) came to fairly similar conclusions in their research that again involved undergraduate Canadian University students who comprised a 115-member sample. The major finding of this research was that 'online social communication appeared to complement or be an extension of traditional social behaviour rather than being a compensatory medium for shy and socially anxious individuals' (Birnie & Horvath, 2002, p. 1). Indeed, they noted that those people with an existing 'large social network and frequent/intimate social communication ... (are) more likely to use the new medium (the internet) for social purposes' (p. 14). In relation to this nexus with sociability and social network, a study by McKenna et al. (2002) of 145 internet users, in a follow up after a 2-year period, that there were 'decreases in loneliness and depression and increases in the size of one's social circle' (p. 29).

In relation to the matter of shyness and the use of an online dating site, in Chapter 1 we noted a study by Scharlott and Christ (1995). Their study comprised a 74-question survey of 102 registered subscribers to the online dating site, Matchmaker. Shyness was assessed using a 5-point scale from a strongly agree to disagree range of questions book-ended with statements such as: 'I don't find it hard to talk to strangers' to 'It is hard for me to act natural when I meet new people' (p. 197). The significant findings were that 'shier users were more likely to agree that Matchmaker allows them to explore new aspects of their personality' and that 'seventy-four percent of the high-shyness users indicated that their main purpose in using Matchmaker was to find a romantic or sexual relationship, while only 46 per cent of the low-shyness users answered that way' (Scharlott & Christ, 1995, p. 199). The size of the cohort described in the study as 'high-shyness users' and 'low-shyness users' were the same. The researchers concluded that 'shy users employ Matchmaker to overcome inhibitions that may prevent them from initiating relationships in face-to-face settings' (Scharlott & Christ, 1995, p. 199). Clearly the nature of the place in cyberspace that was occupied by Matchmaker was significant in attracting shy individuals and a key issue for the attractiveness of this place was anonymity and as such this place constituted a transitional 'safe' place (see Stritzke, Nguyen, & Durkin, 2004) to 'play at love'.

Joinson (2004) conducted a study of self-esteem and its relationship to participants' choice of email versus face-to-face communication. He references a number of other studies that suggested 'that people disclose more, less socially desirable, information about themselves online compared to equivalent FtF (face-to-face) contexts' (p. 479). He goes on to say that 'most explanations... rely on aspects of the media itself to explain any effects. For instance, visual anonymity, lack of identifiability... have all been implicated in heightened self-disclosure on-line' (p. 479). Joinson found that 'LSE (low self esteem) participants showed a greater preference for e-mail over FtF than HSE (high self esteem) participants' (p. 483). Although not studying shyness, Joinson comments that this finding 'experimentally replicates the observation that shy people tend to benefit from computer-based dating systems, and anecdotal evidence that socially anxious people may be more likely to be "pathological" Internet users than the more socially confident' (pp. 483–484).

In the context of the studies on shyness, gender has been raised as a significant variable. In the study by Scharlott and Christ's, they found that males were more likely to initiate the first move on this online dating site and women were more passive. Byrne and Findlay (2004) found that across a number of mediums males were more likely to make the first move when initiating a first date. In this study, when females did initiate the first move, they showed a preference for using SMS (short message service) rather than telephone calls – their male counterparts had no such preference.

Whitty (2004a) also recently found that males were more likely to initiate the first contact when online.

The fact that shy individuals use a service, such as Matchmaker, to pursue social relationships may not come as any great surprise. A more general study on the use of the internet involved 3154 internet users and findings were that over 30 per cent of shy individuals spend between 6 and 11 hours each week on a variety of internet places and do so with the intention of pursuing social relationships (Carducci & Klaphaak, 1999). The nature of the engagement of shy individuals with cyberspace would appear important in terms of understanding what the variety of places in cyberspace has to offer.

Peris, Gimeno, Pinazo, Ortet, Carrero, Sanchiz, and Ibañez (2002) tried to establish whether or not there was a common personality or common social profile among internet users using a double sample consisting of 66 'online chatters', the majority of whom were identified as Spanish; and a second sample of 149 psychology students in a Spanish University. A Spanish version of the *Eysenck Personality Questionnaire* was used in pursuing this research and the profile that emerged was one that 'portrays persons satisfied with their real-world social relations and prone to begin and maintain social interaction' (p. 48). In addition, the sampling was such that 'chatters' were compared to 'nonchatters' on the internet. The researchers found that for chat users, there was no 'distinctive pattern' (p. 49) and 'that shyness or emotional instability is not a feature of chat users as a group' (p. 50).

It is interesting to note that 30 years ago, a study found that 40 per cent of the adult population experiences shyness (Zimbardo, Pilkonis, & Norwood, 1975). The cyberspace studies noted thus far have not considered this finding as a potential reference point in relation to relative shyness in making comparisons between numbers of 'chatters' versus 'nonchatters'. Some may not have considered this issue simply because they are relying upon the research instrument itself to be norm referenced and their focus is to simply reflect upon the relativity within those who are actually engaging the internet. A study of shyness and anxiety as predictors of patterns of internet usage by Scealy, Phillips, and Stevenson (2002) did note this point of comparison between internet and non-internet populations. Scealy et al. were keen to discover whether the use of the internet was correlated in any manner with levels of shyness and social anxiety. The significance of 40 per cent of the normal population as experiencing shyness was, in itself, viewed as a reason to ascertain if the internet represented a type of 'safe-haven'. The sample used in the study by Scealy et al. comprised 177 participants, the majority of whom were recruited from a University in Australia. These respondents were asked to complete three questionnaires: (a) an internet questionnaire about internet usage; (b) one related to the Social Reticence Scale; and (c) one questionnaire related to the Trait Anxiety Inventory. One of the major findings was that 'shyness and anxiety did not specifically pre-dispose people to lower or higher levels of use of the Internet's communicative functions' (Scealy et al., 2002, p. 513). In the finer detail, the researchers did find that shy males were more likely to use the internet for recreation/leisure searches, which indicates that 'shy people may not always seek out online communication, but pursue other interests' (p. 514).

Most recently, two studies have investigated shyness as a predictor of internet dependence or addiction. A study by Chak and Leung (2004) of 722 internet users, located in Hong Kong, required its convenience sample of respondents, 78 per cent of whom were 12–26 years of age and 36 per cent of male gender, to complete five questionnaires that related to: (a) internet usage; (b) the Internet Addiction Test; (c) the revised Cheek and Buss Shyness Scale; (d) the Internality, Powerful Others and Chance Scales; and (e) social demographic variables. This study found that 'the higher the tendency of one being addicted to the Internet, the shier the person' (p. 564) and, in keeping with the findings of Scealy et al. (2002), 'shy males use e-mail, ICQ and chat rooms less' (p. 567). Unfortunately, the study examined only online activity in terms of the number of hours per week individuals spent on the internet rather than or in addition to the purpose of the activity. In the relationship between shyness and internet, findings in relation to cause and effect on 'addiction' remained speculative.

Yuen and Lavin (2004) examined a speculated correlation between internet dependence and interpersonal shyness, both online and offline. Again, a sample of convenience was used that involved 283 students at a private New York University; 204 of whom were female. The methodology involved an online questionnaire that included a group of seven questions adapted from the Diagnostic and Statistical Manual of Mental Disorders as the means to determine 'dependence'. The fundamental finding from the research was that 43 of the sample were shy in offline social interactions but when online, their shyness level was significantly lower than the non-dependent group. Unlike Chak and Leung (2004), Yuen and Lavin found no significant variation in their results due to gender.

The results from the studies by Yuen and Lavin (2004) and Chak and Leung (2004) begin to take us into the issue of cause and effect, which we will comment upon presently, but at this point some of the forgoing research studies appear to be, in some respects, contradictory. As a generic space, it would appear that shy and socially anxious individuals are not more frequently encountered in cyberspace than their counterparts. This, however, is to somewhat miss the point as shy individuals appear attracted to some specific spaces precisely because they are shy and those spaces are 'safe'. It is thus a *differentiated* cyberspace that we need to clearly keep in mind when considering personality traits and character type.

In reviewing the research findings, we found that some spaces in cyberspace provide a safe haven for the shy, socially inept, socially isolated, and depressed. Of course, further research is required to support this claim. When it comes to forming relationships in cyberspace it might be that shy individuals are more comfortable with using an online dating site than mobile phone technology to find a date (more on this in the following chapter). Moreover, there might be something about the nature of the internet that makes it a space and place that has something of a *transformative effect* on human personality and character, at least for some users of the internet. This notion has been partly supported by the literature (e.g., McKenna et al., 2002). The transformative effect upon some aspects of character clearly holds therapeutic potential and significance to those who have some difficulty in developing relationships in face-to-face due to shyness, social anxiety, and poor social skills.

Introvert–Extravert

The level of introversion is something that was noted as very significant in terms of the character types described by Jung (1917/1953, 1921/1989). Our review of the research literature has failed to reveal any research that has explicitly investigated the relationship between the internet users and the notion of 'type' – as used in the Jungian sense of the term. There have, however, been a number of studies that have investigated the relationship of internet users with their level of introversion often using the *Eysenck Personality Inventory* (EPI) as the instrument to measure the level of introversion/extraversion.

In the question of whether cyberspace is a place where introverts are more commonly encountered, the studies thus far seem to indicate that this might not be the case, but again we need to note that cyberspace is not one generic space and some studies in the past have not carefully differentiated the spaces wherein they conducted their research. Moreover, in using the term 'internet' many of the research studies are referring to email and chat room spaces.

In the well-known HomeNet study conducted by Kraut et al. (1998) they found that 'greater social extroversion and having a larger local social circle predicted less use of the Internet...' (p. 1025). Interestingly, in their follow-up study Kraut et al. (2002) found that 'the association of Internet use with changes in community involvement was positive for extraverts and negative for introverts' (p. 61). The researchers noted that 'Holding constant respondents prior community involvement, extraverts who used the Internet extensively reported more community involvement that those who rarely used it; on the other hand, introverts who used the Internet extensively reported less community involvement that those who rarely used it' (p. 64). To the researchers, these findings seemed to support a 'rich get richer' thesis by which those with strong social networks and social skills further enhanced their networks with the internet regarded as an avenue where differences between introverts and extraverts become amplified in terms of their relative abilities to use social resources.

In research that involved 72 Israeli University students, Hamburger and Ben-Artzi (2000) examined the use of 12 internet services with the levels of extraversion and neuroticism. Thus, in this study the internet was not simply regarded as one generic space. Again the EPI was employed and different patterns of association were found for men and for women. Men who scored highly on extraversion appeared to use 'Leisure Services' (e.g., sex web-sites, random surfing) whereas women who scored low on extraversion had a higher uptake of 'Social Services' (e.g., chat, discussion groups, people address seeking). The researchers concluded that the greater use of leisure sites by extraverted men could be attributed to a greater need for stimulation and arousal – in this context the researchers note that a number of studies have found that 'extraversion is positively related to sexual sensation seeking as manifested by higher sexual arousal... because currently most sex sites are aimed at men, the relationship between extraversion and the use of sex sites on the Internet reveals itself only among men' (p. 447). The greater use of social services by introverted women was attributed to a greater need for social support. Although defining 'Leisure Services' to be sex-websites and random surfing is obviously limiting, this research nonetheless deepens our understanding of a differ-ential internet usage for extraverts and introverts and the relationship with gender – information that is particularly valuable for web-designers. This research is firmly suggestive of the proposition that in chat rooms and discussion groups we would tend to find a relatively higher proportion of introverts. Yet, in contrast, Peris et al. (2002), who also used the EPI to examine respondents from chat rooms, found 'no significant differences in extraversion and psychoticism scores' (p. 48) and no differences in these results based on gender (p. 46).

In their study of 220 adult internet users in Oxfordshire, England, and again using the EPI, Hills and Argyle (2003) produced findings that were contradictory to those of Hamburger and Ben-Artzi (2000) but consistent with Peris et al. (2002). Again, Hills and Argyle were interested in which internet services were being accessed. Hills and Argyle found men appeared to use chat rooms more than women and there were no positive correlations with levels of extraversion except 'there was a weak positive association of extraversion with the home based services, which might suggest that extraverts are more willing than introverts to access services from home' (Hills & Argyle, 2003, p. 67). Of course, one of the problems in comparing these studies is that no doubt different personalities are attracted to different types of chat rooms and discussion boards. For example, some are set up for sexual discussions, some for hobbies, others for intellectual discussions, and so forth.

There appears to be a degree of conflict in the findings in respect to detecting any significant correlation between an internet user's level of extraversion with the specific internet service being accessed. Future research on character type will need to look closely at the type of internet services being accessed and explore if there are any intervening variables that may help resolve these conflicting research studies. Again, we also raise the question of whether personality remains static. Can the internet re-mould characters? Do personality styles alter as a consequence of their online interactions?

Psychoticism, neuroticism, and the delusional

Throughout this book we have noted that cyberspace maybe regarded as a place of play in which an illusionary quality is implied. In addition, we have contended that cyberspace is not always liberating and that the boundary between reality and fantasy can be blurred such that it produces certain types of psychopathologies (see Ogden, 1985a). The image of who inhabits cyberspace, and chat rooms in particular, has been portrayed by some sections of the media as being the home of the neurotic, psychotic, and the delusional – fundamentally a place where people come to express and perhaps act out their fantasies. Whilst we have not discussed the psychotic, neurotic, and delusional as being character types as such, in the popular press, it is not uncommon to find these psychopathologies described as though they were character types. In our review of the research literature we did note that some studies included 'measures' for some of these psychopathologies. The overall conclusion was that there was no evidence that would confirm such media speculation. However, some of the finer detail is expository.

In examining the relationship between extraversion and the use of specific internet services, Hamburger and Ben-Artzi (2000) used the EPI with its 24-item neuroticism scale. The findings were that for the general sample, neuroticism was negatively related to information services. The variation on this finding was that for women in the sample, neuroticism (i.e., 'experiencing anxiety, distress and emotional lability', p. 444) was slightly related to internet access of social services. These researchers speculated that women have a higher level of self-consciousness that serves as a stress-resistance resource. It is in such a context that Hamburger and Ben-Artzi (2000) argue that the 'Internet environment provides the platform in which introverted and neurotic women feel secure enough in discussions and chat with other people in order to reduce their emotional loneliness' (p. 447). It also needs to be noted that while the EPI also allows for reporting upon psychoticism, Hamburger and Ben-Artzi did not comment upon this factor in their study.

In 2001, Tuten and Bosnjak concluded that based on a small sample of psychology students, individuals with high scores on a scale of neuroticism appeared to use the internet less frequently. A study of 206 south eastern United States internet users, who were college students, was purposefully conducted by Swickert, Hittner, Harris, and Herring (2002) to test Tuten and Bosnjak's (2001) conclusions, but with a larger and more broadly based sample. Swickert et al. employed the NEO Five-Factor Inventory to ascertain levels of neuroticism and the results were contradictory to those obtained by Hamburger and Ben-Artzi. Specifically, Swickert et al. found that 'both correlation and regression analyses revealed marginally significant negative associations between neuroticism and Information Exchange and neuroticism and Leisure' (p. 447). Swickert et al. (2002) suggest, 'the association between neuroticism and leisure Internet use requires further attention in order to clarify the inconsistencies in the literature' (p. 448). Again, as we have suggested, results might vary due to how one defines leisure activities online (Whitty & McLaughlin, in press).

It might be recalled that the earlier noted studies by Peris et al. (2002) and by Hills and Argyle (2003) also employed the EPI and as such could report upon neuroticism as well as psychoticism. Peris et al. found 'that the subjects' basic scores in extraversion, neuroticism, and psychoticism do not match any distinctive personality pattern, although (and in contrast to Hamburger and Ben-Artzi, 2000) female chatters have been found to have a slightly higher emotional stability (low neuroticism)' (p. 49, first bracketed comment is our insert). Hills and Argyle (2003) found no significant correlations of internet use with neuroticism or psychoticism.

Again, without interrogating the soundness of the research design and methodology, it would seem the popular press version of who inhabits cyberspace is not in accord with the research findings. Neuroticism and psychoticism do not appear to be characteristic of internet users that engage in the mainstream activities of visiting chat rooms, playing games, using email, visiting bulletin boards, and alike.

The review of the research in relation to character type and the internet can be noted to be fairly narrowly conceived and, in some cases, the results appear to be contradictory. Again, clearly, when considering the issue of character type, past research moves us to consider that the internet is not simply one generic space. Whilst past research has not explored the more elaborate psychodynamic approaches and understandings of character, psychodynamic theories of character do raise significant questions in the interrogation of the research data. The *transformational effect* in relation to character that psychodynamic research has noted elsewhere can be detected in the research findings of some studies that have explored the cyberspace – character type relationship. In the context of considering character types as being habitual patterns in responding to others, we would like to conclude this chapter with a brief note in relation to the work of Carl Jung on archetypes and its relevance to relationships in cyberspace.

Jung on archetypes

Another pioneer of psychodynamic theory, in the area of character type, that is significant to our review of the research literature is that of Carl Jung. It might be recalled that Jung viewed the unconscious somewhat differently to Freud. Jung envisaged the unconscious to be comprised of what he called the 'personal unconscious' and the 'collective unconscious', the collective unconscious being primordial images and ideas that have emotions and symbolism 'attached' that are manifest in fantasies, dreams, myths, and our emotional responses in everyday life. These common patterns of psychic perception called *archetypes*, Jung (1935/1969) argued, are 'categories analogous to the logical categories which are always and everywhere present as the basic postulates of reason', akin to Plato's ideal forms, except they are 'categories of the imagination' (pp. 517–518). Archetypes are typical modes of comprehending the world (Jung, 1916/1969). An archetype 'is determined as to its content only when it has become conscious and is therefore filled out with the material of conscious experience' (Jung, 1938/1968, p. 79). This 'content' is an image: archetypes merely hold the possibility of an image. Confusion between the archetype itself and the content of the archetype is in many ways understandable as specific archetypes are often referred to by their symbolic or imaginal manifestations. For example, Jung (1912/1969) talks of the 'Jonah-and-the-Whale' image and says it has 'any number of variants, for instance the witch who eats children, the wolf, the ogre, the dragon, and so on' (p. 419). These images are all variants on the theme of being psychologically engulfed: an experience of being devoured or swallowed. Thus, as one writer notes, 'the archetype is an abstract theme (engulfment), and the archetypal images (whale, witch, ogre, dragon, etc.) are concrete variations on that theme' (Adams, 1997, pp. 102–103).

Many find Jung's work on archetypes difficult to grasp because the archetypal patterns of the psyche are not unveiled through normal linear thought processes, but rather through an impressionistic collection of themes and aspects that seem to cohere in a fashion to reveal a figure with particular definable features. Jung described a number of archetypes whose content was anthropomorphic: for example, the Anima, Animus, the Divine Child, the mother and Great Mother, the Wise Old Man, the

Trickster, and the Kore or Maiden. Jung noted that there are in fact many archetypes whose content was anthropomorphic, but he only wrote extensively about a few examples. The anima, for instance, he contended, is the image of a woman, or the feminine, in a man's dreams, fantasies, and thoughts. The image is not of an actual woman but are a collection of 'ideals' (not necessarily 'good' or 'beautiful') – fantasies that have been influenced by: experiences with women (mother, lover, wife, etc.); the man's own bi-sexual nature in which femininity comes from biological sources such as hormones; and mans' collective experiences of women through the ages. The comparable counterpart to anima in the sense this is the image of a male, or the masculine, in a women's dreams, fantasies, and thoughts. Again these images are 'ideals' or fantasies that include figures such as famous men, father-figures, religious figures, and morally bankrupt male figures. Both males and females incorporate an anima and animus as a component of their psyche as part of their own 'collection' of traits. Clearly the issue of projection of both feminine and masculine sides of the psyche is important in terms of how one might be 'viewed' and wish to be viewed on the internet.

In terms of cyberspace as a place for social interaction, social communication, and relationship formation, it is sensible not only to talk about the possibility of certain character types being more attracted to the internet, but, from a Jungian perspective, to also talk about the manner in which people respond to each other in terms of archetypes. The personal and collective unconscious are both important considerations to a Jungian-based understanding of social interaction. In observing the manner in which people respond to one another in cyberspace and the *resonance* that may give rise to an ongoing relationship, consideration of archetype would seem to have considerable merit.

One paper that explored archetypes in an examination of individual behaviour in cyberspace was that by Childress (1999). In his paper entitled 'Archetypal conceptualization of cyberspace as the Celtic Otherworld', Childress suggests there are 'similarities between the ancient Celtic conceptualization of the Otherworld and the modern, quasi-dimensional cyberspace created by the Internet' (p. 262). Childress argues that the Celts did not commit their mythology and beliefs to writing but instead relied upon an oral tradition. Alternatively, Christian monks did record local legends that revealed Celtic conceptualizations of the 'Otherworld' (or, *sidhe*). A number of themes emerge from these local legends. One underlying theme is that the otherworld is 'a magical domain outside of normal time and space' (Childress, 1999, p. 262). The following aspect of this mythology has particular significance to character type and is thus worthy of extensive quotation:

> The general format of the myth involves a hero who, while hunting, spies a beautiful woman or animal and gives chase. The prey of the hero often turns out to be the fairy queen, either in her human or animal aspect. The beautiful woman or animal leads the hero onward, and he becomes disoriented as he finds himself in an unfamiliar part of the forest. Still he follows the chase and is soon led to the entrance into a fairy mound, or *sidhe*. When he enters he finds himself in a beautiful world of boundless happiness and the source of all wisdom.... In this Otherworld, the hero is immeasurably happy while he participates in abundant feasting, drinking, fighting, and sexual activity. Soon, however, the hero yearns to revisit the human world to see old friends and loved ones and he is ultimately granted permission to leave. When the hero returns to the normal human world he discovers that, while only a year or two had passed inside the fairy mound, hundreds of years have passed in the world of humans and all his friends and loved ones have long been dead.
>
> Although the Celtic Otherworld is depicted as a world of joy and abundance, there is also a dark side to the Otherworld and to the residence of fairy hills generally.... The residents of the *sidhe*, or fairy mound, also express dual aspects of both light and darkness. Although they are described as beautiful, ageless, and magical beings, they are also described as mischievous and dangerous. (Childress, 1999, p. 262)

The description of the Celtic Otherworld would seem to resonate with some of the themes raised in this chapter. The notion of an intoxicating alluring Otherworld that leads one astray from attending to other relationships in the 'real world' would seem akin to the issue of internet addiction and internet dependence. The passage of time that appears to go unnoticed by those who inhabit the Otherworld is not unlike the manner in which some find the internet as a place where one may lose track of time. The initial disorientation described in the myth is also akin to the experience of those who are novices on the internet but once familiar with the software and the variety of places within the internet, the experience of the internet may change from disorientation to 'one of awe and wonder'

(Childress, 1999, p. 263). The 'magical' domain of the internet as a 'domain of beauty, wisdom, and abundance' (Childress, 1999, p. 264) does hold significant potential including psychological benefit but there are also some potential dangers for some groups of people.

The Celtic Otherworld is *one* archetype amongst a number that we may draw upon to help organise our experience of cyberspace. For some, the experience of cyberspace is like that of the Celtic Otherworld that Childress (1999) succinctly describes as 'A world of disembodied voices and ethereal spirits, a world of beauty without age, deformity, or illness, a world of abundance that satisfies refined pleasures and canal lusts' (p. 264). As researchers we struggle to try to comprehend this 'Otherworld' called cyberspace. The mere fact that we may perceive it as being *otherness* should cause us to pause and alert ourselves to the possibility that models we have developed from experiences of the 'real world' may not be appropriate for comprehending this other place. It is also important to remind ourselves of the psychodynamic processes that otherness may trigger. In this book we have argued that object-relations theories suggest one way in which we may respond to otherness is to engage in the regressive behaviour of splitting. While we may note this behaviour in the various posts on the internet, we also need to be attentive to potential for researchers themselves, in their very acts of enquiry, to unconsciously project onto their data and tunnel their observations and commentary in a manner that may bear the hallmarks of splitting. For those readers who are researchers, the tale of the Celtic Otherworld might simply guide them to investigate and concentrate their research into establishing the extent of the dark side while ignoring or neglecting the dynamics of the light side. For others the tale may have the opposite effect. We noted in our earlier discussion that archetypes are typical modes of comprehending the world, which, when read through specific experiences, all have a 'light' and a 'dark' side. Awareness of the 'other' side is important if we are to appropriately benefit from the 'wisdom' of our collective unconscious.

Clearly, in our investigations of how relationships are formed in cyberspace, the issues of character type and of archetype would appear to hold much potential. Revisiting previous studies in the field and surfacing questions from different conceptual lenses is a necessary prelude to further research. A psychodynamic lens, as used in this book, does surface new questions and simultaneously serves to re-frame some of our previous understandings about relationship in cyberspace. In the following chapter we continue to examine how researchers might continue their investigations into understanding online relationships. We also consider how this technology might change and what new appeal it might have for those initiating, maintaining, and developing relationships.

CHAPTER 9

Visions of the Future

> *Smart mobs consist of people who are able to act in concert even if they don't know each other. The people who make up smart mobs cooperate in ways never before possible because they carry devices that possess both communication and computing capabilities. Their mobile devices connect them with other information devices in the environment as well as with other people's telephones. Dirt-cheap microprocessors are beginning to permeate furniture, buildings, and neighbourhoods: products, including everything from box tops to shoes, are embedded with invisible intercommunicating smartifacts. When they connect the tangible objects and places of our daily lives with the Internet, handheld communication media mutate into wearable remote-control devices for the physical world.*
>
> (Rhiengold, 2002, p. xii)

The world has already changed since Howard Rhiengold wrote 'Smart mobs' but the way in which we communicate, develop, and maintain relationships are moving in the same direction as in the world Rhiengold has predicted. Cyberspace is here to stay and we will continue to initiate and develop relationships within this space. However, this space is increasingly becoming a part of our daily lives, and we hop in and out of this space much more quickly than ever before. This final chapter discusses visions of how we might continue developing cyberspace to play at relationships, love, romance, and sex. It also considers how researchers might ethically study these ways of relating.

The future of online dating: Waxing or waning?

The increase in numbers of online dating sites worldwide suggests that online dating is becoming a popular choice for individuals to seek partners.

Dr James Houran, who is the Chief Psychologist for TRUE.com (and online dating site), said the following about the future of online dating:

> I feel the future of the industry is extremely bright for three reasons. First, the rise and success of niche sites has sparked interest from new consumer markets with special needs and interests. They're arguably bringing new people into the fold. Second, new technologies are enhancing the '*tools of online dating and matchmaking*' such as improved personal profiles, chat rooms and webcams, mobile communications linked to dating sites, and scientifically-validated compatibility testing. These features help overcome the past restrictions of online communication and relationship development. They simply make the process more fun and personal – it actually breathes life into the traditional personal ad. Lastly, one could argue there is a singles epidemic in society. Longer life spans, high divorce rate, and the fact that people are putting off marriage till later in life mean there are more singles in society than in decades past. These busy singles are short on time and opportunities, so they are looking for an efficient and cost effective way to look for and cull qualified prospects. Online dating, therefore, is actually a savvy approach to the problem.

Houran's sentiments are also consistent with research conducted by Brym and Lenton (2003), who examined the rise of online dating in Canada, and identified four main social forces that have driven the growth of online dating. These include:

- an increasing number of singles in the population (especially because people are leaving marriage until later in life);
- given that, career and time pressures are increasing, people are looking for more efficient ways of meeting others for intimate relationships;
- single people are more mobile due to demands of the job market, so it is more difficult for them to meet people for dating; and
- workplace romance is on the decline due to growing sensitivity about sexual harassment.

Clearly, there is definitely a demand for services like online dating sites. Another interesting point raised by Houran is that online dating is much more fun and lively than the standard personal ad. For example, online dating sites have developed playful tools to assist online daters to effectively cyber-flirt (e.g., sending virtual kisses or hearts through the sites to another individual, rather than some bland text indicating interest). This reflects the theory developed in this book that argues the case that cyberspace is potentially a playful space to initiate and develop relationships. Making these spaces more 'fun' may take away some of the hurt or upset that might accompany rejection. In saying that, as with any form of play, individuals need to learn the rules and play within these rules. Moreover, as with any game individuals compete to be the best players (as was evident in the interviews outlined in Chapter 7).

Interestingly, some online dating sites are trying to step up the anonymity again – they are doing this by providing a phone service where one can receive phone calls without having to disclose their 'real' phone numbers. Hence, if the dater sounds unsavoury they can simply delete that phone number and not be telephoned again by that particular individual. As noted in Chapter 7, many of the online daters were very keen to meet their dates within a week or so of identifying them on the online dating sites. This means that unlike other spaces online, people do not take advantage of remaining anonymous and gradually getting to know the other person online. In Chapter 7 we identified that one reason why participants were disinterested in spending a great deal of time in chat rooms and emails was because they were savvy shoppers who knew that online daters can be very strategic in regard to their online presentations. By introducing anonymous phone calls, online daters might again take advantage of being somewhat anonymous and might also feel more confident that they are getting to know a more 'real'/unfiltered self through the telephone lines. We are yet to establish the success of this new tool. However, given the background of literature on strategic presentation of self there seems to be both advantages and disadvantages that online daters might like to consider when it comes to utilising anonymous phone calls. First, it allows individuals, as just stated, to get to know more about the 'real' person; however, for themselves it does not allow them to be as strategic as they might like to be.

What is interesting about online dating is the way these sites are developing more effective ways to match individuals through these sites. Online dating sites typically have search tools, a little bit like google, where people put in categories of the person they are searching for and a programme has been written to match the most appropriate people. This is not solely based on characteristics as described in Chapter 7 (e.g., SES, number of children, attractiveness) but also on personality characteristics. These programmes have been written to assist the online dater in their quest to seek out the most appropriate partner. Therefore, online dating is not simply fun, but also becoming quite scientific. Various companies, such as eharmony.com, boast about having the best matching tools available on their site. This is not just a concern for the people running the companies but for academics who are also now starting to question the logistics of these compatibility services. Houran, Lange, Rentfrow, and Bruckner (2004), for example, critique some of these computer programmes and have suggested that matchmaking is not necessarily all about *similarity* and that (as demonstrated in previous studies) sometimes *complementarity* is also an important consideration. These theorists insist that such match-making systems should be properly evaluated. They have argued that:

> Indeed medical patients would not take a drug that has not been approved by the FDA (unless they are desperate) and likewise people looking for relationships should not so willingly trust online psychological tests and matching systems that have not been independently proven to meet professional testing standards. (pp. 15–16)

Does this all mean that online dating is here to stay? Personal ads never disappeared off the scene, so one can hazard a safe guess that online dating sites will remain for the immediate future. However, unlike personal ads they will no doubt improve to become a more successful tool at matchmaking.

Bluetoothing and blogging for love

There are other means of dating in cyberspace, and these are not restricted to just the internet. Bluetooth technology is taking off as a new tool to find a potential mate. For example, a company called *Proxidating* allows individuals to install software in their mobile phone where individuals can create a profile. With Bluetooth technology when a person comes within approximately 15 metres the phone alerts the single person that another single person is in the vicinity and they receive a text and image of the potential date. As they describe on their website: 'Imagine you are crossing the street when the girl/boy of your dreams passes before you, your phone buzzes and their face appears on your phone's screen' (Proxidating, 2005).

Imagine indeed! In this book it has been argued that cyberspace ought not to be treated as one generic space. Moreover, we need to consider where cyberspace and the offline world intersect. Bluetooth technology is a good exemplar of where the two worlds collide. When it comes to dating, using mobile phones gives one the advantage of checking out the chemistry of another person immediately; however, it takes away all of the strategic advantages online daters seem to enjoy. One could also imagine the scenario that on the day they are within 15 metres of their dream date is the day they have their bad – nah, worst hair day!

How might bloggers use their sites to attract a date? Weblogs, or what are also known as blogs, are essentially 'frequently modified web pages in which dated entries are listed in reverse chronological sequence' (Herring, Scheidt, Bonus, & Wright, 2004). Schmidt (2005) extends upon this definition stating that 'most weblogs allow comments on postings as well as advanced linking mechanisms (e.g., trackback), thus facilitating a network of "distributed conversations" (the Blogosphere)'. Schmidt points out that there are several types of blogs, including ones that are personal diaries, blogs that are used as a medium of expert communication, and blogs that are used as a channel of corporate communication (e.g., quasi-journalism). Bloggers are the individuals who create their sites and if their blogs include personal material they might find this a tricky thing to balance while still trying to find a partner. Unlike an online dating profile, which only provides a snap shot of an individual, blogs give a detailed summary of someone's life. In Chapter 7, social penetration theory was outlined, and it was pointed out that on internet dating sites individuals are exposed to more depth and breadth about an individual than they would ordinarily find out after a first date. This is even more likely if individuals date someone with an online diary – available for the world to see. Ben Kepple (2003), who is a blogger, talks about his dilemma of dating and still updating his blog. He imagines the following scenario taking place if after the second date he disclosed to his date that he would blog the event.

ME: You know, I really had a lot of fun tonight. Can I give you a call some-
　　time?
FOXY GIRL: Sure.
ME: Cool. Say, do you mind if I blog this?
FG: What!
ME: You know, blog our date. On my Web site!

FG: You never told me you had a Web site!

ME: Well, I was *meaning* to tell you, and ...

FG: I can't believe it! How could I have been so stupid as to think you were ACTUALLY NORMAL?!

ME: No, no, I'm not going to go into particulars, I just want to ...

FG: You make me want to throw up!

ME: Now look, it's really not what you're thinking. I can close out the comments section, and ...

FG: COMMENTS SECTION? Oh, great, so now you're going to have a committee judge our date?

ME: It's not a committee!

FG: I think I'm going to faint.

ME: What! Well, here, let ...

FG: Why, you! ...

SMACK!

ME: OUCH! Look! I don't have to do this, I just wanted your permission first, that's all!

FG: I'll bet you've already posted about the first date we went on! I can't believe I agreed to go out on a second with ... you.

ME: Well, no one's perfect, are they? (wince)

SMACK!

Like kids in a lolly shop

We have continually emphasised in this book that how we play in cyberspace and the rules of the games we play online are very different depending on which space we are considering. As demonstrated in this chapter, finding a partner via an online dating site, a blog, or via Bluetooth technology can all be very different experiences. Opportunities for how one can present themselves in these spaces vary, and so to do the processes in getting to know one another. Of course, we cannot forget the 'old-fashioned ways' of meeting people in MUDs and MOOs, newsgroups, chat rooms, bulletin boards, and so forth – all of which are again slightly different in the way they are set up to meet and communicate with others. While it is too early to say, one might predict that rather than one of these means of meeting others becoming more popular than others – what is more likely to happen is that different methods will suit different people, and this might vary by age, gender, and personality.

Writing as therapy

James Pennebaker (1997) has emphatically argued that self-disclosure is not only good for one's emotional health, but in turn, boosts individuals' physical health. In particular, Pennebaker (1997) stresses the importance of *writing* about one's emotional experiences. Freud is well-known for his 'talking cure' – where the patient transfers his/her earlier psychosexual conflicts (those conflicts that led to his/her symptoms) onto the relationship between the analyst and the patient. Pennebaker, however, argues that it is not necessary to tell someone else the problem, but rather believes that writing down the problem is just as helpful as telling someone else. In his research, he found empirical support for the notion that writing about one's deepest thoughts and feelings about traumatic events results in improved moods, a more positive outlook, and greater physical health.

Pennebaker has not limited his work to writing offline. In 1997, after the death of Princess Diana, he and his colleague observed an AOL chat room for over 28 days (see Stone & Pennebaker, 2002). They found that writing about Princess Diana's death within the first week was very high, but this dropped dramatically a week later. They also found that during the first week there were fewer positive emotion words, but with time positive emotion words increased. These theorists believed that what they found supports a model of collective coping, which starts with an emergency phase, where everyone constantly discusses the problem, and then moves to an inhibition phase, where the topic is still thought about but discussion is discouraged. Stone and Pennebaker (2002) argued that chat rooms can provide a 24-hour world where individuals can discuss their problems. They suggest that people can benefit from being anonymous and can move to more than one chat room to find release.

Weblogs were not as popular when Stone and Pennebaker (2002) published their paper; however, they are also worthwhile considering as a confessional, therapeutic tool. Those who use weblogs as a diary have the opportunity to express their emotions daily in writing. Perhaps this is cathartic for some and a motivation for keeping an online diary. Hiler (2002), for example, states: 'I blog because I have always enjoyed writing. It's very cathartic.' Interestingly, Mobile phone giant Nokia is soon to release 'Lifeblog' (see www.nokia.com/lifeblog), which is an inexpensive software program (release price of 30 euros) for Nokia phones that allows the user to create a multimedia diary that can later be transferred to a computer, retaining the chronological order in which entries were created, as well as allowing the user to create an online blog. Lifeblog is mostly intended to be a personal multimedia diary that is shared amongst friends and family and moves away from the original 'media' commentary-related aspect of blogging.

Although blogs might have some potential therapeutic benefit one needs to be mindful of the optimal writing conditions that Pennebaker (1997) has identified. Pennebaker stresses the importance that one benefits from being anonymous and not writing for others. He argues that if one writes with an audience in mind (e.g., one's spouse) then this can affect the way an individual construes an event and how they express their emotions. Therefore, blogs, while on the surface might appear to be a therapeutic tool, are perhaps less helpful when compared to chat rooms, where one is more likely to be anonymous.

Online psychotherapy

We have discussed throughout this book the therapeutic value of cyberspace. Therefore, it should come as no surprise that individuals have been finding ways to conduct therapy within this space. In the future, we might find better ways to use this space to conduct psychotherapy; however, in doing so one needs to recognise both the advantages and the limitations of online psychotherapy. We might also question whether the relationships with one's therapist or with one's online client is similar or different to the therapist/client relationship offline.

In the 1960s, Weisenbaum developed an interactive program that became known as ELIZA. It is a program where someone can write normal sentences to interact with the computer without having to know any computer language. Weizenbaum named it ELIZA after the character of Eliza Doolittle in the play *Pygmalion* and in the musical *My Fair Lady*. The program was designed to appear as if a proper conversation was taking place, although, in reality, it did not. Certain words and phrases were programmed to trigger seemingly appropriate responses. The programme appeared very human like – with a semblance of 'Rogerian' psychoanalysis, where the therapist asks questions based purely on what the patient says. There are now various versions of ELIZA, some more sophisticated than others.

John Suler (1999b) reports in his online book how he has asked his students to interact with ELIZA. He requested that his students use the programme in two ways: first, to treat it as a serious way to acquire help by honestly discussing a problem with it, and second, to play with the program in an attempt to trick it, in order to better understand how the programme works. Most students reported that the programme did not help them with their problem. However, interestingly, many did report that they learned something about their personal views and feelings about psychotherapy. Hence, rather than expecting ELIZA to act as a real counsellor, John Suler argues that ELIZA's gross limitations as a psychotherapist is a useful tool to teach students to appreciate what is expected of a good psychotherapist.

While ELIZA has many serious flaws, it has not stopped individuals finding ways to use cyberspace to conduct psychotherapy. Suler (2004b) provides a thorough list of advantages and disadvantages of online and computer-mediated psychotherapy. He also, importantly, points out that this can be carried out in different spaces online and in different ways (for a summary of some of the pros and cons, in these different spaces, see Suler, 2004b).

Overall, the work carried out by Suler suggests that cyberspace provides in some way an attractive space to conduct therapy. This is perhaps no surprise when you consider that when Freud conducted his psychotherapy he typically required his clients lie on a couch and avoided eye contact with them. Not seeing the therapist allowed the analysand to drift off into a space that they felt comfortable and safe in. Such an arrangement also supposedly prevented the analysand from being distracted or inhibited by any facial reaction of the therapist. Cyberspace, arguably, creates an even safer space for the analysand but of course, in agreement with Suler, we acknowledge the limitations as well as the ethical problems associated with using this space for therapy. John Suler (2002) has also discussed his view on the future of psychotherapy in cyberspace. He contends that he expects that people will 'specialise' in different forms of online clinical work. One of these types of therapy is 'avatar therapy'.

Avatar therapy

Kate Anthony is another counsellor who believes that as technology
develops it is likely that this will become a popular space for both clients
and therapists. Anthony and Lawson (2002) argue that 'clients find the
idea of anonymous, safe, comfortable and readily available service provi-
sion empowering and preferable to traditional (usually face-to-face)
therapy'. Anthony is a strong supporter of the development of avatar
therapy. An avatar is the 'visible representation of a human appearing in a
computer generated world' (Anthony & Lawson, 2002). Gross and
Anthony (2002) argue that there are two possible uses for avatar therapy,
these are:

> One is its possible use in conjunction with the current attempts to provide CBT
> by a computer without the aid of a therapist. . . . The second possibility, which is
> perhaps less dependent on creating avatars that are quite so naturally looking,
> might be for group therapy. (p. 14)

While we too acknowledge these strengths of avatar therapy, the draw-
backs also need to be considered in the development of this form of
therapy. For example, as mentioned above, the ethics of conducting this
form of therapy are questionable. Moreover, there are the problems associated with 'acting out' with characters to such an extreme online that the
benefits might not be transferred offline.

The future of sex in cyberspace

> ICTs and the home personal computer (PC) in particular are becoming sexual
> objects of desire for some, enabling the consumer to be the "computer fetishist",
> the producer of and having access to, his/her own sexual predilections, fantasies
> and immersive interactions. (Barber, 2004, p. 142)

In this book, we have not considered in as much detail, as we might,
about how individuals can play and be creative sexually online. Given that
we believe that cyberspace is a place that offers opportunities for people to
be creative and freer than they might be offline, this is certainly worth some

further thought. Cybersex, hotchatting, and cyber-flirting are really just the tip of the iceberg when it comes to sexual activities in cyberspace. Futurists have considered many more ways individuals might utilise cyberspace for sexual pleasure. For example, while teledildonics is currently in its infancy, this form of cybersex will probably become more popular as the technology improves. Teledildonics is essentially a VR application that allows individuals to interactively have sex with people miles away – it will do so by placing individuals in full-body suits which will stimulate all five senses.

Trudy Barber, who is an artist and a sociologist, has put forward some suggestions for how, in the future, cyberspace might be used in sexual gratification. In her PhD she examined Master R's work – who is a homosexual sadomasochist and media IT specialist. He combines the mobile phone, the PC, and internet technology with internally worn vibrators together with other forms of electrical stimulation (e.g., electrically stimulating the nipples and other erogenous zones). Barber (2004) describes Master R's work as 'transitional fetishism in that he is combining and converging both immersive and physically invasive technologies'. She has written that his 'sexuality is the reciprocal transition between experiencing the human and experiencing the machine' (p. 147). Applying Winnicott's object-relations theory again, like the blanket or the teddy bear, vibrators and other such devices might be considered as transitional objects. Linking these objects to cyberspace – a space between reality and fantasy can make sexuality more playful and hence potentially transformative. Activities that individuals might feel forbidden or embarrassing offline might be seen as more acceptable within cyberspace. In reflecting on Master R's work Barber (2004) has argued that:

> It will be important to consider that as communication and computer technologies converge they come together to create new objects and subjects of desire where the consumer also becomes the creator, boundaries between 'reality' and the 'virtual' become blurred, and the audience and the participant become one and the same. (p. 148)

Barber (2004) has also imaginatively suggested future possibilities for combining technology and cyberspace for sexual pleasure. She believes that, not only will the entire body be immersed in VRs, but other senses will also be manipulated, including smell. She imagines, for example, a world with artificial prostitutes – fully interactive life sized, warm sex dolls, personalised 'bolted-on' gadgetry for longer distance communication, vibrators with artificial personalities, glasses connected to software which will enable the individual to be aroused by everything they see, and autoerotic music. While the possibilities that Barber has raised have yet to materialise, even as this book is being written there are some designers working on some of these ideas.

Barak and Fisher (2002) in discussing their vision of the future and technology contend that 'For better and for worse, the future development of Internet sexuality will have individual, relationship, and societal impacts that clinicians must anticipate and acquire the insight and skill to manage' (p. 268). Hence, it might even be the case that sex therapists can utilise cyberspace to assist individuals with sexual problems.

Ethical considerations for future online research

Of course, in addition to considerations of how individuals might conduct their relationships online and explore sexuality in cyberspace in the future, as researchers we should also be interested in how we can best utilise the technology to study online relationships and sexuality. As this book demonstrates, the amount of research into online relationships and sexuality are on the increase. In spite of this, there is little academic literature available on how researchers might best examine this topic area in an ethical manner. Given that the development and maintenance of online relationships, and the engaging in online sexual activities can be perceived as private and very personal, there are potentially ethical concerns that are unique to the study of such a topic area (Whitty, 2004c).

A common form of using the internet for researching online relationships and sexuality is to analyse the text produced by people online. The text can be produced in a number of different forums, including emails, IM, chat rooms, MUDs, and newsgroups. One way researchers collect data is by '*lurking*' in these different spaces in cyberspace.

Lurking

A lurker is a participant in a chat room or a subscriber to a discussion group, listserv, or mailing list who passively observers. These individuals typically do not actively partake in the discussions that befall in these forums. For the purposes of collecting data some social scientists have opted to play the role of lurker. The development of online relationships (both friendships and romantic) and engaging in online sexual activities, such as cybersex, could easily be perceived by those engaging in such activities as a private discourse. Given the nature of these interactions, social researchers need to seriously consider if they have the right to lurk in online settings in order to learn more about these activities – despite the benefits of obtaining this knowledge.

Mehta and Plaza (1997) examined pornography in public newsgroups. They predicted that anonymous, non-commercial users would be more likely to post explicit material compared to commercial distributors (who have a greater awareness of the legal ramifications of posting such material and are more easily traceable). A content analysis was performed on 150 randomly selected pornographic images from 17 alternative newsgroups, which they named. They found that their hypothesis was not supported, and that instead commercial users were more likely to post explicit pornography in public access newsgroups. They suggested that commercial users are perhaps motivated to take risks, such as publishing highly erotic material and sometimes illegal material (such as posting naked pictures of children), because this is a means of attracting new customers to their private pay-per-use bulletin board services.

In a follow-up study, Mehta (2001) visited 32 Usenet newsgroups and randomly selected 9800 pornographic images. These pictures were posted by commercial, anonymous, and non-anonymous individuals and were images of the individuals themselves, their sexual partners, and others. They rated the images according to whether they were: commercial or non-commercial; rarity of a particular pornographic image; number of participants interacting sexually in an image; type of penetration; oral sex; masturbation; ejaculation; homosexual sex; bondage and discipline; and/or whether they involved the use of children and adolescents. Mehta (2001) found some significant changes in the type of material being posted on these newsgroups since his previous study, including a greater proportion of images of children and adolescents.

While both these studies provide important information for psychologists, social scientists, and criminologists, they also raise some important ethical and legal questions in respect to how we conduct our research online. Although it was not discussed, one might wonder if these researchers sought permission to use their institutions' servers to peruse internet sites containing illegal material, and what the legal ramifications are if they did not. Another less obvious question, as social researchers we need to start asking is: Are these public Usenet newsgroups the same type of media as commercially sold erotic videos, pornographic magazines, and comics (as these researchers allude to)? If not, then can we apply the same ethical standards to this media as we would to offline content? Ferri (1999, cited in Mann & Stewart, 2000) has asserted that 'private interactions *do* take place in public places' (p. 46). Sharf (1999) supports this view, stating that 'despite widely announced admonitions concerning the potential for public exposure, there exists the paradox that writing to others via e-mail often feels like a private or, in the case of an on-line group, quasi-private act' (p. 246). Mann and Stewart (2000) make the point that men having sex in beats (public spaces where men have sex with men) are quite private acts occurring within public spaces. Indeed, it would be ethically challenging to justify observing such beats for the sake of our research. As we have argued elsewhere in this book, there are fuzzy boundaries between what constitutes public and private spaces online. This is not a clear-cut issue, and in addressing the issue it would also be counter-productive for social scientists to provide an answer that applies to the entire internet. Instead, we need to acknowledge that there are different places online. For example, a chat room might be deemed a more public space than email. To this end, it is contended here that lurking in public newsgroups might be ethically questionable. We must, as researchers, debate how intrusive a method lurking potentially is. As Ferri (1999, cited in Mann & Stewart, 2000) contends 'who is the intended audience of an electronic communication – and does it include you as a researcher?' (p. 46).

If we are to make divisions between private and public spaces online, the demarcations are possibly not so obvious. As previously raised by Ferri, private interactions can and do indeed occur in public places. As we have argued elsewhere in this book, we believe that cyberspace can be perceived by individuals to be a private space – this has some influence in the way they communicate. For instance, we know that people are more likely to self-disclose in some places online compared to face-to-face. Therefore, even if we conclude that some spaces online are public spaces, the anonymity they afford can give the illusion that these are private spaces. Can we as researchers ethically take advantage of these people's false sense of privacy and security? Is it ethically justifiable to lurk in these sites and download material without the knowledge or consent of the individuals involved? This is especially relevant to questions of relationship development and sexuality, which are generally understood to be private matters. It is suggested here that good ethical practice needs to consider the psychology of cyberspace and the false sense of security the internet affords. It is quite naïve of researchers to simply equate online medium with what, at first thought, might appear to be offline equivalents (such as magazines and videos). In the cases presented above, it is perhaps the commercial material that is more akin to the offline equivalents such as commercially available pornographic magazines and videos.

Deception

At a recent conference, a postgraduate student presented a piece of work that examined online dating relationships. For the sake of her research, she put up profiles of herself on an online dating site – sometimes with photos, sometimes not, giving herself very different characteristics and personalities across the profiles. She was interested in finding which profiles would evoke the most interest. She corresponded via email with some of the men who contacted her; however, she did not tell any of the participants that she was doing this for her research and that she was not in any way interested in finding a date. Listening to her conference presentation the majority of the audience were appalled and sufficiently so to state very clearly that research of this kind should never be undertaken.

One of the interviewees in Whitty's online dating study claimed to be a journalist and that he was married but using the online date site to gather material for an article he was working on. He lied on the site, claiming to be single. Moreover, for some reason, unlike the example above, he also felt the need to meet up with the people he met online and even went as far as sleeping with his dates. While it is unclear as to whether this would have helped him write a 'good' story, it is obvious that this is a very deceptive and firmly, in our view, an unethical way to research a story.

While it might be unclear as to how ethical it is for lurkers to collect data on the internet, there is less doubt as to whether it is acceptable to deceive others online in order to conduct social research, especially with respect to online relationships and sexuality. According to the Australian National Health and Medical Research Council (NHMRC, 1999), which set the ethical guidelines for Australian research:

as a general principle, deception of, concealment of the purposes of a study from, or covert observation of, identifiable participants are not considered ethical because they are contrary to the principle of respect for persons in that free and fully informed consent cannot be given.

They do, however, state that under certain unusual circumstances deception is unavoidable when there is no alternative method to conduct one's research. However, in these circumstances individuals must be given the opportunity to withdraw data obtained from them during the research that they did not originally give consent to. Moreover, the council stipulates that 'such activities will not corrupt the relationship between researchers and research in general with the community at large' (NHMRC, 1999).

Practical considerations

In this next section suggestions are provided for best practice in respect to studying internet relationships and sexuality and can, in many ways, be generalised to other forms of online research. It examines informed consent, withdrawal of consent, confidentiality, and psychological safeguards.

Informed consent

Given the ethical dilemmas researchers are faced with conducting research online, in many cases the better alternative is to set up a reasonable system in place for participants to give informed consent. Informed consent requires researchers to be up front, from the beginning, about the aims of their research and how they are going to utilise the data. In offline research individuals often sign a form to give their consent; however, this is not always achievable online. One way around this is demonstrated in Gaunt's (2002) study. Gaunt was interested in the types of friendships established in online chat rooms. He recruited participants by entering into these rooms and asking whether individuals would be interested in conducting an online interview about their online friendships. If participants were interested in being interviewed and if they were over the age of 16 years, Gaunt directed the participant to a website, which contained information about his project. This website informed the participants about the purpose of the study, the procedure that would be employed and the ethics involved, as well as contact details of the researcher, his supervisor, and the university Human Ethics Committee.

> Participants were informed that if they continued by returning to the private chat room where the researcher was waiting, that this would be taken as being indicative of their informed consent to participate in the research. All this having taken place, the interview would commence. (Gaunt, 2002)

In some cases, spaces on the web are moderated. In these instances, it is probably also appropriate to contact the moderators of the site prior to contacting the participants. This is analogous to contacting an organisation prior to targeting individuals within that organisation. Wysocki (1998) was interested in examining 'how and why individuals participate in sexually explicit computer bulletin boards; and to see if sex on-line is a way of *replacing* face-to-face relationships or a way of *enhancing* them' (p. 426). She researched this by considering the social construction of love and sexuality as constructed by users of a bulletin board service called the '*Pleasure Pit*'. Rather than employ covert methods, Wysocki was up front with her identity as a researcher. She originally approached the systems operators and told them that she was a sociologist who was interested in using *Pleasure Pit* to collect data. The operators were enthusiastic about her research and she was invited to meet them and learn how the bulletin board service operated. She found that the service had a system in place to ensure that no participants were minors. To recruit participants, a sign went up on the bulletin board stating:

> There will be a female here at the Pleasure Pit office to do interviews with anybody who happens to be on-line ... she is doing research on BBS relationships and is interested in what happens to your inhibitions when your [sic] on the key board (we know what happens to them). Watch for more info on her activities. I may call you to set up a voice interview with her. If you volunteer you will be first called and you husband types (with spouses not into this) be sure to let me know that you do or don't want a call. (Wysocki, 1998, p. 430)

Following this announcement she placed her questionnaire, which contained forced choice and open-ended questions, in the *Pleasure Pit*. To ensure confidentiality, when Wysocki collected the respondents' answers she separated the participant's name from the survey and assigned a number to each questionnaire. In addition, Wysocki interviewed some participants online. Participants that read her notices contacted her and she interviewed them in real time in chat mode.

While there are improvements that could have been made to Wysocki's procedure, it does provide a better alternative to downloading text without the participants' consent. The steps that Wysocki carried out could, however, have been ameliorated. In her first notice, participants should have been given more details about the project so that they could make informed consent. The aims of the project and how the data were to be utilised needed to be included. Whether participants' responses were confidential or not should have been made clear in the initial notice. Moreover, Wysocki's contact details and the institution at which she was conducting the research should have been provided from the very beginning of the project so that people could contact her about any questions they had about the project. The respondents should have been informed from the outset that their responses would remain anonymous and that their identities would not be revealed in any publication of the results. A project of this sort, as with many projects on sexuality and relationships, has the potential to cause distress for a participant – even when there is no malice intended from the researcher. Safeguards need to be put into place to ensure the participant has a professional to turn to if for some reason the interview or questionnaire causes some psychological distress. One further question raised by this research is: Should researchers expose the names of the chat rooms, bulletin boards, and newsgroups from which they recruit their participants from?

While the above studies and suggestions potentially deal with consent in a fairly reasonable manner, we should also be aware that some European countries require written consent (Mann & Stewart, 2000). Mann and Stewart suggest that if written consent is required then the participant could download a form and sign it offline and then return it by fax or postal mail. Another alternative is re-considering whether written consent is necessary or whether one can deal with consent electronically.

Withdrawal of consent

We need to also consider the withdrawal of consent. In research about relationships and sexuality, in particular, there is the risk that the internet interview or survey has created too much stress for the participant to continue. As with offline research, we need to consider up until what point a participant can withdraw consent. For example, it is obviously too late to withdraw consent once the results have been published; hence, it is a little naïve to state the participants can withdraw consent at anytime. The end point of withdrawal of consent might be, for instance, after the submitting of the survey, or at the conclusion of the interview the interviewer might find confirmation that the participant is happy to allow the researcher to include the transcript in the study. As social scientists, we should also be aware that the lack of social cues available online makes it more difficult for us to ascertain if the participant is uncomfortable. Thus, we should tread carefully and possibly make an effort to check at different points in an interview if the individual is still comfortable with proceeding.

There are other issues unique to internet research in respect to withdrawal of consent. For example, the computer could crash mid-way through an interview or survey. Mechanisms need to be put into place to allow that participant to re-join the research if desired, and consent should not be assumed if it is not certain why the interview ceased. In addition, in circumstances such as the computer or server crashing, we might need to have a system to enable debriefing, especially if the research is asking questions of a personal nature. A recent work by Nosek, Banaji, and Greenwald (2002) suggests that debriefing can be made available by providing a contact email address at the beginning of the study. They also suggest providing 'a "leave the study" button, made available on every study page, [which] would allow participants to leave the study early and still direct them to a debriefing page' (p. 163). In addition, they state that participants be given a list of FAQs, since they argue that there is less opportunity to ask the sorts of questions participants typically ask in face-to-face interviews.

Confidentiality

There are various ways we might deal with the issue of confidentiality. As with offline research we could elect to use pseudonyms to represent our participants, or alternatively request preferred pseudonyms from them. However, a unique aspect of the internet is that people typically inhabit the web using a screen name, rather than a real name. Can we use a screen name given that these are not real names? While they may not be people's offline identities, individuals could still be identified by their screen names if we publish them – even if it is only recognition by other online inhabitants.

Psychological safeguards

As mentioned earlier in this chapter, research into the areas of relation-ships and sexuality is likely to cause psychological distress for some. It is perhaps much more difficult to deal with psychological distress online and with individuals in other countries. It is difficult to provide names of psychologists in other countries available to counsel the participants. Nevertheless, it is imperative that we ensure that the participant does have counselling available to them if the research has caused them distress – which sometimes might be delayed distress. This could mean that there are limits to the kinds of topics about which we interview participants online or that we restrict our sample to a particular country or region where we know of psychological services that can be available to our participants if required.

On a 'concluding note'

Cyber-relationships and cybersex (of some kind) are here to stay. How we develop online relationships and engage in cyberspace will modify as tech-nology is developed and as people discover new ways to utilise this space. Psychologists and social scientists ought to be interested in how individ-uals relate online, how these relationships might be improved, and how they might impact on our offline relationships. Of course, as illustrated in this book, our online and offline activities are not completely separate, nor are individuals' online and offline relationships. Nonetheless, the theory offered in this book purports that cyberspace is a unique space for playing at love and sexuality. As also highlighted in this book, the way we play at love and sexuality varies depending on which space we are playing in. For instance, if people meet in an online dating site they have different expec-tations about how the relationship will develop when compared to meeting in a newsgroup. As researchers, we need to be mindful of this and not attempt to develop one 'grand' theory to explain all cyber-relationships. Rather than concluding the discussion here, we hope that what we have written in this tome will serve to foster ongoing dialogue within the field that seeks to understand the confluence of cyberspace and human relation-ships.

Notes

3 Playing at Love: Winnicott and Potential Space

1. In this book we prefer to use the term 'psychodynamics' to that of psychoanalysis, as a less 'treatment' oriented synonym that implies the normality and dynamic nature of psychological processes.
2. This is a very significant issue, for much of the psychoanalytic community hold the view that 'even the psychoanalysis of adults has resemblances to play in as much as the clinical situation is set apart from the rest of life, the patient's utterances are not acted upon by the analyst, and free association allows free play for the imagination' (Rycroft, 1995, p. 134; see also Modell, 1996, p. 27, Winnicott, 1971d, p. 38). Further, in the case of play therapy the equivalent of free association is encouraged by allowing the child to design games with toys and in so doing the child might re-enact aspects of disturbed behaviour and give clues to the unconscious. Feelings in this play therapy setting may be revealed which in the real situation are inhibited for example, the child might swear at the rag doll, but not at dad who the doll may represent.
3. It is worthy of note that sometimes you only become aware of the nature of the rules when they are transgressed which is the case in offline play. This said, there are some publications that are emerging that seek to articulate some of the rules of play (e.g., see Fein & Schneider, 1995, 1997, 2002).
4. The actual *how* and *why* identification occurs is an extremely important issue if we are to understand the aberrant behaviour and psychopathologies that can arise from playing in cyberspace. Interestingly, Mason and Carr (2000) have argued that, in contrast to cognitive (and behaviourist) approaches, psychodynamic explanations offer an explanation of both how and why identification occurs. These authors note that a premise that is given by cognitive approaches is that 'identification is caused by self-categorization' (Dutton, Dukerich, & Harquail, 1994, p. 234). This reasoning seems tautological or the nature of the causality is obscure. Thus, while cognitive approaches generally suggest that self-esteem or self-knowledge may be the reasons for identification, there is little in the way of explaining how this occurs.

4 Object Engagement and Dysfunctional Aspects of Relating Online

1. In a very similar process, *play therapy* produces the equivalent of free association in allowing the child to design games with toys and in so doing the child may re-enact aspects of disturbed behaviour and give clues to the unconscious. Feelings in this play therapy setting may be revealed which in the real situation are inhibited for example, the child might swear at the rag doll, but not at dad who the doll may represent. The objects serve as psychic keys to memories and feelings that may not otherwise be so easily released.

References

Abramis, D. (1990). Play in work. *American Behavioral Scientist, 33*, 353–373.

Adams, M. V. (1997). The archetypal school. In P. Young-Eisendrath & T. Dawson (Eds.), *The Cambridge Companion to Jung* (pp. 101–118). Cambridge: Cambridge University.

Aitken, S. C., & Herman, T. (1997). Gender, power and crib geography: Transitional spaces and potential places. *Gender, Place and Culture, 4*, 63–88.

Altman, I., & Taylor, D. A. (1973). *Social penetration: The development of interpersonal relationships*. New York: Holt, Rinehart and Winston.

Andrejevic, M. (2000, June). *Digital aesthetics in the era of cyber-capitalism*. Paper presented at the International Communication Association annual convention, Acapulco.

Anolli, L., & Ciceri, R. (2002). Analysis of the vocal profiles of male seduction: From exhibition to self-disclosure. *Journal of General Psychology, 129*, 149–169.

Anthony, K., & Lawson, M. (2002). The use of innovative avatar and virtual environment technology for counselling and psychotherapy. Retrieved March 5, 2005, from http://www.kateanthony.co.uk/InnovativeAvatar.pdf.

Argyle, K., & Shields, R. (1996). Is there a body in the net? In R. Shields (Ed.), *Cultures of internet: Virtual spaces, real histories, living bodies* (pp. 58–69). London: Sage.

Asch, S. E. (1946). Forming impressions of personality. *Journal of Abnormal and Social Psychology, 41*, 258–290.

Askew, M. W. (1965). Courtly love: Neurosis as institution. *The Psychoanalytic Review, 52*, 19–29.

Baker, A. J. (2000). Two by two in cyberspace: Meeting and connecting online. *CyberPsychology & Behavior, 3*, 237–242.

Baker, A. J. (2002). What makes an online relationship successful? Clues from couples who met in cyberspace. *CyberPsychology & Behavior, 5*, 363–375.

Balint, M. (1968). *The basic fault*. London: Tavistock.

Barak, A. (2005). Sexual harassment on the Internet. *Social Science Computer Review, 23* (1), 77–92.

Barak, A., & Fisher, W. A. (2002). The future of Internet sexuality. In A. Cooper (Ed.), *Sex & the internet: A guidebook for clinicians* (pp. 263–280). New York: Brunner-Routledge.

193

Barber, T. (2004). Deviation as key to innovation: Understanding a culture of the future. *Foresight – The journal of future studies, strategic thinking and policy,* 6 (3), 141–152.

Bargh, J. A., McKenna, K. Y. A., & Fitzsimons, G. M. (2002). Can you see the real me? Activation and expression of the 'true self' on the Internet. *Journal of Social Issues, 58,* 33–48.

Baruch, E. (1991). *Women, love, and power: Literary and psychoanalytic perspectives.* New York: New York University.

Bassols, R., Bea, J., & Coderch, J. (1985). La identitat i els seus limits [Identity and its limits]. *Revista Catalana de Psicoanalisi, 2,* 173–188.

Becker, D., Sagarin, B., Guadagno, R., Millevoi, A., & Nicastle, L. (2004). *Personal Relationships, 11,* 529–538.

Ben-Ze'ev, A. (2004). *Love online: Emotions and the internet.* Cambridge, UK: Cambridge University.

Birnie, S. A., & Horvath, P. (2002). Psychological predictors of Internet social communication. *Journal of Computer Mediated Communication, 7* (4), Retrieved March 25, 2005, from http://jcmc.indiana.edu/vol7/issue4/horvath.html.

Bocij, P. (2004). *Cyberstalking: Harassment in the internet age and how to protect your family.* Westport, Connecticut: Praeger.

Bollas, C. (1978). The transformational object. *International Journal of Psycho-Analysis, 60,* 97–107.

Bollas, C. (1987). *The shadow of the object: Psychoanalysis of the unthought known.* London: Free Association Books.

Bollas, C. (1992). *Being a character: Psychoanalysis and self-experience.* New York: Hill & Wang.

Brabant, E., Falzeder, E., & Giampieri-Deutsch, P. (Eds.). (1993). *The Correspondence of Sigmund Freud and Sándor Ferenczi: Volume 1, 1908–1914.* Cambridge, Massachusetts: Belknap.

Brym, R. J., & Lenton, R. L. (2003). *Love at first byte: Internet dating in Canada.* Retrieved March 25, 2005, from http://www.societyinquestion4e.nelson.com/Chapter33Online.pdf.

Buss, D. M., & Barnes, M. (1986). Preferences in human mate selection. *Journal of Personality and Social Psychology, 50,* 559–570.

Buss, D. M., & Shackelford, T. K. (1997). Susceptibility to infidelity in the first year of marriage. *Journal of Research in Personality, 31,* 193–221.

Buss, D. M., Larsen, R., Westen, D., & Semmelroth, J. (1992). Sex differences in jealousy: Evolution, physiology, and psychology. *Psychological Science, 3,* 251–255.

Byrne, R., & Findlay, B. (2004). Preference for SMS versus telephone calls in initiating romantic relationships. *Australian Journal of Emerging Technologies and Society, 2* (1), Retrieved April 15, 2005, from http://www.swin.edu.au/ajets.

Capellanus, A. (1969). *The art of courtly love* (J. Parry, Trans.). New York: Norton. (Original work published around 1174)

Carducci, B. J., & Klaphaak, K. W. (1999, August). *Shyness, internet usage and electronic extraversion: Patterns and consequences.* Poster session presented at the annual meeting of the American Psychological Association, Boston MA.

Carr, A. N. (1993). The psychostructure of work: 'Bend me, shape me, anyway you want me, as long as you love me it's alright'. *Journal of Managerial Psychology, 8* (6), 3–6.

Carr, A. N. (1994a). For self or others? The quest for narcissism and the ego-ideal in work organisations. *Administrative Theory & Praxis, 16,* 208–222.

Carr, A. N. (1994b). Anxiety and depression among school principals: Warning, principalship can be hazardous to your health. *Journal of Educational Administration, 32* (3), 18–34.

Carr, A. N. (2001). Organisational and administrative play: The potential of magic realism, surrealism and postmodernist forms of play. In J. Biberman & A. Alkhafaji (Eds.), *Business research yearbook: Global business perspectives* (Vol. 8, pp. 543–547). Michigan: McNaughton & Gunn.

Carr, A. N. (2002). Managing in a psychoanalytically informed manner: On overview. *Journal of Managerial Psychology, 17,* 343–347.

Carr, A. N. (2003a). Thanatos: The psychodynamic conception of the 'death instinct' and its relevance to organizations. In J. Biberman & A. Alkhafaji (Eds.), *Business research yearbook: Global business perspectives* (Vol. 10, pp. 803–807). Michigan: McNaughton & Gunn.

Carr, A. N. (2003b). The psychodynamic conception of the 'death instinct' and its relevance to organisations. *Journal of Psycho-Social Studies, 2* (1), 1–15.

Carr, A. N., & Downs, A. (2004a). Transitional and quasi-objects in organization studies: Viewing Enron from the object-relations world of Winnicott and Serres. *Journal of Organizational Change Management, 17,* 352–364.

Carr, A. N., & Downs, A. (2004b). Enron: Taking our cue from the world of object relations. *Journal of Critical Postmodern Organization Science, 3* (2), 1–15.

Carr, A. N., & Gabriel, Y. (2001). The psychodynamics of organizational change management. *Journal of Organizational Change Management, 14,* 415–420.

Cate, R., & Lloyd, S. (1992). *Courtship.* Newbury Park, CA: Sage.

Chak, K., & Leung, L. (2004). Shyness and locus of control as predictors of Internet addiction and Internet use. *CyberPsychology & Behavior, 7,* 559–570.

Cheating wife stories – cheating husband stories. Retrieved August 2, 2005, from http://www.chatcheaters.com/cheating-stories/cheating-stories.html.

Childress, C. A. (1999). Archetypal conceptualisation of cyberspace as the Celtic otherworld. *CyberPsychology & Behavior, 2,* 261–265.

Civin, M. A. (2000). *Male, female, email: The struggle for relatedness in a paranoid society.* New York: Other Press.

Clark, J. M. (1997). A cybernautical perspective on impulsivity and addiction. In C. Webster & M. Jackson (Eds.), *Impulsivity: Theory assessment and treatment* (pp. 82–91). New York: Guilford.

Cloyd, J. (1976). The marketplace bar: The interrelation between sex, situations, and strategies in the pairing ritual of homo ludens. *Urban Life, 5,* 293–312.

Coleman, L. H., Paternite, C. E., & Sherman, R. C. (1999). A re-examination of deindividuation in synchronous computer-mediated communication. *Computers in Human Behavior, 15,* 51–65.

Collins, S., & Missing, C. (2003). Vocal and visual attractiveness are related in women. *Animal Behaviour, 65,* 997–1004.

Constant, D., Sproull, L., & Kiesler, S. (1997). The kindness of strangers: On the usefulness of electronic weak ties for technical advice. In S. Kiesler (Ed.), *Culture of the internet* (pp. 303–322). Mahwah, NJ: Lawrence Erlbaum Associates.

Coontz, S. (1988). *The social origins of private life: A history of American families 1600–1900.* New York: Verso.

Cooper, A. (1998). Sexuality and the Internet: Surfing into the new millennium. *CyberPsychology & Behavior, 1,* 181–187.

Cooper, A. (2002). *Sex & the internet: A guidebook for clinicians.* New York: Brunner-Routledge.

Cooper, A., & Sportolari, L. (1997). Romance in cyberspace: Understanding online attraction, *Journal of Sex Education and Therapy, 22* (1), 7–14.

Cooper, A., Delmonico, D. L., & Burg, R. (2000). Cybersex users, abusers, and compulsives: New findings and implications. *Sexual Addiction & Compulsivity, 7,* 5–29.

Cooper, A., Scherer, C., & Marcus, I. D. (2002). Harnessing the power of the Internet to improve sexual relationships. In A. Cooper (Ed.), *Sex & the internet: A guidebook for clinicians* (pp. 209–230). New York: Brunner-Routledge.

Cooper, A., Putnam, D. E., Planchon, L. A., & Boies, S. C. (1999). Online sexual compulsivity: Getting tangled in the net. *Sexual Addiction & Compulsivity, 6,* 79–104.

Cramer, R., Manning-Ryan, B., Johnson, L., & Barbo, E. (2000). Sex differences in subjective distress to violations of trust: Extending an evolutionary perspective. *Basic & Applied Social Psychology, 22* (2), 101–109.

Crook, J. H. (1972). Sexual selection, dimorphism, and social organization in the primates. In B. Campbell (Ed.), *Sexual selection and the descent of man 1871–1971* (pp. 238–239). Chicago: Aldine.

Cuciz, D. (n.d.) *The history of MUDs: Part II. Gamespy articles.* Retrieved February 16, 2005, from http://archive.gamespy.com/articles/january01/muds1/index4.shtm.

Cummings, J., Sproull, L., & Kiesler, S. (2002). Beyond hearing: Where real-world and online support meet. *Group Dynamics: Theory, Research, and Practice, 6,* 78–88.

Cupach, W., & Spitzberg, B. (1998). Obsessive relational intrusion and stalking. In B. Spitzberg & W. Cupach (Eds.), *The dark side of close relationships* (pp. 233–263). Hillsdale, NJ: Lawrence Erlbaum Associates.

Cupach, W., Spitzberg, B., & Carson, C. (2000). Toward a theory of obsessive relational intrusion and stalking. In K. Dindia & S. Duck (Eds.), *Communication and personal relationships* (pp. 131–146). New York: John Wiley & Sons.

Curtis, P. (1992, May). Mudding: Social phenomena in text-based virtual realities. *Proceedings of the 1992 conference on the Directions and Implications of Advanced Computing*, Retrieved February 16, 2005, from ftp://ftp.lambda.moo.mud.org/pub/MOO/papers.

Daft, R., & Lengel, R. (1986). Organizational information requirements, media richness and structural design. *Management Science, 32* (5), 554–571.

Danet, B., Ruendenberg, L., & Rosenbaum-Tamari, Y. (1998). Hmmm... Where's that smoke coming from? In F. Sudweeks, M. McLaughlin & S. Rafaeli (Eds.), *Network & netplay: Virtual groups on the internet* (pp. 41–75). Menlo Park: AAAI/MIT.

Davis, S. (1990). Men as success objects and women as sex objects: A study of personal advertisements. *Sex Roles, 23*, 43–50.

DeBurgher, J. (1972). Sex in troubled marriages. *Sexual Behavior, 2*, 23–26.

Degeling, P., & Carr, A. N. (2004). Leadership for the systemization of health care: The unaddressed issue in health care reform. *Journal of Health Organization and Management, 18* (6), 399–414.

Deirmenjian, J. (1999). Stalking in cyberspace. *The Journal of the American Academy of Psychiatry and the Law, 27* (3), 407–413.

Dion, K., Bercheid, E., & Walster, R. (1972). What is beautiful is good. *Journal of Personality and Social Psychology, 24*, 285–290.

Donahue, E., Robins, R., Roberts, B., & John, O. (1993). The divide self: Concurrent and longitudinal effects of psychological adjustment and social roles on self-concept differentiation. *Journal of Personality and Social Psychology, 64*, 834–846.

Donner, L., & Ephron, N. (Producers), & Ephron, N. (Director). (1998). *You've got mail* [Film]. Warner Bros.

Downey, J. L., & Vitulli, W. F. (1987). Self-report measures of behavioural attributions related to interpersonal flirtation situations. *Psychological Reports, 61*, 899–904.

Dunn, R. (1998). *Identity crisis: A social critique of postmodernity.* Minneapolis: University of Minnesota Press.

Dutton, J., Dukerich, J., & Harquail, A. (1994). Organizational images and member identification. *Administrative Science Quarterly, 39*, 239–263.

Eibl-Eibesfeldt, I. (1971). *Love and hate.* New York: Holt, Rinehart and Winston.

Ellis, B., & Symons, D. (1990). Sex differences in sexual fantasy. *Journal of Sex Research, 27* (4), 527–555.

Elron Software, I. (2001). *The year 2001 corporate web and email usage study.* Retrieved March 1, 2005, from http://www.elronsw.com/pdf/NFOReport.pdf.

English, H., & English, A. (1966). *A comprehensive dictionary of psychological and psychoanalytical terms* (2nd ed.). New York: David McKay. (Original work published 1958)

Erikson, E. (1959). Identity and the life cycle. *Psychological Issues* (Monograph 1 [1], 13–117). New York: International Universities.

Fein, E., & Schneider, S. (1995). *The rules: Time tested secrets for capturing the heart of Mr. Right.* New York: Warner.

Fein, E., & Schneider, S. (1997). *The rules II: More rules to live and love by.* New York: Warner.

Fein, E., & Schneider, S. (2002). *The rules for online dating: Capturing the heart of Mr. Right in cyberspace.* New York: Pocket Books.

Feinberg, L. S. (1996). *Teasing: Innocent fun or sadistic malice?* USA: New Horizon.

Feingold, A. (1990). Gender differences in the effects of similarity and physical attractiveness on opposite-sex attraction: A comparison across five research paradigms. *Journal of Personality and Social Psychology, 59*, 981–993.

Feingold, A. (1991). Sex differences in the effects of similarity and physical attractiveness on opposite-sex attraction. *Basic and Applied Social Psychology, 12*, 357–367.

Feldman, M. (2000). Munchausen by Internet: Detecting factitious illness and crises on the Internet. *Southern Medical Journal, 93*, 669–672.

Feldman, S., & Cauffman, E. (1999). Sexual betrayal among late adolescents: Perspectives of the perpetrator and the aggrieved. *Journal of Youth and Adolescence, 28* (2), 235–258.

Ferenczi, S. (1994). *First contributions to psycho-analysis.* London: Karnac. (Original work published 1916)

Feuer, A., & George, J. (2005, February). Internet fame is cruel mistress for a dancer of the Numa Numa. *The New York Times*, Retrieved February 26, 2005, from http://www.nytimes.com/2005/02/26/nyregion/26video.html?ex=1110085200&en=2dc7acb2f0f91b71&ei=5070.

Fitness, J. (2001). Betrayal, rejection, revenge and forgiveness: An interpersonal script approach. In M. Leary (Ed.), *Interpersonal rejection* (pp. 73–103). New York: Oxford University.

Freud, S. (1977). Three essays on sexuality. In J. Strachey (Ed. and Trans.), *On sexuality* (Vol. 7, pp. 31–169). Harmondsworth, England: Penguin Freud Library. (Original work published 1905)

Freud, S. (1977). Fetishism. In J. Strachey (Ed. and Trans.), *On sexuality* (Vol. 7, pp. 345–357). Harmondsworth, England: Penguin Freud Library. (Original work published 1927)

Freud, S. (1983). Inhibitions, symptoms and anxiety. In J. Strachey (Ed. and Trans.), *On psychopathology* (Vol. 10, pp. 229–333). Pelican Freud Library, Great Britain: Pelican. (Original work published 1926)

Freud, S. (1984). On narcissism: An introduction. In J. Strachey (Ed. and Trans.), *On metapsychology: The theory of psychoanalysis* (Vol. 11, pp. 59–97). Harmondsworth: Pelican Freud Library. (Original work published 1914)

Freud, S. (1984). The ego and the id. In J. Strachey (Ed. and Trans.), *On metapsychology: The theory of psychoanalysis* (Vol. 11, pp. 339–408). Pelican Freud Library, Great Britain: Pelican. (Original work published 1923)

Freud, S. (1985). Psychopathic characters on the stage. In J. Strachey (Ed. and Trans.), *Art and literature* (Vol. 14, pp. 119–127). Harmondsworth, England: Penguin Freud Library. (Original work published 1905–6)

Freud, S. (1985). Creative writers and day-dreaming. In J. Strachey (Ed. and Trans.), *Art and literature* (Vol. 14, pp. 129–141). Harmondsworth, England: Penguin Freud Library. (Original work published 1908)

Freud, S. (1985). Thoughts for the times on war and death. In J. Strachey (Ed. and Trans.), *Civilization, society and religion* (Vol. 12, pp. 57–89). Harmondsworth, England: Penguin Freud Library. (Original work published 1915)

Freud, S. (1985). Group psychology and the analysis of the ego. In J. Strachey (Ed. and Trans.), *Civilization, society and religion* (Vol. 12, pp. 91–178). Harmondsworth: Pelican Freud Library. (Original work published 1921)

Freud, S. (1985). Splitting of the ego in the process of defence. In J. Strachey (Ed. and Trans.), *On metapsychology: The theory of psychoanalysis* (Vol. 11, pp. 461–464). Harmondsworth, England: Penguin Freud Library. (Original incomplete work published 1940)

Freud, S. (1986). *The interpretation of dreams* (J. Strachey, Ed. and Trans., Vol. 4). Great Britain: Pelican Freud Library. (Original work published 1900)

Freud, S. (1986). An outline of psychoanalysis. In J. Strachey (Ed. and Trans.), *Historical and expository works on psychoanalysis* (Vol. 15, pp. 371–443). Harmondsworth, England: Pelican Freud Library. (Original work published 1940)

Freud, S. (1988). *New introductory lectures on psychoanalysis* (J. Strachey, Ed. and Trans., Vol. 2). Harmondsworth, England: Penguin Freud Library. (Original work published 1933)

Freud, S. (1990). Delusions and dreams in Jensen's 'Gradiva'. In J. Strachey (Ed. and Trans.), *Art and literature* (Vol. 14, pp. 27–118). Harmondsworth, England: Penguin Freud Library. (Original work published 1906)

Friedman, J. (1989). Therapeia, play and the therapeutic household. In C. Oakley (Ed.), *Thresholds between philosophy and psychoanalysis: Papers from the philadelphia association* (pp. 56–75). London: Free Association Books.

Fromm, E. (1970). Die psychoanalytische charakterologie und ihre bedeutung für die sozialpsychologie. In *The crisis of psychoanalysis*. New York: Holt, Rinehart and Winston. (Original work published 1932)

Fromm, E. (1994). *Escape from freedom*. New York: Owl books, Henry Holt and Company. (Original work published 1941)

Fromm, E., & Maccoby, M. (1970). *Social character in a Mexican village.* Englewood Cliffs, NJ: Prentice Hall.

Gaunt, N. (2002, April). *Doing it live in cyberspace: Online interviewing for social psychological research?* Paper presented at SASP, Adelaide.

Gibson, W. (1986). *Neuromancer.* London: Grafton Books.

Gibson, D., Malerstein, A., Ahern, M., & Jones, R. (1989). Character structure and performance on the MMPI. *Psychological Reports, 65,* 1139–1149.

Givens, D. (1978). The nonverbal basis of attraction: Flirtation, courtship, and seduction. *Psychiatry, 41,* 346–359.

Glass, J. (1993). *Shattered selves: multiple personality in a postmodern world.* Ithaca, NY: Cornell University.

Glass, G., & Wright, T. (1985). Sex differences in type of extramarital involvement and marital dissatisfaction. *Sex Roles, 12,* 1101–1120.

Grammer, K. (1990). Strangers meet: Laughter and nonverbal signs of interest in opposite-sex encounters. *Journal of Nonverbal Behavior, 14,* 209–236.

Grammer, K., Kruck, K., Juette, A., & Fink, B. (2000). Non-verbal behaviour as courtship signals: The role of control and choice in selecting partners. *Evolution and Human Behavior, 21,* 371–390.

Green, N. (2001). Strange yet stylish headgear: Virtual reality consumption and the construction of gender. In E. Green & A. Adam (Eds.), *Virtual gender: Technology, consumption and identity* (pp. 150–172). London: Routledge.

Griffiths, M. (1998). Internet addiction: Does it really exist? In J. Gackenbach (Ed.), *Psychology and the internet* (pp. 61–75). New York: Academic Press.

Griffiths, M. (1999). Internet addiction: Fact or fiction. *Psychologist, 12,* 246–250.

Griffiths, M. (2000). Internet addiction – Time to be taken seriously? *Addiction Research, 8,* 413–418.

Grohol, J. (1998). Response to the HomeNet study. *PsychCentral,* Retrieved October 27, 2004, from http://psychcentral.com/homenet.htm.

Grohol, J. (1999). Too much time online: Internet addiction of healthy social interactions? *CyberPsychology & Behavior, 2* (5), 395–401.

Gross, S., & Anthony, K. (2002). Virtual counsellors – Whatever next? *Counselling Journal, 13* (2), 14–15.

Gumbel, A. (1999). Techno detectives net cyber-stalkers. *Independent on Sunday,* January 31, 17.

Gwinnell, E. (1998). *Online seductions: Falling in love with strangers on the internet.* New York: Kodansha International.

Hamburger, Y. A., & Ben-Artzi, B. (2000). The relationship between extraversion and neuroticism and the different uses of the Internet. *Computers in Human Behavior, 16,* 441–449.

Hancock, J., Thom-Santelli, J., & Ritchie, T. (2004). Deception and design: The impact of communication technologies on lying behavior. *Proceedings, Conference on Computer Human Interaction,* New York, *6* (1), 130–136.

Hansen, G. (1987). Extradyadic relations during courtship. *Journal of Sex Research, 23* (3), 382–390.

Herring, S. C. (1993). Gender and democracy in computer-mediated communication. *Electronic Journal of Communication, 3* (2), Retrieved February 7, 2005, from http://ella.slis.indiana.edu/~herring/ejc.txt.

Herring, S. C., Scheidt, L. A., Bonus, S., & Wright, E. (2004, January). Bridging the gap: A genre analysis of weblogs. *Proceedings of the 37th Hawaii International Conference on System Sciences (HICSS-37)*, Los Alamitos: IEEE Computer Society Press (CD-ROM).

Higgins, E. T. (1987). Self-discrepancy theory. *Psychological Review, 94*, 1120–1134.

Hiler, J. (2002) *Saltire*. Retrieved March 3, 2005, from http://saltire.weblogger.com/2002/04/02.

Hills, P., & Argyle, M. (2003). Uses of the Internet and their relationships with individual differences in personality. *Computers in Human Behavior, 19*, 59–70.

Hiltz, S., Johnson, M., & Turoff, M. (1986). Experiments in group decision making: Communication process and outcome in face-to-face versus computerized conferences. *Human Communication Research, 13*, 225–252.

Holland, N. (1995). The Internet regression, *Free Association*, Retrieved October 1, 2004, from http://www.human-nature.com/free-associations/holland.html.

Houran, J., Lange, R., Rentfrow, P. J., & Bruckner, K. H. (2004). Do online matchmaking tests work? An Assessment of preliminary evidence for a publicized 'predictive model of marital success'. *North American Journal of Psychology, 6*, 507–526.

Huizinga, J. (1980). *Homo Ludens: The study of the play-element in culture*. London: Routledge & Kegan Paul. (Original work published 1944)

Joinson, A. N. (2001). Self-disclosure in computer-mediated communication: The role of self-awareness and visual anonymity. *European Journal of Social Psychology, 31*, 177–192.

Joinson, A. N. (2003). *Understanding the psychology of the Internet behaviour: Virtual worlds, real lives*. Basingstoke: Palgrave Macmillan.

Joinson, A. N. (2004). Self-esteem, interpersonal risk, and preference for e-mail to face-to-face communication. *CyberPsychology & Behavior, 7* (4), 479–485.

Jordan, A. (2005, February). Budding cyber love ends in divorce. *Sydney Morning Herald*, February 7, 2005, Retrieved February 17, 2005 from http://www.smh.com.au/articles/2005/02/07/1107625114716.html.

Jung, C. G. (1953). *The collected works of C. G. Jung: Two essays on analytical psychology* (R. F. C. Hull, Trans.) (Vol. 7). Princeton: Princeton University. (Original work published 1917)

Jung, C. G. (1968). Psychological aspects of the mother archetype. In R. F. C. Hull (Trans.), *The collected works of C. G. Jung: The archetypes and the collective unconscious* (2nd ed., Vol. 9, Part 1, pp. 75–110). Princeton University: Princeton University. (Original work published 1938)

Jung, C. G. (1969). *The collected works of C. G. Jung: Symbols of transformation* (R. F. C. Hull, Trans. 2nd ed., Vol. 5). Princeton: Princeton University. (Original work published 1912)

Jung, C. G. (1969). The transcendent function. In R. F. C. Hull (Trans.), *The collected works of C. G. Jung: The structure and dynamics of the psyche* (2nd ed., Vol. 8, pp. 67–91). Princeton: Princeton University. (Original work published 1916)

Jung, C. G. (1969). Psychological commentary on 'The Tibetan book of the dead'. In R. F. C. Hull (Trans.), *The collected works of C. G. Jung: Psychology and religion, West and East* (2nd ed., Vol. 11, pp. 509–526). Princeton: Princeton University. (Original work published 1935)

Jung, C. G. (1989). *The collected works of C. G. Jung: Psychological types* (R. F. C. Hull, Trans. Rev. ed.) (Vol. 6). London: Routledge. (Original work published 1921)

Kendon, A. (1975). Some functions of the face in a kissing round. *Semiotica, 15,* 299–334.

Kenrick, D. T., Sadalla, E. K., Groth, G., & Trost, M. R. (1990). Evolution, traits, and the stages of human courtship: Qualifying the parental investment model. *Journal of Personality, 58,* 97–116.

Kepple, B. (2003). *Blogging and dating.* Retrieved March 25, 2005, from http://www.benkepple.com/archives/000046.html.

Kiesler, S. J., Siegel, J., & McGuire, T. W. (1984). Social psychological aspects of computer-mediated communication. *American Psychologist, 39,* 1123–1134.

Kitzinger, C., & Powell, D. (1995). Engendering infidelity: Essentialist and social constructionist readings of a story completion task. *Feminism & Psychology, 5* (3), 345–372.

Klein, M. (1944). The emotional life and ego-development of the infant with special reference to the depressive position. In J. Riviere (Ed. and Trans.), *Developments in psycho-analysis* (pp. 198–236). London: Hogarth.

Klein, M. (1975a). *The writings of Melanie Klein I: 'Love, guilt and reparation' and other works 1921–1945.* London: Hogarth.

Klein, M. (1975b). *The writings of Melanie Klein II: The psychoanalysis of children.* London: Hogarth.

Klein, M. (1975c). *The writings of Melanie Klein III: 'Envy and gratitude' and other works 1946–1963.* London: Hogarth.

Klein, M. (1975d). *The writings of Melanie Klein IV: Narrative of a child analysis.* London: Hogarth.

Klein, M. (1986). *The selected works of Melanie Klein* (J. Mitchell, Ed.), London, UK: Penguin Books.

Koller, M. R. (1951). Some changes in courtship behavior in three generations of Ohio women. *American Sociological Review, 16,* 266–370.

Kraut, R., Kiesler, S., Boneva, B., Cummings, J. N., Helgeson, V., & Crawford, A. M. (2002). Internet paradox revisited. *Journal of Social Issues, 58,* 49–74.

Kraut, R., Patterson, M., Lundmark, V., Kiesler, S., Mukopadhyay, T., & Scherlies, W. (1998). Internet paradox: A social technology that reduces social involvement and psychological well-being? *American Psychologist, 53,* 1017–1031.

La Bier, D. (1983). Emotional disturbance in the federal government. *Administration and Society, 14,* 403–448.

La Bier, D. (1986). *Modern madness: The emotional fallout of success.* Massachusetts: Addison-Wesley.

Laplanche, J., & Pontalis, J. (1988). *The language of psycho-analysis* (D. Nicholson-Smith, Trans.). London: Karnac. (Original work published 1967)

LaRose, R., Eastin, M. S., & Gregg, J. (2001). Reformulating the Internet paradox: Social cognitive explanations of Internet use and depression. *Journal of Online Behavior, 1* (2), Retrieved October 27, 2004, from the World Wide Web: http://www.behavior.net/JOB/v1n2/paradox.html.

Lea, M., & Spears, R. (1995). Love at first byte? Building personal relationships over computer networks. In J. T. Wood & S. W. Duck (Eds.), *Understudied relationships: Off the beaten track* (pp. 197–233). Newbury Park, CA: Sage.

Lea, M., Spears, R., & DeGroot, D. (2001). Knowing me, knowing you: Effects of visual anonymity on self-categorization, stereotyping and attraction in computer-mediated groups. *Personality and Social Psychology Bulletin, 27* (5), 526–537.

Lenhart, A., Rainie, L., & Lewis, O. (2001). *Teenage life online: The rise of the instant message generating and the Internet's impact on friendships and family relationships.* Retrieved March 3, 2005, from http://www.pewinternet.org/pdfs/PIP_Teens_Report.pdf.

Levine, D. (2000). Virtual attraction: What rocks your boat. *CyberPsychology & Behavior, 3,* 565–573.

Levitt, E. (1980). *The psychology of anxiety.* New Jersey: Lawrence Erlbaum Associates.

Livingstone, S. (2001). *Online freedom: Safety for children.* Retrieved March 2, 2005, from http://www.lse.ac.uk/collections/media@lse/pdf/free_safety_children1.pdf.

Lupton, D. (1995). The embodies computer/user. *Body & Society, 1,* 97–112.

Maccoby, M. (1976). *The gamesman.* New York: Simon and Schuster.

Maheu, M., & Subotnik, R. (2001). *Infidelity on the internet: Virtual relationships and real betrayal.* Naperville, USA: Sourcebooks, Inc.

Mann, C., & Stewart, F. (2000). *Internet communication and qualitative research: A handbook for researching online.* London: Sage Publications.

Mason, S., & Carr, A. N. (2000). The construction of identity in organizations: Beyond the cognitive lens. In A. Rahim, R. Golembiewski, & K. Mackenzie (Eds.), *Current topics in management* (Vol. 5, pp. 95–116). Stanford, Connecticut: JAI.

McCown, J. A., Fischer, D., Page, R., & Homant, M. (2001). Internet relationships: People who meet people. *CyberPsychology & Behavior, 4,* 593–596.

McKenna, K. Y. A., & Bargh, J. A. (1998). Coming out in the age of Internet: Identity 'de-marginalization' through virtual group participation. *Journal of Personality and Social Psychology, 75*, 681–694.

McKenna, K. Y. A., & Bargh, J. A. (2000). Plan 9 from cyberspace: The implications of the Internet for personality and social psychology. *Journal of Personality and Social Psychology, 4*, 57–75.

McKenna, K. Y. A., Green, A. S., & Gleason, M. E. J. (2002). Relationship formation on the Internet: What's the big attraction? *Journal of Social Issues, 58*, 9–31.

McRae, S. (1996). Coming apart at the seams: Sex, text and the virtual body. In L. Cherny & E. Weise (Eds.), *Wired women: Gender and new realities in cyberspace* (pp. 242–263). USA: Seal Press.

Mehta, M. D. (2001). Pornography in Usenet: A study of 9,800 randomly selected images. *CyberPsychology & Behavior, 4*, 695–703.

Mehta, M. D., & Plaza, D. E. (1997). Pornography in cyberspace: An exploration of what's in usenet. In S. Kiesler (Ed.), *Culture of the internet* (pp. 53–67). Mahwah, NJ: Lawrence Erlbaum Associates.

Mitchell, S. A., & Black, M. J. (1995). *Freud and beyond: A history of modern psychoanalytic thought*. New York: Basic Books.

Modell, A. H. (1996). *Other times, other realities: Toward a theory of psychoanalytic treatment*. Cambridge, MA: Harvard University. (Original work published 1990)

Moller, H. (1959). The causation of the courtly love complex. *Comparative Studies in Society & History, 1*, 137–163.

Mongeau, P. A., Hale, J. L., Johnson, K. L., & Hillis, J. D. (1993). Who's wooing whom? An Investigation of female initiated dating. In P. J. Kabfleisch (Ed.), *Interpersonal communication: Evolving interpersonal relationships* (pp. 51–68). Hillsdale, NJ: Lawrence Erlbaum Associates, Inc.

Moore, M. M. (1985). Nonverbal courtship patterns in women: Context and consequences. *Ethology and Sociobiology, 6*, 237–247.

Moore, M. M. (1998). Nonverbal courtship patterns in women – Rejection signalling: An empirical investigation. *Semiotica, 118*, 201–214.

Morahan-Martin, J. (1999). The relationship between loneliness and Internet use and abuse. *CyberPsychology & Behavior, 2*, 431–439.

Morahan-Martin, J. (2005). Internet abuse: Addiction? Disorder? Symptom? Alternative Explanations? *Social Science Computer Review, 23* (1), 39–48.

Morahan-Martin, J., & Schumacher, P. (2003). Loneliness and social uses of the Internet. *Computers in Human Behavior, 19*, 659–671.

Morton, L., Alexander, J., & Altman, I. (1976). Communication and relationship definition. In G. R. Miller (Ed.), *Explorations in interpersonal communication* (pp. 105–125). Beverly Hills, CA: Sage.

Murstein, B. (1974). *Love, sex and marriage through the ages*. New York: Springer.

NetAccountability. (n.d.) Retrieved March 5, 2005, from the World Wide Web: http://www.netaccountability.com/ver2/index.cfm.

NHMRC (1999). *National statement on ethical conduct in research involving humans.* Retrieved September 25, 2002, from http://www.health.gov.au/nhmrc/publications/humans/part17.htm.

Nosek, B. A., Banaji, M. R., & Greenwald, A. G. (2002). E-research: Ethics, security, design, and control in psychological research on the Internet. *Journal of Social Issues, 58* (1)*,* 161–176.

Ogden, T. H. (1985a). On potential space. *The International Journal of Psychoanalysis, 66,* 129–141.

Ogden, T. H. (1985b). The mother, the infant and the matrix. *Contemporary Psychoanalysis, 21,* 346–371.

Ogden, T. H. (1991). Analysing the matrix of transference. *The International Journal of Psychoanalysis, 72,* 593–605.

O'Hara, D. (2000). *Courtship and constraint: Rethinking the making of marriage in Tudor England.* Manchester: Manchester University.

Parks, M. R., & Floyd, K. (1996). Making friends in cyberspace. *Journal of Communication, 46,* 80–97.

Parks, M. R., & Roberts, L. D. (1998). 'Making MOOsic': The development of personal relationships online and a comparison to their off-line counterparts. *Journal of Social and Personal Relationships, 15,* 517–537.

Paul, L., & Galloway, J. (1994). Sexual jealousy: Gender differences in response to partner and rival. *Aggressive Behavior, 20,* 203–211.

Paul, L., Foss, M., & Galloway, J. (1993). Sexual jealousy in young women and men: Aggressive responsiveness to partner and rival. *Aggressive Behavior, 19,* 401–420.

Pennebaker, J. W. (1997). *Opening up: The healing power of expressing emotions.* New York: Guilford Press.

Peris, R., Gimeno, M. A., Pinazo, D., Ortet, G., Carrero, V., Sanchiz, M., & Ibañez, I. (2002). Online chat rooms: Virtual spaces of interaction for socially oriented people. *CyberPsychology & Behaviour, 5,* 43–51.

Perper, T. (1985). *Sex signals: The biology of love.* Philadelphia: ISI.

Pontalis, J. (1981). *Frontiers in psychoanalysis: Between the dream and psychic pain.* London: Hogarth.

Proxidating (2005). Retrieved March 25, 2005, from http://www.proxidating.com/index.php?code_pays=UK&code_lang=EN.

Reicher, S. (1994). Social influence in the crowd: attitudinal and behavioural effects of de-individuation in conditions of high and low group salience. *British Journal of Social Psychology, 23,* 341–350.

Rheingold, H. (1993). *The virtual community: Homesteading on the electronic frontier.* Cambridge: The MIT.

Rheingold, H. (2002). *Smart mobs: The next social revolution.* Cambridge, MA: Basic Books.

Rice, F. P. (1996). *Intimate relationships, marriages, and families.* Mountain View, CA: Mayfield Publishing.

Rice, R. E., & Love, G. (1987). Electronic emotion: Socioemotional content in a computer mediated communication network. *Communication Research, 14*, 85–108.

Rogers, C. (1951). *Client-centered therapy*. Boston: Houghton-Mifflin.

Rogers, P., & Lea, M. (2005). Social presence in distributed group environments: The role of social identity. *Behaviour & Information Technology, 24*, 151–158.

Rollman, J., Krug, K., & Parente, F. (2000). The chat room phenomenon: Reciprocal communication in cyberspace. *CyberPsychology & Behavior, 3* (2), 161–166.

Roscoe, B., Cavanaugh, L., & Kennedy, D. (1988). Dating infidelity: Behaviors reasons, and consequences. *Adolescence, 23*, 35–43.

Rycroft, C. (1995). *A critical dictionary of psychoanalysis* (2nd ed.). Harmondsworth, England: Penguin.

Scealy, M., Phillips, J. G., & Stevenson, R. (2002). Shyness and anxiety as predictors of patterns of Internet usage. *CyberPsychology & Behavior, 5*, 507–515.

Scharlott, B. W., & Christ, W. G. (1995). Overcoming relationship-initiation barriers: The impact of a computer-dating system on sex role, shyness, and appearance inhibitions. *Computers in Human Behavior, 11*, 191–204.

Schmidt, J. (2005, March). *Blogging as social action: The trias of practice, rules and relations*. Paper presented at German Online Research Conference, Zurich.

Schneider, J. P. (2003). The impact of compulsive cybersex behaviours on the family. *Sexual and Relationship Therapy, 18*, 329–354.

Schwartz, H. (1990). *Narcissistic process and corporate decay: The theory of the organization ideal*. New York: New York University.

Seabrook, J. (1994, June). My first flame. *New Yorker*, 70–79.

Serres, M. (1982). *The parasite* (L. Schehr, Trans.). Baltimore: John Hopkins University.

Serres, M. (1995). *Angels: A modern myth* (F. Cowper, Trans.). Paris: Flammarion. (Original work published 1993)

Shackelford, T., & Buss, D. (1996). Betrayal in mateships, friendships, and coalitions. *Journal of Personality and Social Psychology, 22*, 1151–1164.

Sharf, B. F. (1999). Beyond netiquette: The ethics of doing naturalistic discourse research on the Internet. In S. Jones (Ed.), *Doing internet research: Critical issues and methods for examining the net* (pp. 243–256). Thousand Oaks: Sage Publications.

Shaw, J. (1997). Treatment rationale for Internet infidelity. *Journal of Sex Education and Therapy, 22* (1), 29–34.

Sheppard, V., Nelson, E., & Andreoli-Mathie, V. (1995). Dating relationships and infidelity: Attitudes and behaviors. *Journal of Sex and Marital Therapy, 21* (3), 202–212.

Simmel, G. (1984). *Georg Simmel: On women, sexuality, and love* (K. Wolff, Ed. and Trans.). New York: The Free Press.

Spears, R., & Lea, M. (1992). Social influence and the influence of the 'social' in computer-mediated communication. In M. Lea (Ed.) *Contexts of computer-mediated communication* (pp. 30–65). Hemel Hempsted: Wheatsheaf.

Spears, R., Lea, M., & Lee, S. (1990). De-individuation and group polarization in computer-mediated communication. *British Journal of Social Psychology, 29*, 121–134.

Spector Soft, Inc. (n.d.) *Stop infidelity with Spector.* Retrieved March 3, 2005, from http://www.spywaredirectory.com/spector_win.asp.

Spitzberg, B., & Hoobler, G. (2002). Cyberstalking and the technologies of interpersonal terrorism. *New Media & Society, 4* (1), 71–92.

Sproull, L., & Kiesler, S. (1986). Reducing social context cues: Electronic mail in organizational communication. *Management Science, 32*, 1492–1512.

Standage, T. (1987). *The Victorian internet.* New York: Walker and Company.

Stone, A. R. (1995). Sex and death among the disembodied: VR, cyberspace, and the nature of academic discourse. In S. Star (Ed.), *Cultures of computing Sociological Review Monograph* (pp. 243–255). Oxford: Blackwell Publishers.

Stone, L. D., & Pennebaker, J. W. (2002). Trauma in real time: Talking and avoiding online conversations about the death of Princess Diana. *Basic and Applied Social Psychology, 24*, 172–182.

Stratton, J. (1997). Not really desiring bodies: The rise and rise of email affairs. *Media International Australia, 84*, 28–38.

Stritzke, W. G. K., Nguyen, A., & Durkin, K. (2004). Shyness and computer-mediated communication: A self-presentational theory perspective. *Media Psychology, 6* (1), 1–22.

Stryker, S., & Statham, A. (1985). Symbolic interaction and role theory. In G. Lindzey and E. Aronson (Eds.), *Handbook of social psychology* (3rd ed., pp. 311–378). New York: Random House.

Suler, J. (1998). Mom, dad, computer: Transference reactions to computers. *Psychology of cyberspace* (Internet book). Retrieved March 9, 2005, from http://www.rider.edu/~suler/psycyber/comptransf.html.

Suler, J. (1999a). Do boys (and girls) just wanna have fun: Gender-switching in cyberspace. *Psychology of cyberspace* (Internet book). Retrieved March 9, 2005, from http://www.rider.edu/~suler/psycyber/genderswap.html.

Suler, J. R. (1999b). *Computerized psychotherapy.* Retrieved March 7, 2005, from http://www.rider.edu/~suler/psycyber/eliza.html.

Suler, J. R. (2002). The future of online clinical work. *Journal of Applied Psychoanalytic Studies, 4*, 265–270.

Suler, J. R. (2004a). The online disinhibition effect. *CyberPsychology & Behavior, 7*, 321–326.

Suler, J. R. (2004b). Psychotherapy in cyberspace: A 5-Dimension model of online and computer-mediated psychotherapy. *Psychology of cyberspace* (Internet book). Retrieved March 7, 2005, from http://www.rider.edu/~suler/psycyber/therapy.html.

Suttie, I. (1935). *The origins of love and hate*. New York: The Julian Press, Inc.

Swickert, R. J., Hittner, J. B., Harris, J. L., & Herring, J. A. (2002). Relationships among Internet use, personality, and social support. *Computers in Human Behavior, 18*, 437–451.

Tarbox, K. (2000). *Katie.com*. Sydney, Australia: Hodder.

Taxén, G. (2002). Guilds: Communities in Ultima Online. *TRITA-NA-D0208, CID*. Retrieved February 17, 2005, from http://cid.nada.kth.se/pdf/CID-167.pdf.

Taylor, C. (1986). Extramarital sex: Good for the goose? Good for the gander? *Women and Therapy, 5*, 289–295.

Thibaut, J., & Kelley, H. (1959). *The social psychology of groups*. New York: Wiley.

Thomson, R., & Murachver, T. (2001). Predicting gender from electronic discourse. *British Journal of Social Psychology, 40*, 193–208.

Townsend, J. (1993). Sexuality and partner selection: Sex differences among college students. *Ethology and Sociobiology, 14*, 305–330.

Townsend, J., & Levy, G. (1990). Effects of potential partners' costume and physical attractiveness on sexuality and partner selection. *Journal of Psychology, 124*, 371–389.

Townsend, J., & Wasserman, T. (1997). The perception of sexual attractiveness: Sex differences in variability. *Achieves of Sexual Behavior, 26*, 243–268.

Trevino, L., Lengel, R., & Daft, R. (1987). Media symbolism, media richness, and media choice in organizations: A symbolic interactionist perspective. *Communication Research, 14*, 553–574.

Turkle, S. (1995). *Life on the screen: Identity in the age of the Internet*. London: Weidenfeld & Nicolson.

Tuten, T., & Bosnjak, M. (2001). Understanding differences in web usage: The role of need for cognition and the five factor model of personality. *Social Behavior and Personality, 29*, 391–398.

Utz, S. (2000). Social information processing in MUDs: The development of friendships in virtual worlds. *Journal of Online Behavior, 1* (1), Retrieved February 7, 2005 from http://www.behavior.net/JOB/v1n1/utz.html.

Voiskounsky, A., & Smyslova, O. (2003). Flow-based model of computer hacker' motivation. *CyberPsychology & Behavior, 6* (2), 171–180.

Voiskounsky, A., Mitina, O., & Avetisova, A. (2004). Playing online games: Flow experience. *Psychology Journal, 2* (3), 259–281.

Walker, B. M., Harper, J., Lloyd, C., & Caputi, P. (2003). Methodologies for the exploration of computer and technological transference. *Computers in Human Behavior, 19*, 523–535.

Walther, J. B. (1992). Interpersonal effects in computer-mediated interaction: A relational perspective. *Communication Research, 19*, 52–90.

Walther, J. B. (1995). Relational aspects of computer-mediated communication: Experimental observations over time. *Organizational Science, 6*, 186–203.

Walther, J. B. (1996). Computer-mediated communication: Impersonal, interpersonal and hyperpersonal interaction. *Communication Research, 23*, 3–43.

Walther, J. B., Slovacek, C., & Tidwell, L. (2001). Is a picture worth a thousand words? Photographic images in long-term and short-term computer-mediated communication. *Communication Research, 28*, 105–134.

Wedekind, C., Seebeck, T., Bettens, F., & Paepke, A. J. (1995). MHC-dependent mate preferences in humans. *Proceedings of the Royal Society of London. Series B. Biological science, 260* (1359), 245–249.

Wellman, B. (1997). An electronic group is virtually a social network. In S. Kielser (Ed.), *Culture of the internet* (pp. 179–205). Mahwah: Lawrence Erlbaum Associates.

Wellman, B. (2004). Connecting communities: On and off line. *Contexts, 3* (4), 22–28.

Wellman, B., & Gulia, M. (1999). Net surfers don't ride alone: Virtual communities as communities. In M. Smith & P. Kollock (Eds.), *Communities in cyberspace* (pp. 167–194). London: Routledge.

Whitty, M. T. (2001, July). *Tangled web of deceit*. Paper presented at the Society for Australasian Social Psychologists, Melbourne.

Whitty, M. T. (2002). Liar, liar! An examination of how open, supportive and honest people are in Chat Rooms. *Computers in Human Behavior, 18*, 343–352.

Whitty, M. T. (2003a). Cyber-flirting: Playing at love on the Internet. *Theory and Psychology, 13*, 339–357.

Whitty, M. T. (2003b). Pushing the wrong buttons: Men's and women's attitudes towards online and offline infidelity. *CyberPsychology & Behavior, 6*, 569–579.

Whitty, M. T. (2004a). Cyber-flirting: An examination of men's and women's flirting behaviour both offline and on the Internet. *Behaviour Change, 21*, 115–126.

Whitty, M. T. (2004b). Should filtering software be utilised in the workplace? Australian employee's attitudes towards Internet usage and surveillance of the Internet in the workplace. *Surveillance and Society, 2* (1), 39–54.

Whitty, M. T. (2004c). Peering into online bedroom windows: Considering the ethical implications of investigating Internet relationships and sexuality. In E. Buchanan (Ed.), *Readings in virtual research ethics: Issues and controversies* (pp. 203–218). Hershey, USA: Idea Group Inc.

Whitty, M. T. (2005). The 'realness' of cyber-cheating: Men and women's representations of unfaithful Internet relationships. *Social Science Computer Review, 23* (1), 57–67.

Whitty, M. T., & Carr, A. N. (2003). Cyberspace as potential space: Considering the web as a playground to cyber-flirt. *Human Relations, 56*, 861–891.

Whitty, M. T., & Carr, A. N. (2005a). Taking the good with the bad: Applying Klein's work to further our understanding of cyber-cheating. *Journal of Couple and Relationship Therapy: Special issue on Treating infidelity, 4* (2–3), 103–115.

Whitty, M. T., & Carr, A. N. (2005b). Electronic bullying in the workplace. In B. Fisher, V. Bowie, & C. Cooper (Eds.), *Workplace violence* (pp. 248–262). Devon, UK: Willan Publishing Ltd.

Whitty, M. T., & Carr, A. N. (2006). New rules in the workplace: Applying object-relations theory to explain problem Internet and email behaviour in the workplace. *Computers in Human Behavior, 22* (2), 235–250.

Whitty, M. T., & Gavin, J. (2001). Age/sex/location: Uncovering the social cues in the development of online relationships. *CyberPsychology & Behaviour, 4,* 623–630.

Whitty, M. T., & McLaughlin, D. (in press). Online recreation: The relationship between loneliness, Internet self-efficacy and the use of the Internet for entertainment purposes. *Computers in Human Behavior.*

Wilkins, L. (2003, May). Stalker had sophisticated cyber plan. *BBC News, UK edition,* May 20, 2003, Retrieved March 2, 2005, from http://news.bbc.co.uk/1/hi/uk/3040623.stm.

Winnicott, D. W. (1953). Transitional objects and transitional phenomena: A study of the first not-me possession. *The International Journal of Psycho-analysis, 34,* 89–97.

Winnicott, D. W. (1958). *Collected papers.* New York: Basic Books.

Winnicott, D. W. (1971a). *Playing and reality.* New York: Basic Books.

Winnicott, D. W. (Ed.). (1971b). Transitional objects and transitional phenomena. *Playing and Reality* (pp. 1–25). New York: Basic Books. (Original work published 1951)

Winnicott, D. W. (Ed.). (1971c). Dreaming, fantasying and living. *Playing and reality* (pp. 26–37). New York: Basic Books.

Winnicott, D. W. (Ed.). (1971d). Playing: A theoretical statement. *Playing and reality* (pp. 38–52). New York: Basic Books.

Winnicott, D. W. (Ed.). (1971e). The use of an object and relating through cross identifications. *Playing and reality* (pp. 86–94). New York: Basic Books. (Original work published 1968)

Winnicott, D. W. (Ed.). (1971f). The location of cultural experience. *Playing and reality* (pp. 95–103). New York: Basic Books. (Original work published 1967)

Winnicott, D. W. (Ed.). (1971g). The place where we live. *Playing and reality* (pp. 104–110). New York: Basic Books.

Witmer, D., & Katzman, S. (1997). On-line smiles: Does gender make a difference in the use of graphic accents? *Journal of Computer Mediated Communication, 2* (4), Retrieved February 7, 2005, from http://ascusc.org/jcmc/vol2/issue4/witmer1.html.

Woll, S., & Cozby, P. C. (1987). Videodating and other alternatives to traditional methods of relationship initiation. In W. Jones, & D. Perlman (Eds.), *Advances in personal relationships* (pp. 69–108). J. Greenwich, CT: JAI.

Wright, E. (1998). *Psychoanalytic Criticism* (2nd ed.). Cambridge, UK: Polity.

Wysocki, D. K. (1998). Let your fingers to do the talking: Sex on an adult chat-line. *Sexualities, 1,* 425–452.

Yarab, P. E., & Allgeier, E. (1998). Don't even think about it: The role of sexual fantasies as perceived unfaithfulness in heterosexual dating relationships. *Journal of Sex Education and Therapy, 23* (3), 246–254.

Yarab, P. E., Allgeier, E., & Sensibaugh, C. C. (1999). Looking deeper: Extradyadic behaviors, jealousy, and perceived unfaithfulness in hypothetical dating relationships. *Personal Relationships, 6,* 305–316.

Yarab, P. E., Sensibaugh, C. C., & Allgeier, E. (1998). More than just sex: Gender differences in the incidence of self-defined unfaithful behavior in heterosexual dating relationships. *Journal of Psychology & Human Sexuality, 10* (2), 45–57.

Young, K. S. (1996). *Internet addiction: The emergence of a new clinical disorder.* Paper presented at the 104th Annual Convention of the American Psychological Association, Toronto, Canada.

Young, K. S. (1998a). *Caught in the net: How to recognise the signs of internet addiction and a winning strategy for recovery.* New York: John Wiley & Sons.

Young, K. S. (1998b). Internet addiction: The emergence of a new clinical disorder. *CyberPsychology & Behavior, 1,* 237–244.

Young, K. S. (1999). Internet addiction: Evaluation and treatment. *Student British Medical Journal, 7,* 351–352.

Young, K. S., Griffin-Shelley, E., Cooper, A., O'Mara, J., & Buchanan, J. (2000). Online infidelity: A new dimension in couple relationships with implications for evaluation and treatment. *Sexual Addiction & Compulsivity, 7,* 59–74.

Young, K. S., Pistner, M., O'Mara, J., & Buchanan, J. (1999). Cyber disorders: The mental health concern for the new millennium. *CyberPsychology & Behavior, 2* (5), 475–479.

Yuen, C. N., & Lavin, M. J. (2004). Internet dependence in the collegiate population: The role of shyness. *CyberPsychology & Behavior, 7,* 379–383.

Zimbardo, P. G., Pilkonis, P. A., & Norwood, R. M. (1975). The social disease called shyness. *Psychology Today, 8,* 68–72.

Zuckerman, M., & Miyake, M. (1993). The attractive voice: What makes it so? *Journal of Nonverbal Behavior, 17,* 119–135.

Author Index

Subject Index

215